BEER

ACROSS

AMERICA

**A REGIONAL GUIDE
TO BREWPUBS AND MICROBREWERIES**

by Marty Nachel

A Storey Publishing Book

Storey Communications, Inc.
Schoolhouse Road
Pownal, Vermont 05261

Dedication

For teaching me, the sixth of eight children, to appreciate the small things in life and to enjoy all good things in moderation, I'm proud to dedicate this book to my parents, Robert (1923–1991) and Germaine Nachel.

The mission of Storey Communications is to serve our customers by publishing practical information that encourages personal independence in harmony with the environment.

Conceived and produced by Ettlinger Editorial Projects

Edited by Pamela Lappies
Cover design by Meredith Maker
Cover photograph by Nicholas Whitman
Text design and illustration by Greg Imhoff
Text production by Therese G. Lenz
Indexed by Northwind Editorial Services

Note: Much of the material contained herein originally appeared in slightly different form in the Beer Across America® monthly newsletter, written and edited by Marty Nachel.

Printed in Canada by Interglobe, Inc.
First Printing, June 1995

Library of Congress Cataloging-in-Publication Data

Nachel, Marty, 1958-
    Beer across America : a regional guide to brewpubs and microbreweries / by Marty Nachel.
       p.   cm.
    "A Storey Publishing book."
    Includes bibliographical references and index.
    ISBN 0-88266-902-8 (pbk.)
    1. Brewing industry—United States—Directories. 2. Breweries—United States—Directories.
3. Bars (Drinking establishments)—United States—Directories. 4. Beer industry—United States—Directories. I. Title.
HD9397.U52N33   1995
338.7'6633'02573—dc20
                                      95-17212
                                        CIP

Table of Contents

About Beer Across America

Called "the Big Daddy of beer clubs" by *BEER: the magazine*, Beer Across America is the original microbrewery beer-of-the-month club, in operation since 1992. It offers its members a monthly newsletter that provides interesting information about beer and microbreweries, recipes featuring various beers, as well as selections for that month.

For more information or to sample some of the beers featured in this book, please call 1-800-854-BEER.

PREFACE

After too many years of quaffing mediocre beers imposed upon me by American corporate brewhouses, my quest for the perfect beer began. A visit to Toronto's Molson Brewery in 1982 opened my eyes to foreign and ancient concepts of beer consumerism not then commonly practiced in the United States: quality and diversity. Subsequent pilgrimages to breweries in North America, the United Kingdom, and Europe confirmed my suspicion that there is no one perfect beer, but there are scores of exceptionally well-made, personal favorites. Over 100 breweries and brewpubs later, and after tasting well over 1,000 beers, I am convinced that American microbrewers are crafting beer with the best of them.

So how does a welder and steel fabricator of 15 years come to write a book about American beer? When I was not traveling in search of good beer, I was busily brewing my own at home and learning from my mentors in the field. Recognizing the beer consumer's need for accurate and updated information, I began to freelance for a few of the rapidly expanding beer publications. In 1992, a decade after my first trip to Canada, Beer Across America started a trend in microbrewed beer distribution. I was one of their charter members. After a few months of receiving rather thin newsletters with my beer, I approached them about contributing some writing. As of October, 1992, I became the newsletter's writer and editor. This book is the culmination of my efforts. (As for Beer Across America, they've grown to more than 100,000 members as of press time and seem to be growing exponentially.) It seems that a lot of people share my excitement and enthusiasm about discovering this world of microbrewed beer.

On a less personal note, an understanding of the microbrewing movement and of the exceptional products being made by these craft brewers is needed in order to fully appreciate this book.

This movement, favorably recognized as a renaissance, is purely grassroots. It is a consumer-generated response rather than a slickly produced, big-bucks effort foisted upon us by Madison Avenue marketing experts, though they are moving in on us quickly with nationally distributed, mass-produced and widely advertised brands masquerading as true microbrews.

The microbrewing movement is a backlash against the corporate giants in the industry, a classic David and Goliath confrontation. The Goliaths in the industry, producing millions of barrels of beer every year, are referred to alternately as national brewers, industrial brewers, and megabrewers. The role of David is played by the brewers who are producing less than two percent of the entire market. They are deferentially called microbrewers, craft brewers, pub brewers, and "boutique" brewers.

The maximum quantity of beer that a microbrewery could produce (and still be called a microbrewery) was originally considered to be 10,000 barrels per year. This arbitrarily chosen limit sufficed until the popularity of the industry grew, and some of the earliest microbrewers began to exceed that threshold. Brewers' associations quickly raised the limit to 15,000 barrels, which was just as quickly surpassed by the more prolific brewers. As a few very popular craft brewers continue to expand and distribute their product on a national scale, barrelage in some cases is pushing 50,000 annually. While the upper echelon of the microbrewers continue to break barriers, the vast majority of them still produce under 5,000 barrels each year and maintain the traditional emphasis on local consumption.

Presently, no one speaks in absolutes regarding the amount of beer a brewer can produce and still be considered a microbrewery, and numbers are becoming less of an issue. Far more important than the quantity produced by these craft brewers is the quality of their product. These passionate gourmets and artisans have returned to the Old World ways of producing small batches of pure, fresh, distinctive, and flavorful beers. They have truly created their own renaissance.

Beer Across America: A Regional Guide to Brewpubs and Microbreweries, is a celebration of this renaissance.

For those so inclined, it will provide an excellent springboard for a beer education, but the highly technical aspects of beer and brewing have been downplayed in favor of writing something that the reader will simply find fun and interesting to read. I hope that I have succeeded in that.

Cheers!

— Marty Nachel

Reader Take Note

The lists of selected microbreweries — both craft brewers and brewpubs — include those registered at press time with the Association of Brewers. While every effort was made to make the list as complete and accurate as possible, the microbrewing industry is in a constant state of flux.

Names can change, breweries may come and go, and there is the strong likelihood that the listing of beers produced will change considerably. Because this is the nature of the industry, it is strongly recommended that you call in advance of any visit.

ACKNOWLEDGMENTS

No labor of love is complete without acknowledging those who labored or loved enough to make it all possible. My sincere thanks go to the mastermind of this project, book producer Steve Ettlinger, and his staff of one, Jamie Winnick, who kept this train on track and on time; the good people at Storey Communications for their great support and enthusiasm, especially Pam Art, Amanda Haar, and Pamela Lappies; Todd Holmes and Louis Amoroso, for creating big opportunities; Stan Galloway, George Akin, and Pat Wheeler at the American Breweriana Association Beer Label Exchange; Michael Jackson for bringing the world of beer into my living room; Steve Johnson for continued support; Cupric Rotondo for continual inspiration; and Kristi Boss — a neighbor, a friend, and a trusted assistant when needed.

Last but not least, a big thank you to my wife and copilot, Patti, who has spent more time than she cares to remember on family vacations searching out little known breweries, pubs, and liquor stores. She never believed that I would make a career of it.

INTRODUCTION

How To Use This Book

This book is designed as a guide. The serious beer lover wishing to visit the hundreds of brewery locations across the country will be well served. So will the millions of armchair travelers who won't be leaving the comforts of home (indeed, many of the beers listed are distributed widely, thanks to savvy storekeepers, and, of course, the mail order business called Beer Across America). Finally, this book should answer all those questions about beer that are bound to arise when someone begins exploring the fascinating world of microbrewed beer for the first time.

Included in the guide is a section of background information on beer basics (About Beer), which newcomers to the beer world should read first. Features on various aspects of microbrewed beer are found throughout the book and cover such interesting aspects as pairing beer with food, beer glassware, and beer names, among others.

Profiles of intriguing breweries and brewers are found in each regional section, along with the listings of breweries, brewpubs, and festivals found in that region. These are, of course, subject to much change, and readers should phone breweries prior to visiting them; local chambers of commerce should be able to provide information about festival dates and places. This book is a virtual compendium of information providing readers with an insider's view of the craft brewing industry, whether or not they travel. The 50 or so breweries profiled were chosen by simple but important criteria: regionality, stylistic diversity, relevance and/or influence on the industry, and, above all else, the quality of their products. The beer personalities who are profiled were, likewise, chosen for their individual contributions and influence on the industry. While some may, indeed, be the biggest and/or best in the field, my goal was to present a cross section of modern microbrewing, not a collection of reviews or ratings. (That's the reader's job!)

How This Book Is Organized

The guide has been arranged by region, consisting of four semi-longitudinal divisions of the United States. While these may, in some cases, reflect established time zones, that was not the intent. In fact, we added a fifth, composite region for the nationally and regionally distributed contract brews that are not necessarily considered microbrews but share many of the same characteristics.

Part 1

ABOUT BEER

Beer Styles

I t's time to define this beverage we call beer. Simply put, *beer* is a generic term used to describe any beverage fermented with cereal grain. All beers fall into two categories. They are either ales or lagers. The difference between them is the yeast used to ferment the beer, and the ambient temperature ranges of their fermentation, which result in slightly different tastes. *Ale* is the top-fermenting variety and is fermented at warm temperatures. *Lager* is the genetically engineered, bottom-fermenting variety and is fermented at cold temperatures. Just as wines can be classified simply as reds and whites, so, too, can beer. The lager category is the equivalent of white wine: generally lighter in body and color, with a narrower flavor profile that tends to appeal to a wider audience. The ale category is the red equivalent: darker, rounder, more complex and more expressive, appealing to a more experienced palate.

All of the world's approximately 30 recognizable brewing styles fall more or less into these two categories. The following is a list of the most frequently reproduced styles. Included is a description of each style and its accepted parameters. Bear in

mind that handcrafted brews are subject to regional variations and certainly to individual interpretations, no matter how traditional and ancient the recipe.

Barleywine

The term *barleywine* sounds contradictory, in that there is no relationship between barley, which is a grain, and wine, which is made from grapes. So what gives? The name is meant to imply a beverage made from barley that has the strength and character of wine. This brewing style, though obscure, is enjoying a resurgence in the microbrewing industry.

Barleywine is a classic English style of old ale. With its huge body, almost overwhelming malty flavor, and with the kick of a mule, barleywine is not for the weak-kneed. These complex and alcoholic brews pack a one-two punch of flavor and strength. The high level of fermentable sugars, creating a high density, or *gravity,* is responsible for this combination.

The color range for barleywine starts at amber and works its way to browns and reds. The nose (the combination of fragrances, aroma, and bouquet) is pungent:

an olfactory cornucopia of fruit and malt, ethanol (alcohol), and hops. In order to properly balance the bold, malty character, copious amounts of hop bitterness are required, which may further intimidate the novice beer drinker. The finish, or aftertaste, is always long, complex, and warming in the throat.

Bitter

English bitter can be respectfully considered an "everyman's" beer. It is a simple, consumer-friendly style that was betrayed by the name given it centuries ago, with the advent of hop usage in the British Isles.

Bitter is a low gravity, highly attenuated pale ale that is carbonated without the aid of injected carbon dioxide. It is traditionally drawn by hand pumps from wooden casks, rather than pushed with inert gasses from metal kegs. This "all natural" concept became the battleground on which the recent British beer revolution was fought.

Ordinary bitter is at the lowest end of the gravity scale, followed by special bitter and extra special bitter. All three substyles utilize the same basic ingredients, allowing for graduated increases in grain and corresponding hop ratios. Bitters run the color spectrum from gold to burnished copper. Hop bitterness ranges from subdued to aggressive, but always in appropriate balance with the malt. The flavor profile of the malt is fairly complex, allowing for additional fermentation characteristics such as fruitiness and diacetyl (a volatile yeast compound characterized by

a buttery or butterscotchlike aroma and taste). The extra special bitter is particularly robust and complex, finishing with ample alcohol content.

Bock Beer

The northern German city of Einbeck was the first center of commercial brewing in the thirteenth century. Beer from Einbeck became known as "beck beer" (no relation to Beck's beer). At that time, beck beer was famous throughout the Hanseatic League, those cities that openly traded on the North and Baltic Seas. But it was completely unknown in the south of Germany. The eventual introduction took place several hundred years later, in the early 1600s, at the wedding of the Duke of Brunswick to the daughter of a wealthy aristocrat from the south. The wedding was in Bavaria and was attended by nobility from distant states. The beer style from the north was embraced by the Bavarians and was adopted as the beer of choice in the state-commissioned Hofbrauhaus in Munich. It soon became known as "bock" beer — a corruption of "beck" in the Bavarian accent.

Bavarians like to downplay the Einbeck connection in favor of local versions of the beer's origin. *Bock* means billygoat, which is the symbol of the astrological sign Capricorn (December 22–January 19). This is the time when brewers start making bock beer. Another version of the bock beer story uses the goat as the symbol of fertility. (Contrary to a well-known and often-repeated rumor, bock beer is not what is cleaned out of the bottom of the vat once a year!)

The bock style is a medium- to full-bodied lager; very malty, with chocolaty, dark grain flavors. It has a creamy mouthfeel, and the finish is lengthy and malty sweet. Hop bitterness is subdued; just enough to cut the cloying character of the malt. The color can run the spectrum from deep burnt orange to mahogany. A true German bock beer must have a minimum alcohol content of 6.5 percent in order to be called a bock beer.

The style's popularity has inspired many derivations:

Helles bock: A pale version of regular bock. The difference is the deletion of the chocolate grain, which, in essence, removes the chocolate flavors and most of the dark color.

Maibock (May bock): This style is brewed for consumption in the month of May. It is basically a helles bock with a more pronounced hop character in the aroma and on the palate. Some brands are even *dry-hopped* for added bouquet. *Dry-hopping* is a method of imbuing the beer with a fresh hop aroma (without the bitterness) by adding hops directly to the beer while in the aging tank or barrel, instead of during the boiling process as is usually done.

Weizenbock: A regular bock beer that has a portion of its malted barley replaced by a portion of malted wheat; usually not exceeding 25 to 40 percent of the total amount of grain.

Eisbock: Long before today's North American brewers jumped on the ice beer bandwagon, German brewers were producing an eisbock. The method of partially freezing the beer and straining out the ice crystals leaves behind a maltier, more alcoholic product. This process has been in use in Germany since the dawn of artificial refrigeration.

Doppelbock (double bock): This name refers to the doubling of ingredients for a more intense taste and higher achohol content (8.5 to 9 percent). (The most intrepid brewers offer the difficult-to-brew triple bock that is made with stronger yeasts and aged longer than usual, which packs a 17 percent alcohol content wallop.) Oddly enough, it was a religious order of Italian monks who introduced this style of bock beer. The Order of St. Francis of Paula, cloistered high in the Bavarian Alps, developed this distinctive brew. They named this high-test double bock "Salvator," in honor of the Savior; thus, Paulaner Salvator was born. In reverence to the original, all subsequent German doppelbocks have been given names that end in "-ator". American microbrewers continue the tradition of using the "-ator" suffix, making doppelbocks easy to spot on the menu.

Brown Ale

Brown ale is a close relative of pale ale. Aside from the obvious color difference, brown ales are slightly maltier than the pale ales but are less aggressively hopped. The water used for brewing traditional brown ale is chalky, and this hardness in the water tends to accentuate the hop's bitter qualities.

Brown ales are relatively low-gravity beers that yield low alcohol content after quick fermentations. Chocolate malt is used to impart the brown color and chocolaty palate. Some brewers add small quantities of molasses or brown sugar to lend other flavor and aroma nuances. The nose may also hint of fruit and toffeelike aromas.

The brown ale category includes a substyle known as English mild. This working class favorite, though made with the same principal ingredients, is of even lower gravity, lower alcohol and lower carbonic content, making it the perfect session beer (see glossary) that it is.

Once again, Americans have taken a foreign beer style and adapted it to local tastes. The American rendition of brown ale maintains similar color and gravity profiles, but it is dryish rather than sweet and has far more hop presence in both the aroma and taste.

Flanders Brown Beer

Flanders, with its stretch of coastline on the North Sea, is the westernmost region of Belgium. It has a rich brewing tradition, and its breweries produce beers unlike anything brewed anywhere else.

Reddish-brown in color, Flanders beers are noted for being complex, with an assertive sour character. The beer's complexity comes from its grain content, which includes four distinct types of malted grain and an addition of corn grits. The ale's tartness is derived from indigenous yeast strains and an extended aging process. The yeast has been identified as a combination of 20 different strains. After a primary and secondary fermentation in metal tanks, the beer is further aged from 18 to 24 months in uncoated oak tuns. It is during this stage that the beer's distinctive, acetic character is created.

Fruit Beer

Surprising though it may seem, beer and fruit do make a good match and their harmonious relationship is nothing new. While some beer styles invite the imbiber to put fruit slices, juices, or syrups into their beer just prior to drinking, a real fruit beer is one in which the fruit is added long before the beer leaves the brewery.

Fruit beer is not a common style because making it can be a real pain in the mash! To begin with, fresh fruits can not be boiled with the rest of the beer, because boiling can cause the fruit to release *pectin*, a carbohydrate which yields a gel. If this pectin "sets," or congeals, it creates a cloudy beer that is difficult to clarify. On the other hand, if the fruit is not heated in some way, there is the risk of contamination from the natural bacteria that reside in or on the fruit. One way to produce fruit beer without the headaches is to use fruit extracts instead of the real thing. This is a more sensible and relatively risk-free method of making fruit beer. Most craft-brewed fruit beers are found on tap rather than in bottles, since they are still somewhat of an anomaly to regular beer consumers.

The Belgians are widely recognized as the masters of brewing fruit beers. The spontaneously fermented lambic beers from the Senne River Valley have macerated fruit sitting in the aging vessels along with the fermenting beer. These beers undergo a long secondary fermentation and are aged a full two years before being bottled — certainly not a viable option for small brewers with limited tankage.

German Ales

Recognized as the world leaders in the production of lager beers, it is hard to imagine German brewers creating indigenous ale styles. Neither single yeast cell isolation nor artificial refrigeration were at anyone's disposal in the early days of brewing, so brewers were left to work with what they had: top-fermenting yeast strains.

One of these ale styles is known as *altbier*. The style is strongly associated with the city of Dusseldorf, though it also has lesser ties to Munster and Dortmund. The word "alt," contrary to popular belief, does not mean ale, but rather "old," a reference to Old World brewing styles.

As is common to ale styles, modern day altbiers are fermented warm, but they are aged cold like lager beer. The altbier profile is deep amber to copper in color, light- to medium-bodied, with an assertive palate and somewhat aggressive hop levels. The hop mix is complex and differs from one brewery to the next. German hop varieties such as Hallertau, Tettnang, and Spalt are usual, but American domestic varieties like Perle or Northern Brewer will suffice.

The second and even lesser known German ale is *Kölschbier*, pronounced "kelsh." The name is a controlled appellation. Kölsch is a derivation of the city of Köln (in French, "Cologne"). The name is only used commercially for beers of this

Cooking with Beer

In the past, chefs and gourmands have rarely used beer in the preparation of food. These days though, food preparers everywhere are discovering the joy of cooking with beer. Just about anywhere water or wine is called for in a recipe, beer can be used as a substitute. This is particularly true in the preparation of sauces, marinades, soups, and gravies. Professional and domestic cooks alike are finding the quality and variety of microbrewed beer a welcome addition to their kitchens. Beer has now found a place of favor among other ingredients used to enhance food.

Most of the foods that are prepared with beer are fairly unsophisticated, but beer, by its mere presence, can lend a touch of sophistication. Brewpub chefs are finding new and interesting ways of incorporating their house brews into their food, with menu items as eclectic as the beers themselves. (One example, a beer vinaigrette salad dressing, is served in a midwestern brewpub.)

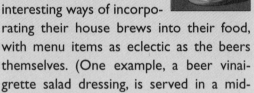

Despite its elevated presence in brewpub cuisine, beer still lends itself best to simple, basic food. This includes that ever-present staple, beer batter on fish, shrimp, and sundry seafood items; beer-cheese soups; chili with stout; beer bread; ale gravy; baked beans with beer; and the perennial favorite, bratwurst boiled in a mixture of beer and onions.

style brewed in Cologne by members of the Köln Brewer's Union. This ensures that only members of the Köln Brewer's Union may produce and market a Kölschbier.

The appearance of the beer is noticeably pale and slightly hazy, due partly to the addition of wheat, but mostly to the fact that the beer is unfiltered. Kölschbier is clean on the palate, with a slight lactic character. It is low in gravity and alcohol content. Hop bitterness is fairly high, and the overall profile is that of a refreshing, summery-type beer. Citizens of Köln proudly swear by its qualities as a digestive aid.

Altbiers and Kölschbiers are few and far between, but American microbrewers now reintroducing these German ales are finding an enthusiastic audience for them.

Munchener Helles

The original pale lager beer was brewed in Munich in 1928, the year that the famous Paulaner Brewery introduced a helles (pale) lager, known as Munchener helles (or Munich pale). This style is meant to be imbibed as an everyday libation. It is quaffed (or guzzled!) by the liter throughout Bavaria.

Munchener helles, sometimes referred to as "continental lager," is pale yellow to brilliant gold in color and light- to medium-bodied. The accent is on the maltiness with just enough hop bitterness extracted from "noble" hop varieties (see glossary) to balance the malt. The downplayed hop character is the principal difference between pale lager and Pilsner, and one to look out for when buying American microbrews.

Munchener Dunkel

The classification alone seems to cause fear and trepidation among thousands of American beer drinkers. "Dunkel," or "dark," has always been synonymous with "sinister," "menacing," and other foreboding adjectives. This simple beer style has been unjustly warded off by the psychological silver crosses: ignorance and misinformation.

Dark beer is merely a lager beer that has an additional roasted malt thrown in to add complexity to the aroma and palate. These dark versions of the Munich helles style tend to be somewhat sweeter and only marginally heavier on the palate. Most of the style's reputation as being heavy and strong is exaggerated. Confusion reigns when any malt beverage is branded a dark beer.

Ironically, the original Munchener beers were fairly dark until the introduction of helles lager in 1928. Due to its popularity, many other Bavarian brewers began making helles lager, thus making the dunkel style even less popular. There is also another style of dark beer virtually unheard of here in the United States, called *schwarzbier* (black beer), which is basically a dark Pilsner (see page 10). This style is associated with the Kulmbach region of Germany.

Most European dark beers imported to the United States fall more or less in between these styles and cater to mass market appeal. European darks and big brewery domestic dark beers generally are produced in smaller quantities because of the belief that most American beer drinkers are still afraid of the dark!

Oktoberfest

Oktoberfest beer is an offshoot of another lager style known as *Märzen* or *Märzenbier,* a fairly heavy, malty style brewed in the spring and named for the month of March ("Marz" in German). Before artificial refrigeration, it was often the last batch of beer brewed before the warm summer months, when brewing was ill-advised. It was a higher gravity beer than the "regular" beer, which was brewed throughout the rest of the year, stored in caves, and consumed throughout the summer. All of the beer left in storage at harvest time (the beginning of the new brewing season) was hauled out and consumed ceremoniously.

There was already a party atmosphere rooted in the Oktoberfest celebration, but in 1810 it took on a more reverent slant. In late September of that year, Bavaria's crown prince was married to Theresa Von Sachsen-Hildburghausen, a public event that happened to coincide with the rollout of the stores of Märzenbier. Munich and its citizenry so enjoyed the statewide celebration that all agreed to commemorate the nuptial feast and its pageantry annually. More than a million people attend the event every year. It is held on the *Theresienwiese* (Theresa's meadow), so named for the royal bride.

Today, Munich's Oktoberfest begins on a Saturday in mid-September with the Lord Mayor's proclamation, *"O'zapft ist!"* (It is tapped!) as he taps the ceremonial first keg of beer. The festival lasts 16 days and ends on the first Sunday in October.

Oktoberfest beer traditionally is copper-orange in color, with a dense, white head.

The nose is very malty with low hop aroma and no fruity esters or buttery compounds (see glossary). The round, malty palate is medium-full bodied with a creamy mouth-feel. Hop bitterness is low — just enough to cut the malty sweetness which lasts well into the finish.

Pale Ale

This style of beer was developed in the 1700s because pale malt, which is needed to brew a pale ale, was difficult to produce prior to that time. The parameters of the style are fairly loose, allowing for a generous range of color and a fair fluctuation in gravities. Two things are certain: fruity esters in the nose and a big hop presence in both the flavor and the aroma. In fact, hops are the key to developing a good pale ale. The classic pale ale uses a hop from England known as Kent goldings, but Northern Brewer, Galena, or Brewer's gold varieties are perfectly acceptable. Pale ales are often dry-hopped. They usually have a medium body and low-to-medium maltiness, and alcohol should not be obvious in the flavor or the sensation.

There is one particular style of pale ale known as *India pale ale* (I.P.A. for short). The beer derives its name from Britain's colonialism of India during the 1800s. British royal subjects living in India demanded their favorite ales be shipped to them, but the month-long journey on the open sea could prove devastating to the average cask of beer. A British brewer named Hodgson recognized this problem and decided to brew an ale of greater strength in order to withstand the rigors of oceanic transit. The antiseptic properties of the increased alcohol volume, coupled with a high concentration of hop acids, assured the colonialists of a palatable product at journey's end. A surprising dividend was realized also, upon receipt of the beer. The gentle, rocking motion of the ship on water caused the beer within the casks to pick up some of the oaky character of the barrels, much like red wine. Some brewers today maintain that link with the past by using oak barrels for the aging process.

Brew Pub Poets Society

During the Depression era, a literary luncheon group met at New York's Algonquin Hotel. The diverse group of writers included Dorothy Parker, Robert Benchley, George Kaufman, and Harold Ross. This group, known for its incisive wit and snappy repartee, became the celebrated Algonquin Round Table.

Fostering a 1990s style of wit and wisdom, the Brew Pub Poets Society of Charlotte, North Carolina, is a modern-day Round Table — on a beer budget. The idea for the Brew Pub Poets Society was conceived, appropriately enough, over a couple of late night beers at the Dilworth Brewing Company in August, 1991. Founders Jack Dillard and Bruce Hensley were lamenting the lack of a creative outlet in Charlotte. The Dilworth Brewery was receptive to the idea of hosting this prospective group of local wits, and, by September, a list of 70 interested individuals had been compiled. The only requirement for membership was the composition of an original poem about beer and/or its associated pleasures, to be recited at a monthly club meeting.

The kindred spirits who form the Brew Pub Poets Society are an eclectic group, both male and female. Among their ranks are a sportswriter, a radio DJ, a sound engineer, an editor, a publisher, a humor columnist, a movie critic, several copywriters, public relations publicists, local TV personalities, a couple of actors, a designer, and an assortment of others. Now numbering more than 100, members in good standing are considered members for life.

The "BPPS" commits all original works (now numbering in the hundreds) to the club archives for safekeeping. They have published a short compilation of their best pub poetry, *Once Upon a Frothy Brew,* which was released in the spring of 1993 and was two years in the making. This tome contains at least one verse from 20 different members and multiple contributions from some of the club's more prolific beer bards. There are parody poems, haiku verses, a limerick, an ode, a tribute poem, an anniversary poem, and other surprises. A future volume of pub poetry promises to highlight the best of the rest.

In addition to continued monthly meetings and a second book, the Brew Pub Poets Society plans to take their act on the road. The first stop will be the Great American Beer Festival in Denver, where members hope to provide entertainment to a captive (and hopefully captivated) beer-loving audience.

If you are a poet but are loath to
    show it,
to hell with all propriety,
just pen some curses in
    metered verses
and send to the Pub Poets Society!

Pilsner Beer

This style, more than any other, is what most Americans think of when the subject turns to beer. Small wonder. Most major breweries in the world produce something akin to this style. Unfortunately, most pay the original no homage.

The original Pilsner beer (still the standard bearer in the industry) is from the town of Plzen in the Czech Republic. The name, Pilsner Urquell, makes note of the fact that it is the original; urquell means "original source." The Pilsner name in all its many forms — Pils, Pilsner, Pilsener, Plzensky — comes from the Bohemian town where the brewery was built in 1842. The golden-colored, bottom-fermented lager brewed there quickly became popular in Europe, and, eventually, all over the world.

The style is golden, malty, and well-hopped. The bouquet has the unmistakable kiss of the Saaz hop from the Zatec region in Bohemia. Caramel notes are often observed as is a hint of diacetyl, rounding out the sweetness and mouthfeel. One key ingredient in a real Pilsner beer is the extremely soft water, similar to that which is pumped from the aquifers under the Urquell Brewery.

Many breweries in Germany have adopted the Pilsner style of beer. Although close to the Czechoslovakian exemplar, the German Pils has a narrower taste profile: cleaner, crisper, lighter in color, with less body and sweetness. Bitburger Pils is one of the finest examples of the Germans' adaptation of this style.

Sadly, the American industrial brew-eries have diluted the style almost beyond recognition. The flagship brands of Anheuser-Busch, Coors, Stroh's, Miller, and lesser known brands are nothing but innocuous and unimpressive imitations of the original Pilsner beer.

Porter

Porter is a style that has been "rescued" by the American microbrewing industry. Prior to the resurgence of microbreweries, it was virtually extinct in this country and had diminished considerably in its homeland, the United Kingdom.

The name *porter* comes from the porters at London's Victoria Station, who were known to consume large quantities of this beer. Technically, it did not exist as a single style. The porters ordered portions of several different beers, which were mixed together in the same drinking glass. This concoction became known as "entire." One enterprising brewer marketed a beer that closely approximated this mix of brews, and the name "porter" was used to identify it.

Today, there are two basic styles of porter: brown and robust. The robust version is a cousin of stout, very dark, but not opaque. It often takes on a reddish appearance in the presence of light. Dark grain aromas dominate the nose. Robust porter is medium- to full-bodied with an alcohol content that ranges between 5 and 7 percent. The most noticeable characteristic is the dark grain flavors derived from the chocolate malt and/or black malts in the grist. Hop bitterness, combined with mild grain astringency, balance the sweetness of the crystal malt.

Brown porter is a meeker version of its big brother; body and color are lighter, though still maintaining a minimized dark grain flavor and hue. Both the malty sweetness and hop bitterness are downplayed, lowering the resulting alcohol to between 4 and 6 percent, which makes this more of a *session* beer, a light-bodied, low alcohol beer. Generally speaking, American microbrewers favor the robust style of porter while the brown porter remains the forte of the British brewers.

Rauchbier

Where there's smoke there's . . . beer? There is — in the city of Bamberg, Germany. This Franconian town, in north Bavaria, is famous for its *rauchbier,* or smoked beer. This style, while very popular in this region, is rarely seen elsewhere in the world. Many beers are said to be an acquired taste, but none is so aptly described as rauchbier.

A beer gets its smoked character when a brewer kilns the malt over a wood fire, usually beechwood. The grain retains the smoky flavor and imparts this quality to the beer, when the grain is mashed. How smoky the beer will be depends both on how long the malt is allowed to smoke, and how much of the grain bill is comprised of smoked malt. The smoked character of the beer varies from one brewer to the next, but it is always noticeable and often assertive.

If you could clear away the smoke, the underlying beer is similar in style to an Oktoberfest. The color ranges from coppery orange to amber-brown, depending on the degree of kilning of the malt. Like Oktoberfest beer, the accent is on the malty sweetness — both the hop aroma and bitterness is subdued. The trick to making a good rauchbier is achieving the perfect balance between the malt and the smoke.

Any beer style can be given a smoky character, but some styles are better suited to it than others. The flavor profile of the underlying beer should always show through the smoke. Porter is one style in particular that lends itself to a smoky aroma and taste. The Alaskan Brewing Company in Juneau has won numerous awards for its smoked porter, and produces one of the few commercially bottled examples of this style.

One German brewer, Rauchenfels, has perfected a very different method of creating a smoked beer. By heating stones over a very hot fire, then dropping them into the boiling wort, the brewer achieves two objectives. First, the stones impart a smoky character to the brew. Second, the superheated stones carmelize the wort as they are dropped in the kettle. These stones, with their coating of carmelized malt sugars, are then placed in the fermenters where the carmel flavors are imparted into the beer. This is how Rauchenfels *steinbiere* (stone beer) is created.

Red Beer

Rojo, rouge, rot. They all mean red. It's too bad color is the whole basis for this style, which actually is no style at all. Red beer, as it is presently made and marketed, is nothing more than a couple of extra grains of malt and a lot of marketing hype.

The only true red beer is the burgundy-colored Belgian Flanders red beer. Rodenbach and Rodenbach Grand Cru, brewed in Roeselare, are the standard-bearers for this style. These beers' sharply sour palate is derived from a lactic fermentation which can last as long as two years. The red cast of the beer is a result either of the use of Vienna malts, or the aging of the beer, which takes place in uncoated oak tuns. Unquestionably, there is no relation whatsoever between this style and the style that American brewers are disgorging from their brew kettles.

Vienna-style lager, which originated long ago in that Austrian city, may also have sown the seeds for the hype surrounding red beer. When the new generation of pale beers — both the Pilsner style and the pale ale style — were introduced, the beer-drinking public preferred the bright, golden-colored beers over these old amber beers with the red tinges. One of the last survivors of this style is the Mexican-made Dos Equis.

Why did American brewers decide to create a new style? It had a lot to do with the success of Killian's Red, made by Coors. The Coors Brewing Company bought the rights to the name of George Killian's Red Ale of Ireland, and promoted the brand heavily here in the United States. Unfortunately, Coors' version of Killian's is a lifeless interpretation of the big, bountiful, malty ale produced on the Auld Sod (notice that Coors dropped the word ale from the name). Today, all a brew-er has to do is add an extra scoop of Vienna or caramel malt to his brew and slap a "red" label on his packaging.

Scottish Ale and Scotch Ale

These are two distinct beer styles that often are thought to be one and the same. Because there are so few examples of either in the marketplace, their scarcity adds to the confusion.

Scottish ale is the Caledonian equivalent of English ale. The main differences are that Scottish ales are generally darker, maltier, and softer on the palate. The low hopping rates contribute to this soft, malty character. The cause of the darker appearance is the inclusion of small amounts of roasted barley not found in English ales. Low levels of carbonation are also an important characteristic and help to maintain the aforementioned softness.

The Scots have a unique system of classifying their ales. The antiquated *shilling* designation is a throwback to a time when beer was taxed according to its gravity and strength. The Scottish light is called 60 shilling, Scottish heavy is 70 shilling, and the even stronger Scottish export is referred to as 80 shilling. When in a Highland pub, one orders a beer by its shilling designation.

Scotch (Scots) ale is traditionally known as a *wee heavy*, and, like the Scottish ales, is categorized by shillings. Due to the higher gravities, the corresponding numbers are greater. Scotch ales usually start at 90 shilling and can go as high as 120 shilling. These strong ales share the same flavor characteristics as the Scottish ales, but to an exaggerated degree. Scotch ales typically are overwhelmingly malty, almost to the point of cloyingly sweet, and the low hopping rates do little to cut the intense maltiness. Regrettably, the lack of protective hop resins also tends to diminish the brew's shelf life, leaving only the alcohol to fend off the inevitable stale, off flavors. Scotch ale often is roused during the fermentation process to keep the yeast active. This results in relatively low final gravities and alcohol potentials as high as 8 percent by volume.

Although Scotland is famous for some of the world's finest Scotch whisky, the only correlation between the beer and the whisky is their country of origin.

Steam Beer

Steam beer has long been a brewing tradition in Great Britain. The name comes from the inevitable hiss that emanated from the barrels of warm beer when they were tapped. The Germans developed a similar style called *dampfbier*, which translated literally is *steam beer*. In early twentieth-century America, the style varied considerably from one brewery to the next, and was known by several names: swankey, small beer, and common.

The United States brewery that revived the style and developed the modern recipe also trademarked the name. This makes for some confusion. The Anchor Brewing Company of San Francisco registered the steam beer designation as its own, and the style is now known simply as California common, or Cal-com, beer.

One of the most obvious identifiable features of steam beer is its hybrid style. While ales use a top-fermenting yeast and ferment at warm temperatures, Cal-com beers are fermented warm, but use lager yeasts designed for cold fermentation. Why the "against-the-grain" approach? Artificial refrigeration was not in widespread use on the West Coast when this style was developed. The new German lager yeast was abundant and less contaminated with the bacteria that reside in ale yeast cultures. High-hopping rates were also used to combat spoilage and delay its unpleasant effects on beer.

Today, there are few legitimate examples of this style, although many other beers have similar profiles. All-malt amber ales and lagers that have a percentage of caramel malt in the *mash* (the porridgelike substance consisting of grain and water, which is created in the early stages of the brewing process) will simulate the palate. Hop bitterness achieved with the use of the Northern Brewer variety of hop, along with a pungent hop bouquet, will closely resemble the hop profile of this style.

Stout Beer

Stout. Most people think immediately of Guinness when they see that word, which is perfectly understandable, seeing that Guinness Stout is the best-selling example of the style, worldwide. It is, more correctly, just one of the stout styles. Guinness's version is known as an Irish-style stout, and not just because it originated in Dublin. The Irish-style stout is drier than its English counterpart (known as London style), which is a sweeter stout. While there are many similarities between the two, the principal difference is how their roasted character is achieved. The Irish dry stout is defined by the roastiness of the unmalted roasted barley, while the sweet London stout uses chocolate malt in its place. Aside from the obvious contrast between the stouts' sweet and dry character, the London style has a creamier texture — a slightly higher gravity and sweetness across the palate — that is the result of the use of milk sugar (lactose), which is unfermentable. In rare instances, this style is also referred to as milk stout.

Both of these stout styles share common ingredients such as the highly-kilned black patent malt, used for its coloring and its bitter, almost charred, grain flavor. Top-fermenting ale yeasts are also used by brewers of both styles.

There is a rare style of stout strongly associated with pre-Bolshevik Russia.

British brewers found favor among the czars of Russia, particularly for their brand of stout. Unfortunately, the English-made stout did not travel well to St. Petersburg and other points east. To compensate for the short shelf life of their beer, the British brewers did as they had done for the India pale ale that had been shipped to Bombay and Calcutta. They raised the gravity and increased the hop content. This complex brew, with resulting high alcohol, was greatly admired by the Russian rulers. The style has since come to be known as Russian stout, imperial stout, or Russian imperial stout.

There are devotees of all the stout styles, but they are small in number, particularly here in the United States. The coffeelike, roasty character of stout is an acquired taste that average beer drinkers haven't attained, which is quite understandable for those who quaff beer to sate a thirst; stout is no thirst quencher. It is, in fact, the "steak and potatoes" of the beer world.

Trappist/Abbey Beer

The word *Trappist* does not so much denote a type of beer as it does a type of brewery. A Trappist beer can only be made at one of six Trappist Abbey breweries in Europe. There are five in Belgium and one in the Netherlands. Any brewer wishing to market a version of one of these breweries' products must use the term "Abbey beer," because the Trappist name is a *controlled appellation* — the exclusive domain of a town or region — much the same as Champagne and Bordeaux are in France.

While the beers made by these Cistercian monks vary in style, there are common qualities about them. They all feature high gravities, warm fermentation, a rare type of top-fermenting yeast propagated at the abbeys, and bottle conditioning. Some brewers add candy sugar during the boiling process. The high fermentation temperatures produce a full range of fruity and buttery aromas and flavors.

Some abbeys produce ales of three graduated strengths. The *single,* usually made for the monks' personal consumption; the dark *dubbel,* a stronger version of the single; and the golden *trippel,* the most potent.

With regard to microbrewed abbey beers, since much of the Trappist beers' character is a result of their indigenous yeast, it is necessary for the microbrewer to obtain these strains in order to replicate the style properly. Only some are succeeding.

Wassail

Wassail is a traditional style of spiced ale that is brewed for the holiday season (Thanksgiving through New Year's). It is also referred to as holiday beer, yule ale, winter warmer, and, if fruit is contained, mulled ale.

The word *wassail* (rhymes with *fossil),* comes from the Old English *waes hael* — *be hale* or *be whole* — both of which mean *be of good health,* a proper toast in those days. The drink of choice was usually mulled ale, a strong ale laden with spices and sweetened with sugar or pieces of

Specialty Beers

This ambiguous grouping of beers really can't be considered a singular style since there are no parameters for the brewer to follow, and that is precisely the attraction. Asking a brewer to create a specialty beer is like giving a kid the keys to the funhouse.

Concocting a specialty beer allows wide latitude in terms of ingredients. The underlying beer is usually very simple. It is the choice of specialty ingredients that gives the beer its individuality. While smoked beers and fruit beers qualify as specialty beers, this is an amalgam of all the rest.

The simple act of using unusual grains like millet or rye in a brew can constitute a specialty beer. Different natural fermentables (other sources of sugars for the yeast to eat) such as honey, molasses, brown sugar, maple syrup, and sorghum, are always a popular detour. Brewer's chocolate and brewer's licorice can also create uniquely flavored beers. Don't count out the possibility of using starchy vegetables as fermentable additives. Potatoes, yams, and pumpkins have also been used to create different-tasting beers.

The use of herbs in beer provide the brewer with an almost unlimited array of choices. Coriander seems to be very popular these days. So is ginger. Don't be surprised to find out that your favorite beer contains anise, allspice, lemongrass, cumin, cardamom, or mint. One of the most popular specialty beers in today's market — Chili Beer — contains a hot pepper floating in the bottle!

fruit. The spices used were nutmeg and ginger, while the fruit was usually roasted crab apple. The concoction was warmed by the fire before being served in a bowl, which came to be known as the wassail bowl and was traditionally cut from the wood of the maple tree.

These pagan practices eventually became an accepted part of Christian ritual. Merry groups of revellers (made all the merrier by the ale nog) would visit the houses of friends and neighbors to sing carols of the season. This came to be known as "wassailing."

What started centuries ago as a simple toast to good health became the beverage we drink, the bowl we drink from, and the ritual celebration itself.

Wheat Beer

Although we drink it year-round, summer is typically the season for *wheat beer*, a thirst-quenching ale that has become quite popular in the United States since the 1980s. Its popularity could be due to the 17-ounce bottles in which wheat beer is imported, or the vitamin-charged, yeasty sediment left in it. Or it could be due to its wheaty flavor and zesty effervescence. Some people just like drinking beer with a lemon in it! Whatever the reason, wheat beer is neither new nor unique.

Wheat beer in America is alternately known as *weizenbier* or *weissbier*. Of these two designations, *weizen* (meaning wheat) is the more correct; *weiss* actually means white. A traditional German weizenbier must use at least 50 percent malted wheat. The rest of the grist is malted barley.

Weizenbier clones made elsewhere use anywhere between 25 to 75 percent wheat malt, depending on the whims of the brewer. Traditional weizenbiers also have a dose of yeast added at bottling time for a secondary fermentation in the bottle. This is called *hefe-weizen,* or yeast-wheat. If you prefer a wheat beer without the yeast, a filtered *kristallklar* (crystal clear) weizenbier is also widely marketed.

As with other beer styles, there are variations on the wheat beer theme. There are *dunkelweizens* (dark wheat) and *wiezenbock* (wheat bock) beers. While those are pretty self-explanatory, Berliner Weisse is altogether different. Dubbed "the champagne of the Spree" by Napoleon, Berliner Wiesse is a pale, tart, and crisply effervescent beer of mild strength that makes the ultimate summer thirst quencher. The pronounced sour taste is the intended result of adding lactobacillus bacteria during fermentation. For those unaccustomed to this taste, Berliner Weisse may be ordered *mit schuss* — a dollop of raspberry syrup or essence of woodruff — to offset the beer's sharp acidity.

Witbier

Because witbier is rarely brewed anywhere except Belgium, it is a relatively unknown style in the United States and, therefore, underappreciated. However, there are a couple of microbreweries producing it here and its popularity is growing, if only in small circles.

Belgium is a linguistically divided nation, and this has created some confusion regarding this ale. In the French-speaking provinces it is called *biere blanche* and in the Flemish-speaking regions it is known as *witbier*. Both terms translate as "white beer." It is not actually white, but a very pale yellow, and is often cloudy (the cloudiness helps to create the white appearance). Both the paleness and the cloudiness can be partly attributed to the high percentage — 45 percent — of unmalted wheat that goes into the beer. The balance of the grist is barley malt.

This style is brewed in the Brabant town of Hoegaarden, which is known for its wheat beers. Although witbier is made with wheat, it is not referred to as a wheat beer because of the inclusion of such ingredients as rind of the bitter Curacao orange, the perfumey coriander seed, and another "secret" spice believed to be grain of Paradise (also known as alligator seed). The beer is generally hopped with the English Kent hop and Styrian variety of hop. After a relatively short and cool fermentation, the beer is given another dose of yeast, prior to being bottled for additional conditioning.

The Belgian product is never filtered or pasteurized, and the yeast remains in the bottle. Newer, American versions are similar, although they may undergo a flash pasteurization process before shipping. Witbier, when young, can be sharply refreshing. Even when aged, it makes a wonderful summer thirst quencher, even though it is soft on the palate.

How Beer is Made

In order to fully understand and appreciate the quality and diversity of the beers now being produced by the microbrewers, it helps to have a rudimentary knowledge of beer — the ingredients, equipment, and processes involved.

The Ingredients

At its most basic, beer is made from four principal ingredients: barley, hops, yeast, and water. These are the only allowable ingredients as stipulated by the *Reinheitsgebot,* or German Purity Law (see page 23). Each one of these ingredients plays an integral part in the brewing of beer.

Barley, a cereal grain, is essential to beer. Its natural sugars feed the yeast during the fermentation process. Before the barley can be used for brewing, it must undergo a malting process. In microbreweries, this is performed by a maltster, the person who supplies grain to the breweries. In the beginning of the malting process, the grain is moistened to start germination. During this time, the starchy insides of the kernel are transformed into complex, soluble, malt sugars

called *maltose.* The grain is then heated and dried with hot air to halt the germination process. Some of this grain also will be kilned (baked) in order to make the roasted malts needed for darker beer styles. Barley also gives the beer flavor, body, and the proteins essential for head retention.

Hops are the flowers of a viney plant called *humulus lupulus.* These flowers, which bear a great resemblance to small, green pine cones, are prized for their unique contribution to the flavor of beer. The minute, waxy lupulin glands rupture at high temperatures, releasing acids that account for the malt-balancing bitterness and an herbal hop flavor in the beer. Hops are also critical to the aromatic profile of the beer, lending a pungent floral or spicy character to the nose. In addition, additional acids and resins in the hops have been found to protect beer from microbial contamination, leading to a longer shelf life (see page 136). This discovery, centuries after hops were first used in brewing, was a welcome surprise to brewers.

Yeast is a voracious, single-cell organism with a renowned sweet tooth. Prior to the invention of the microscope, yeast was not even recognized as an ingredient in beer. The hard-working yeast is the catalyst of fermentation, consuming all the fermentable sugars. In return for its meal, yeast gives off alcohol and carbon dioxide. Yeasts are categorized simply as top-fermenting or bottom-fermenting. The former prefers to work in warm temperatures for short periods of time; the latter is designed to perform in cold temperatures over extended periods of time. All yeast types can work in a wide temperature range, though some work better under certain conditions. Lager and ale yeasts were genetically engineered to work best in cold temperatures.

Water is often overlooked by the consumer as a key element in making beer, but never by the brewer. Beer is more than 90 percent water. Modern technology allows today's brewers to alter and adjust acidity and alkalinity, and otherwise manipulate the water's makeup to suit their individual needs.

These, then, are the four primary ingredients in a Reinheitsgebot beer. There are many others that can be, and are, incorporated into the brewing process by intrepid craft brewers. The use of additional ingredients such as fruit flavorings or spices by no means dishonors the brewer or his beer. Breaking the confinements of the German Purity Law is an acceptable practice, as long as it is not done in an effort to cheapen the beer or defraud the consumer. Most microbrewers are very willing to disclose the contents of their products with pride.

The Equipment

Brewers are justifiably proud of their brewhouse equipment and their mastery over it. When showing it to visitors, they often run out of breath long before they run out of enthusiasm! Though brewing equipment for small brewhouses and pubs comes in all shapes and sizes and is made by an ever-increasing list of manufacturers, it all works toward a common goal: to make good beer.

A pub's brewing area, if it is within sight of the customer, is shielded behind panes of glass for several reasons. First, a brewhouse is a semi-sterile, "look, but don't touch" environment; even brewers don't needlessly touch or handle equipment. Second, a brewhouse is often located in cramped quarters, has wet floors, and has hoses the size of boa constrictors lying about the floor. In other words, it's a lawsuit waiting to happen.

Breweries generally are either divided by partitions into different rooms, or are comprised of multiple levels. Aside from the availability of space, there are several practical reasons for this. The milling room, where the grain is crushed, tends to be full of grain dust which, if not kept under control, can become an airborne contaminant. The brewhouse itself can be very hot and steamy, requiring a specialized ventilation system. The floor is perpetually wet, requiring troughs or large drains to draw off rinse water or spillage. The fermentation room and the aging cellars are kept at cool temperatures, and, of course, any packaged product has to be refrigerated separately.

The Brewing Process

There are seven steps in the brewing process: milling, mashing, boiling, cooling, fermenting, aging, and packaging.

Milling The first step in the process is the milling (crushing) of malted barley and most other grains. This is done with a grain mill with adjustable rollers. The idea is to break open the outer husk of the grain kernel to expose the inner endosperm, while being careful not to mill it into flour. It is then dumped into a large kettle called the *mash tun.*

Mashing In the mash tun, the milled grain is infused with the hot water that makes up the bulk of the beer. Through a series of rigid time and temperature controls, the heated water leeches the soluble malt sugars and proteins out of the grain, turning the mash into a thick, porridgelike soup called the *wort.* This unfermented beer is then drained in the mash tun through a screen called a *false bottom.* It is sparged with warm water to

A Bear of a Brew?

Wildlife is of great interest to craft brewers. Wild Goose and Wild Boar breweries have dedicated themselves to a particular animal, while others, such as the Mendocino Brewing Company and the Fish Brewing Company, have entire stables of beer named for birds and creatures of the sea. There are numerous references to nonhuman mammals and various feathered, finned, and furry animals: There is Bad Bear ale, Black Bear ale, and Bruin pale ale; Panther Tail ale, Alley Cat ale, and Cheshire Cat ale; Falcon pale ale, Condor lager, Meadowlark ale, and Red Rooster Beer; Orca pale ale, Blue Whale ale, and Red Shark ale. There's Sea Lion stout, Black Cow stout, Desert Bighorn stout, Bullfrog stout, and Rainbow Trout stout. There is Blind Pig dunkelweizen, Jack Rabbit pale ale, Copperhead pale ale, Woodchuck porter, and Killer Bee Honey ale. As if proof of dogs' status as man's best friend is in question, witness this kennel of beers: Bulldog stout, Black Dog bitter, Moon Dog ale, Rin Tin Tin brown ale, Ol' Yeller golden ale, Turbodog, Red Dawg, and Laughing Lab Scottish ale. There is a Doggie Style amber, but its canine connection is tenuous, at best. For whatever reason, three brewers have felt the need to entice us with such names as Duck's Breath Bitter Ale, Moose Juice Stout, and Dog Spit Stout — yum!

Speaking of stouts, check out these outlandish names: Hogsback, Dirty Face, Thunderhead, Sledgehammer, and Paddy Whacker. But these can't compare with barleywines for their humor. In true British tradition, most can be immediately identified by the "old" prefix in the name. There's Old Woolly, Old Foghorn, Old Curmudgeon, Old Dipsea, Old Bawdy, Old Crustacean, Old Winkie, Old Knucklehead, Old Chucklehead, and Old Abeerration. There are still other barleywines not following the "old" tradition: Bucksnort, Big Boris, Belly Up, Chicken Killer, Bigfoot, and — in an overt attempt at one upsmanship — Dremo Tibetan Bigfoot, complete with the subtitle "Watch out Sasquatch, here's the Tibetan Yeti."

rinse out any leftover sugars in the *grain bed.* The hot wort is pumped over to the brew kettle for the boil.

It should be noted that some breweries produce what is called *extract beer.* These brewers buy a malt syrup that is the equivalent of the wort produced during a full grain mash, only it has been dehydrated, reduced to only 20 percent of its original water content. The sweet, sticky extract can simply be mixed with water in the brew kettle, effectively bypassing the need for the milling and mashing equipment and the time those processes require. Generally speaking, extract beers do not maintain the same high standard of quality found in all-grain beers. Certain flavor components, obvious to those with educated palates, often are lost in the extract-production process.

Boiling After the mashing process is complete, the wort is brought to boiling temperature in the brew kettle. Intermittently throughout the boil, the brewer adds measured quantities of hops, both the quantity and the variety of which are determined by the desired beer style. Hop varieties added early in the boil are considered *bittering hops,* chosen for their bittering properties. Hop varieties added late in the boil, usually within the last 15 minutes, are *aroma hops,* chosen for their aromatic properties. Other ingredients, such as spices or fruit flavorings, are also added during the boil.

Cooling Since the hot, sweet wort is a perfect medium for bacteria to flourish, it is important to cool it as quickly as possible, which is usually done with a *counterflow wort chiller.* This efficient device not

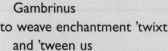

The King and His Quart

We invoke the spirit of King
  Gambrinus
to weave enchantment 'twixt
  and 'tween us

as we sup our fill on flesh of beast
and bib aplenty on broth of yeast

gently inspired by the barley's ghost,
blessings on the brewer and our
  publican host.

— Marty Nachel

only cools the wort, but it also allows the brewer to recapture the hot water at the other end, for future use in the brewery. Once the wort is cooled properly, yeast is *pitched* into the wort as it is pumped into a *fermentation vessel.*

Fermentation The cooled wort, freshly impregnated with a slurry of yeast, is sealed within an airtight fermentation tank. The active and insatiable yeast cells feast on the abundance of malt sugars, producing carbon dioxide and ethyl alcohol. The build-up of carbon dioxide is vented off, while the alcohol remains in solution. As the amount of available sugars decreases, the yeasts slow down, clump into small masses, and eventually fall dormant. This primary phase of fermentation lasts anywhere from seven to 14 days, depending upon the beer style. Then the beer is sent to the *aging tanks.*

Aging On its way to the aging tanks, the beer is filtered to remove most of the yeast still in suspension. This phase is also called *secondary fermentation* — and *lagering* — if, in fact, the beer is bottom-fermented. In the aging tanks, the beer is cooled and allowed to mature for two to six weeks, depending on whether it is an ale (usually a shorter time) or a lager (usually a longer time). Because the turn-around time is considerably shorter, brewers with limited tank space tend to prefer ale production.

Packaging Craft brewers who package their beers are outnumbered by pub brewers who don't by a margin of approximately two to one. Even those brewers whose entire annual production is bottled and kegged are still not challenging the megabrewers. Many small brewers still rely on antiquated bottling equipment or have fashioned their own labor-intensive, hands-on packaging systems. Of the few pub brewers who offer carry-out beer, usually it is drawn from the tap, and either bottled by the half gallon, in hand-filled, hand-capped containers, or produced on contract at another brewery.

Reinheitsgebot, the Beer Purity Law

Reinheitsgebot — pronounced *rine-HITES-ga-boat* — is a term heard frequently by those who follow the growth of the microbrewing industry. The official name for the vaunted "German Purity Law," it is the oldest consumer protection law on the books, and breweries large and small have been quick to align themselves and their products behind it.

The Reinheitsgebot was drafted by the Duke of Bavaria in 1516, when Bavaria was still a free state. It was then honored again in 1919, when Bavaria agreed to join the Weimar Republic. It is believed that the Reinheitsgebot was preceded by a pure beer law passed in Nürnberg in 1303, but its effects on the brewing industry are not nearly as well documented.

More readily recognized as the Beer Purity Law, the Reinheitsgebot guarantees that a true German beer is made with nothing other than malted barley, hops, yeast, and water. This means no adjuncts (cheaper sources of fermentable sugars like corn or rice), no additives, and no preservatives. Actually, the original law stipulated that only barley, hops, and water were allowed. This was prior to the invention of the microscope, when the importance of yeast to beer was not recognized and therefore was not considered an ingredient. Later, the law was amended and wheat malt became an acceptable ingredient within the parameters set by the Reinheitsgebot. (This, no doubt, was because of the Germans' love of weizenbier.)

It should be noted that the question of allowable ingredients constituted only half of the subject matter of the original decree. The other issue dealt with the pricing structure of beer and was spelled out in the first half of the document. The cost was pre-set, according to measure (quart, half quart) and the time of year. Apparently, beer in Bavaria in the sixteenth century was more expensive in the summer months, when demand was greater. To put some teeth into the law, the good Duke spelled out, in no uncertain terms, the penalty for failure to adhere to the beer law. The following is a literal translation of the final paragraph:

"We hereby declare that hereafter, in the country, in our towns, and in our markets, nothing other than barley, hops, and water shall be used to brew beer. He who intentionally violates this order and shows no respect for same, shall be made to surrender this barrel of beer by the court authorities as punishment as many times as this may happen."

Duke Wilhelm IV, saddled with rising military campaign debts, needed another source of revenue to cover governmental expenditures. He realized that the well-regarded Bavarian brewing industry was a potential taxable powerhouse. History has proved him right. Today, two other European countries besides Germany follow the original decree. In Norway, it is a national law and in Switzerland it is practiced voluntarily. Finland also has instituted a similar law for its brewers. In these days of trade imbalances and unstable economies, the Reinheitsgebot is viewed as an unfair trade barrier and the European economic community has had to address the subject on several occasions. Whatever is to become of the law, the Reinheitsgebot and its author laid down the gauntlet for the brewer and left the beer drinker a legacy of pure and healthful beverages.

The First Consumer Protection Law

In 1516, Duke Wilhelm IV of Bavaria penned the Reinheitsgebot, known as the German Purity Law, which set the parameters for the pricing of beer, and, more importantly, the ingredients allowed in it. The German Purity Law carried such weight that when Bavaria joined the Wiemar Republic in 1919, the rest of Germany adopted the Reinheitsgebot as its own.

It should be noted, though, that the Reinheitsgebot, for all its good intentions, places unreasonable restrictions on brewers if it is followed to the letter of the law. In order for craft brewers to expand their beer horizons, it becomes necessary to bend the rules a bit. If done responsibly and with respectability — not using adjuncts, additives, and preservatives — we will all win in the end.

Additives and Preservatives

While fans of microbrewed beer are concerned with what ingredients go into their favorite brews, they should, in fact, also be rejoicing about what doesn't go into their beer. One of the hallmarks of craft-brewed beers is that they are made without the use of *adjuncts*. Adjuncts are alternative sources of fermentable sugars, such as rice and corn, which are cheaper to use than malted barley. Large, corporate brewers are famous for this sort of frugality. Rice and corn do not imbue the beer with the fullness of flavor and wonderful complexity that comes from brewing with malted barley alone. Far worse than the megabrewers' cost-cutting efforts, however, is their use of other adjuncts, otherwise known as additives and preservatives.

The brewing industry is one of the few consumable-producing industries that is not required by the government to list ingredients on the labels of their products. Surprisingly, consumers have not demanded that they do so. Be aware that among additives and preservatives, there are as many as 50 antioxidants, foam enhancers, colorings, flavorings, and miscellaneous enzymes that are legally allowed in the production of beer. For a complete listing of the polysyllabic chemicals that the government considers safe to drink, see Appendix A.

Yaba-Daba-Doo Brew

The longevity of man's relationship with beer should accord it a place of great honor: It is, after all, estimated to be nearly 10,000 years old. Some anthropologists have hypothesized that Neolithic man made a transition from the nomadic lifestyle of the hunter-gatherer to the relatively sedentary lifestyle of an agriculturist in order to cultivate grain for brewing beer. This Stone Age beer, crude though it may have been, was an important source of nutrients in the diet of these early hominids. While grain also was used in the baking of bread, it was rendered more nutritious after having undergone the beer-making process, in which the starchy insides of the kernel were transformed into proteins and soluble sugars that were not otherwise available.

Evaluating Beer

Not so long ago, beer drinkers could find humor in this hypothetical scenario: Young, upwardly mobile people would get together for a monthly wine and cheese soiree. Gathered around a cutting board, sipping Pouilly Fumé from spotless crystal stemware, they would offer obtuse pronouncements about the wine along the lines of ". . . amiable, perhaps, but just a tad obsequious . . ." or "pretentious, yet not too flatulent . . ."

This mental imagery produced endless snickers and guffaws for those of us who drink beer. But times have changed and so has our beer. We now find ourselves in an uncomfortably similar position as we sip and swirl our way through an ever-increasing number of well-made, handcrafted beers. These microbrews are deserving of our thoughtful observations, and are every bit as good as their vinous counterparts. You'd be hard-pressed to convince a wine drinker of this, but much of the beer produced at the microbrewing level has as much depth and complexity as most wines. It is only fair that we extend the same considerations to the art of the brewer as we do to the art of the vintner.

We need not become beer snobs, but "cold, wet, and fizzy" is an assessment that should be relegated only to the blandest of national beers. Proper taste evaluations require a rudimentary knowledge of the product, including the ingredients and processes that effect the taste and overall quality of the final product (see pages 18–25). It is much too simplistic to take a slug of beer and carelessly declare it either "good" or "bad." What makes one a good consumer is the ability to discern what it is about the product that makes it good or bad. In beer evaluation, certain criteria should be addressed. In addition to taste, beer should have a certain appearance, a certain aroma, and it should possess qualities as defined by its style (see pages 2–17).

There are four basic steps to the proper evaluation of beer: *look, smell, taste, and reflect.*

Evaluating the aroma should come first, as the more subtle aromatics will dissipate quickly after pouring. All beers should have a pleasant nose that includes malt aroma and hop bouquet in varying degrees of intensity. There also should be evidence of positive fermentation characteristics such as fruity or citric esters (citric compounds which contribute to fruity aroma), diacetyl (a buttery or butterscotch aroma or taste) and ethanol (ethyl alcohol). Negative fermentation characteristics might include vegetal, sulphury, enteric, or phenolic odors (see Glossary). Other negatives such as oxidized, skunky, or musty aromas also indicate imperfection in the product.

In terms of appearance, attention should focus on the color, the clarity, and the head retention of the beer. All beers should hold a head, and it should last at least as long as the liquid in your glass. The carbonation bubbles should be small and tightly knit to form a creamy head. The color is dictated by the brewing style and can range from pale straw to gold, amber, copper, red, brown, and opaque black. Clarity, like color, can vary from style to style. In certain brews, cloudiness is intentional, or at least unavoidable.

As with aroma, beer should offer malt and hop flavors in varying degrees of intensity. The malt character can be sweet or dry, simple or complex, caramelly, chocolaty, roasty or toasty. The hops, though primarily used for their bittering properties, can also lend a "green" herbal taste as well as a spicy or cheesy tang, and, occasionally, a metallic tincture can be traced to certain hop varieties. Additional flavors are melded into the beer during the fermentation phase. These can include clove, fruit, and diacetyl essences. Sometimes the ethanol can be obvious. Negative tastes that can develop in beer after fermentation include oxydation, skunkiness, and metallic notes not attributable to hops.

The balance of the malt and hop flavors must also be evaluated. While it is customary for certain beer styles to accentuate the attributes of either the malt or the hops, neither should completely obliterate the other. Finally, you

Nectar of Ancient Gods and Goddesses

There is evidence that early beer making was not limited to a singular geographic location. Wherever the cultivation of grain crops was possible, beer making was possible. Using the grain source indigenous to their surroundings, inhabitants of locations as diverse as Mesopotamia (barley), Egypt (wheat), South America (corn), and China (rice) have left behind artifacts related to their ancient brewing practices. In addition to earthenware pots, petrified grain stores, and golden drinking straws recovered from sarcophagi, archaeologists and anthropologists have decoded hieroglyphics found in tombs and on clay tablets that related to

beer. One of these tablets describes the brewing processes and sings the praises of a Sumerian beer goddess. The "Hymn to Ninkasi" has been studied not only by students of ancient history, but also more recently by brewers wishing to learn more about brewing in the past. Beer gods and goddesses, dieties of high rank and honor, received regular praise and offerings in Babylon and Mesopotamia. These spiritual beings wielded power and authority over the sun, the rain, and the soil — all things necessary to provide a bountiful harvest of grain.

will arrive at the aftertaste, or finish. Long forgotten, and even disregarded by the megabrewers, aftertaste is an integral part of the beer-tasting experience. Balance should again be scrutinized, as a beer's balance can tilt sharply at the finish. The grain's astringent properties can conspire with the hop bitterness to constrict the gullet prematurely, and the alcohol's once pleasant warmth in the throat can turn to searing heat. Also pay attention to the nontaste characteristics of the beer. The body, or fullness, of the beer is more of a sensation than a taste, as is the conditioning (carbonation). Is the beer too watery or does it go down like molasses? Carbonation can be prickly but should not explode on your tongue.

Reflection calls all of your subjective observations to the forefront. It is at this point, after putting the beer through the ringer, that you must form an overall impression of it. All good beer, regardless of style, must have an inherent drinkability. Here, ultimately, is where you get to christen the beer in the name of quality (or not). One question cuts to the chase: would I spend my hard-earned dollars on this product again? End of conversation.

Part II

PACIFIC REGION

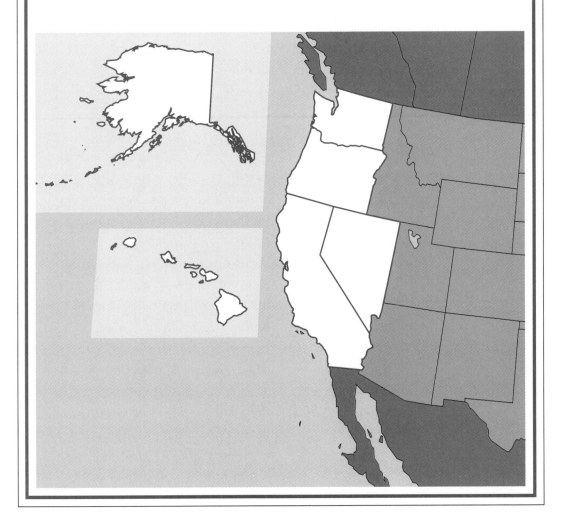

Pacific Brewery Profiles

Alaskan Brewing & Bottling

Somehow, a frosty glass of beer does not strike one as something that would be produced in the subarctic state of Alaska. Such an attitude is naive, because the fact is that although Alaska is our least populous state, 38 breweries have operated on Alaskan soil since it became our 49th state in 1959. Unfortunately, all have fallen victim to the boom or bust cycles that have plagued Alaska's industries. It would seem a serious lack of hindsight for anyone to open another brewery here, but don't tell that to Juneau residents Geoff and Marcy Larson.

The Larsons had solid backgrounds on which to build their brewing venture. Marcy had business management experience, and her father was a supervisor for the Pabst (Georgia) canning plant. Her husband, Geoff, was a chemical engineer working on the design and manufacture of alcohol processing plants for large agriculture companies. The early 1980s signaled the beginning of the microbrewery renaissance, and this encouraged the Larsons to follow their instincts. After attending the Microbrewer's Conference in Denver in 1984 and meeting with a variety of like-minded people, they became firm in their decision. The first step was to set up a limited partnership under the title Chinook Alaskan Brewing & Bottling Company in order to begin raising capital. Originally, 100 investors came forward with $5,000 dollars each. These Alaskan capitalists were backing the first locally brewed beer since the ill-fated Prinz Brau disappeared from the scene in 1976.

The brewery was under construction by the summer of 1986, and test batches were under way by October of that year. The recipe for their beer came about as a result of Geoff and Marcy's painstaking research of old Alaskan breweries. A recipe from the turn-of-the-century Douglas Brewing Company was discovered. This, along with an old shipping invoice for the beer's ingredients, presented enough information to recreate the beer that became known as Chinook Alaskan Amber Beer.

The new beer, brewed in the altbier style (see page 6), is a unique beer with strong ties to Dusseldorf, Germany. It is fermented with ale yeast but is matured at cold temperatures like most lager beers (see page 2). The ingredients for Chinook Alaskan Amber Beer include pale and caramel malts, Cascade and Saaz varieties of hops, and city water from the glacial ice melt held in the Salmon Creek reservoir. Geoff Larson likes to say that "we pre-age our water for ten thousand years." As a testimonial to this creamy, full-bodied gem of a beer, its awards include gold medals (1987, 1988, 1990) in the altbier category at the Great American Beer Festival (see page 97) and the consumer award in 1989. Not content to rest on their laurels, the Larsons have also created other award-winning brews, which include an autumn ale (silver medal, 1989 and 1990) and an ambrosial smoked porter (gold medal, 1994).

I regret to report that these Alaskan beers are not widely distributed. Whether this is due to the brewery's inability to produce a supply equal to the demand or to the locals' selfish hoarding of their hometown brew is unclear. Meanwhile, distribution is limited to their home state and the already microbrew-rich state of Washington.

It should be noted that in order to avoid a legal confrontation with another nonbrewing company over the use of the Chinook name, the Juneau-based brewery dropped the "C" word and is now known simply as Alaskan Brewing & Bottling Company.

Anderson Valley Bottling Company

"Demand only the bahlest" — whatever that means. Visitors to Boonville and Anderson Valley will be perplexed by the peculiar local dialect, Boontling, still spoken in these parts. The dialect is used frequently in advertising for the valley's only resident brewery, the Anderson Valley Brewing Company. One gets a sense of the peculiarity of it all on first sight of the company's logo of "The Legendary Boonville Beers," showing a California black bear with an eight-point rack of deer antlers.

Back in the 1870s, Mendocino County's Anderson Valley was an isolated logging and sheep ranching center. (This isolation helped, no doubt, in creating and preserving the indigenous patois.) Men and women worked laboriously in this rustic and remote community, which was in great need of a local social center and watering hole. In 1873, the Buckhorn Saloon opened in the heart of Anderson Valley on the present-day site of the Boonville brewery. Borrowing from its past, the Anderson Valley Brewing

Company opened the new Buckhorn Saloon 114 years later.

The owners did not initially intend to reincarnate the old saloon. Dr. Kenneth Allen, a chiropractor, and his wife, Kimberley, became Anderson Valley residents in 1980. They purchased the property where the old Buckhorn once stood with the intention of opening a chiropractic office. Along with the deed to the land came ownership of one of the best water supplies in Anderson Valley. This wellspring of good fortune posed a dilemma: what to do with this abundance of pure water. Eventually it was discovered that the unique makeup of the water held potential for the brewing of high quality beer. The rest is (modern) history.

As the first brewpub in California to be built specifically for this purpose, Anderson Valley was painstakingly designed to be a contemporary American setting. A three-story cedar and glass structure with surrounding redwood decks, the building appears to float above street level. Large glass windows frame views of the valley's hillsides as they are pictured on the brewery's distinctive labels. Intimate dining tables are dwarfed below the high, open ceilings. Patrons dine on country cuisine, either on the main level, in the open loft area, or in the warm outdoor beer garden.

The brewery is located on the lower level of the building, adjacent to the gift shop. The brewing equipment was specially designed, according to the Allens' needs. Anderson Valley brews are traditionally handcrafted in the now famous "California style." All are made from two-row malt, specialty grains, Pacific northwest hops, and their own pristine well water, which is high in bicarbonates and is chemical free. The brewing is done by Eric Taylor with help from Ken and Kimberley's son, Loren.

The name of each of the Boonville beers is in the Boontling dialect. Poleeko Gold is a crisp and clear pale ale with an abundance of hops, a floral bouquet, and a lively bitter finish. Boont Amber is a medium-bodied, pale ale with the rich flavor of caramel malt. Barney Flats is a complex, full-bodied, sweet stout (it's not just shy sluggin' gorms neemer!). High Rollers Wheat Beer has a delicate tangy flavor and a crisp, clean finish (it's a slow lope 'n a beeson tree!). Deependers Dark Porter is a dark brown, medium-bodied porter with a roasted coffee character and a chocolaty finish. Belk's Extra Special Bitter Ale (E.S.B.) is full-bodied and malty, finishing with an arousing hoppy bite. Barney Flats won a gold medal at the Great American Beer Festival in 1990, and Belk's won a gold medal at the 1994 Great American Beer Festival.

BridgePort Brewing Company

It is interesting to note that, of the more than 450 microbreweries now in operating in the United States, the top five in terms of barrelage are from the Pacific northwest, and three of those are from Oregon.

Checking in at the number five spot is BridgePort Brewing Company in Portland — the mecca of microbrewing.

The BridgePort Brewing Company was established in 1984, making it the oldest microbrewery in Oregon. It was founded by pioneers in Oregon's wine industry, Dick and Mary Ponzi. And ten years after opening, their company is one of the largest and fastest growing microbreweries in the country.

The BridgePort Brewing Company brew team is dedicated to preserving the integrity and authenticity of regional handcrafted ales. Their British-style (see Beer Styles, page 2) top-fermenting BridgePort Pale Ale and BridgePort Coho Pacific Light Ale offer a choice of light- to medium-bodied beers that have a distinctive full flavor and aroma. The Pale Ale (alcohol 4.2 percent by weight) is a regional favorite. It is medium- to full-bodied, amber-hued, and has a bitter character. The Pale Ale is brewed from four-malted barleys and balanced with local hops, giving it an herbal tang and aroma. The Light Ale (alcohol 3.6 percent by weight) is a light ale in the traditional style. It is smooth, light-bodied, and delicately hopped. Coho Pacific is a honey- to amber-hued, low gravity bitter (see glossary). This sociable, refreshing ale is also a fine complement to light meals.

Brewing high quality ales requires high quality ingredients. All efforts are made to search out the premium ingredients that go into BridgePort ales. Two-row malted barley from Oregon and Washington is supplemented by English specialty roasted barley malts. The hops are locally grown in the Pacific Northwest. Willamette Valley hops give a spicy aroma. Other bittering and aromatic varieties include Nugget, Northern

Brewer, and Kent Goldings. The yeast is a specially selected and well guarded strain of top-fermenting yeast that is propagated at the brewery. As in all beers, the primary ingredient is water. BridgePort Brewing uses only Cascade Mountain water. These ingredients, combined with thoughtful brewing and handling techniques, gives BridgePort ales their distinctive colors, flavors, and aromas. At BridgePort Brewing, they brew "to demand," meaning that they maintain a low inventory, thereby assuring freshness in their products.

Brewing at BridgePort involves three phases: brewing, cellaring, and dispensing. The first phase takes place in the brewhouse. After carefully measuring and crushing the grain, it is mixed with water and boiled to convert starches to sugars. The sweet wort (see glossary) is then transferred to the 80-barrel stainless steel brew

BRIDGEPORT

COHO PACIFIC
—EXTRA PALE ALE—

kettle to boil for one and a half hours. After cooling, the beer is transferred to 180-barrel, stainless steel fermenters. In the cellar, yeast is pitched and the beer undergoes a vigorous five-day fermentation. The beer is then transferred to conditioning tanks, where it matures for seven more days at 45°F (7°C). When it is properly aged, it is filtered, chilled, and carbonated for packaging. For dispensing, the bottled and kegged beer is stored in a refrigerated room until it is shipped for distribution and released into the market. Current production is 60 percent bottles and 40 percent kegs, and is distributed to Oregon, Washington, Alaska, Idaho, Colorado, and Montana.

Here are some BridgePort statistics for the "bean-counters": The new 80-barrel brewhouse gives BridgePort an annual production potential of 50,000 barrels. One day's production is equivalent to 240 barrels — or 480 kegs — or 7,440 gallons — or 59,520 pints — or 79,372 (12-ounce) bottles.

Full Sail Brewery

This Hood River, Oregon, brewing facility was set up in a renovated section of the historic Diamond Fruit Cannery, situated high on a bluff overlooking the Columbia River. The brewpub features large viewing windows, both into the brewhouse and out over the Columbia River Gorge. The pub section of the building was once used as the press room in the Diamond Fruit Cooperative's fruit juice operation.

The brewing equipment at the Hood River location was manufactured by J. V. Northwest of Wilsonville, Oregon. The equipment includes a total of 14 stainless steel tanks, one mash tun, one brew kettle, a whirlpool tank, nine fermenters, and two bright beer tanks. This equipment is capable of producing the 26,000 barrels of beer every year. This is actually the second brewhouse. The original brewing equipment was shipped down river to the second brewery's location.

Portland, Oregon, is home to the Full Sail Brewing Company and Riverplace Brewery, situated in the nautical heart of the city at Riverplace Marina. The seven stainless steel tanks in use here were manufactured by J. V. Northwest for use at the original Hood River facility. They were reconditioned and reinstalled at the Portland location and are now cranking out about 5,000 barrels per year.

Both breweries produce a similar line of beers, which includes Full Sail Golden Ale, Full Sail Amber Ale, and Full Sail Brown Ale. These are the first microbrewed beers from Oregon available in bottles year-round. Also produced at both locations, but on a seasonal basis, are Main Sail Stout, Top Sail Porter, Old Boardhead Barleywine, and WasSail Winter Ale.

You may have noticed the capitalized "S" in the middle of the last beer mentioned. While the second syllable of that word conveniently ties into the brewery's brand-naming scheme, serendipity played a big part. According to Full Sail Brewing Company's promotional material, their WasSail Winter Ale is a heavy ale in the traditional British "winter warmer" style. Wassail is a traditional ale drunk during the winter season. WasSail has a dark, garnet color with a 16.5° Plato starting gravity (see page 166), to produce a strong, full-bodied ale. It is highly hopped with a blend of imported and domestic hops. This hopping combination gives WasSail its complex aromatics which balance and refine the flavors of the four types of malt used to create this brew.

WasSail should be savored in much the same manner as a fine brandy. Because this beer has an alcohol content of 5.2 percent by weight, it is suggested that you enjoy it in moderation. The best way to do that is to share it with friends during the holiday season.

Hart Brewing

The Hart Brewing Company of Kalama, Washington, was founded by the husband and wife team of Tom Baune and Beth Hartwell in the spring of 1984. It had been 104 years since a brewery was last in operation there. Baune and Hartwell were dedicated to crafting truly unique ales, using only the finest natural ingredients.

The brewery began in a turn-of-the-century building, originally the general store for the southwest Washington town of Kalama, just up Interstate 5 from Portland, Oregon. Kalama is on the Kalama River, which provides some of the finest fly fishing in the Cascade Mountain range. The river, fed by glacial waters from Mount St. Helens, is also an excellent source of water for brewing handcrafted beers.

Production in the first year was 200 barrels of full-bodied, top-fermented beer, called Pyramid Pale Ale. The next year's volume topped 500 barrels of all-draught beer. By the end of 1988, the brewery was producing nearly 5,000 barrels annually. At this time, Hart Brewing, Inc. went through significant changes. Five new owners took on the task of managing the market demand. They constructed a new brewery in Kalama on the shores of the Columbia River, more than doubling the work space and increasing the annual brewing capacity to over 20,000 barrels. Though there were con-

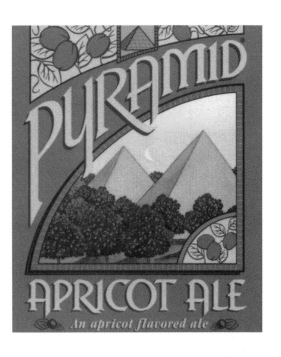

cerns that the level of quality would decline with the new equipment and facilities, those concerns were quickly dispelled when the brews from the new location received both gold and silver medals at the Great American Beer Festival in 1990 and 1991.

True to the original mission, Pyramid Ales are made with all natural local ingredients and are unpasteurized. They are produced in accordance with the German Beer Purity Law of 1516 (see page 23). The water comes from the run-off of Mount St. Helens, the grain is from eastern Washington and Montana, the hops are from the Yakima Valley of Washington State, and the yeast is a special strain maintained at the brewery.

Currently, Hart Brewing offers a full line of distinctive ales meant to be enjoyed with or without the accompaniment of food. There is a Pyramid Pale Ale (also known as Special Bitter) on draught, Wheaten Ale (the first draught wheat beer in the United States since Prohibition), Hefe-weizen (wheat beer with yeast in the

bottle), Sphinx Stout (with hints of chocolate and expresso), Wheaten Bock (bock beer with wheat malt in the grist), Best Brown Ale (toffeelike palate), Amber Wheat Beer (with a hint of tartness, and an excellent aperitif), and Snow Cap Ale (a classic northwest barleywine). More recently, a newer brew, Pyramid Apricot Ale, won a 1994 gold medal at the Great American Beer Festival in the fruit beer category.

Humboldt Brewery

Just a block from the historic plaza in downtown Arcata stands the Humboldt Brewery. Opened in 1987, this brewpub, serving northern California, has taken a decidedly Californian approach to the microbrewing industry. Owner Mario Celotto has created an eating and drinking establishment that successfully links the traditional to the modern day.

Tradition is upheld in several ways, but none is more obvious than in the range and quality of beers brewed at Humboldt. All of the offerings are of the ale variety. Gold Rush Pale Ale, Red Nectar (amber) Ale, Storm Cellar Porter, and Oatmeal Stout are considered the regular beers. The seasonal beers include Appleton Brown Ale, Moonstone Ale, Freshwater Mild, Holidaze Ale, and a wheat beer brewed for summer consumption. The porter and stout are cask-conditioned, as in the Old World, and all of their beers are aged for a minimum of 30 days. All of these brews are made from 100 percent malt, with no adjuncts or additives, and they are not filtered or pasteurized. The beers are

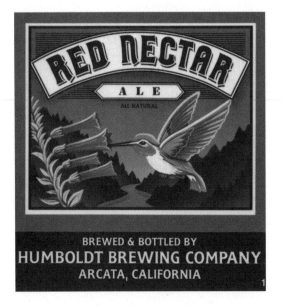

pumped to the bar with traditional English hand pumps or "beer engines" and served at 48°F (9°C).

Brewmaster Steve Parks is especially proud of his Red Nectar Ale. At the 1993 Great American Beer Festival, this brew won a major award. The largest number of entries were found in the mixed category of American pale ale/American amber ale. Humboldt Brewing Company's Red Nectar Ale was awarded the silver medal in this category. Since the gold medal was presented to a pale ale, this essentially makes Red Nectar the number one amber ale in the country. Here's how they describe it: "A robust red, fruity, flower of a beer you will find well-named. Its fiery copper color comes from the generous use of imported crystal malt. The 'nectar' sweetness is offset by the bitterness and bouquet of Eroica, Cascade, and Willamette hops in an aromatic amalgamation."

The brewpub itself consists of a dining area, a bar, and a middle room of rustic wood with a cozy stone fireplace. The decor is a mix of historical artifacts and photos of Humboldt County. There is also a smattering of sports memorabilia from Mario Celotto's playing days as a linebacker for the Oakland Raiders. The brewery, visible behind the bar, has a seven-barrel brewing capacity, and there are 25 aging and serving tanks, visible by the use of viewing mirrors.

Humboldt Brewery's cuisine can best be described as eclectic. Their menu offers a variety of salads, appetizers, sandwiches, and burgers, including Chainsaw Chili Cheeseburger. Fresh

pasta is made on the premises and served as a daily special. Pub fare includes fish and chips (fresh local fish and their own beer batter) and spinach cheese pie. For dessert they suggest cream cheese apple cake served with oatmeal stout!

A recent annex to the brewery houses the 570-seat International Beer Garden and dance hall/concert venue, which offers live music on Friday and Saturday nights.

Thomas Kemper Brewing Company

All microbreweries are unique, but unique is the *very least* you can say about Thomas Kemper Brewing Company. If all the microbreweries in the Pacific Northwest could be thought of as round holes, Thomas Kemper would be a square peg. If all the others were black tuxedoes, Kemper would be a pair of brown shoes. If . . . well, you get the idea. The states of Washington and Oregon

combined form a great bastion of American ale breweries. In their midst stands one lone lager brewery — Thomas Kemper. Kemper is the only microbrewery in the region dedicated to brewing nothing but traditional lager style beers (see Beer Styles, pages 2–17).

The brewery's inaugural brew, Thomas Kemper Helles, was introduced to the Puget Sound market in January 1985. *Helles* (pronounced *HELL-iss*) is German for light or pale, not low calorie. This beer is handcrafted in the truest sense and was well received by the real beer enthusiasts that reside in the area. This is no small feat, mind you — Seattle area residents practically cut their teeth on local micro-brewed beer, and due to their regular exposure to high quality beer, they are tough customers.

The Thomas Kemper brewery is located on a three-acre site in a pastoral setting northeast of Poulsbo, Washington, about a half-hour's ferry ride from Seattle. The brewery is set up in an old meat-packing plant. It has the ambience of a German *bierstube* (beer bar) and features a small tap room and grill, as well as a beer garden for warm weather relaxation.

The food menu offers basic pub fare with English and German specialties.

Since 1985, the brewery has expanded its line of beers considerably. Today, Thomas Kemper brews four beers on a regular basis and three seasonal offerings. The regulars include Thomas Kemper Pale Lager, Pilsner, Hefeweizen, and Integralé. The seasonal specialties include Oktoberfest, Winterbrau, and Rolling Bay Bock. All of these beers are brewed in the classic style and are in adherence with the Reinheitsgebot of 1516 (see page 23). Most of the raw materials used in the brews are from the Pacific Coast states. The hops come from the famed Yakima Valley, the malted grain from eastern Washington State, and the water source is the snowmelt from the Olympic Mountain range.

Winterbrau is brewed with a blend of five different malts, which give it a complex and assertive character. The intensity of the malt is balanced by generous amounts of Nugget, Styrian, and Cascade hops that are added at three stages during the boil. The grain bill, or list of grains, includes pale malt, caramel malt, Munich malt, black-roasted, and cara-Pils. The resulting brew is mahogany in color, rich and creamy in texture, and very malty, with a firm hop accent in the finish. Winterbrau is brewed in small batches during the winter months.

Regular tours of the brewing facility are conducted on the weekends. Weekday tours are given by appointment only and require reservations one to two weeks in advance.

Pacific Hop Exchange

A March 1994 issue of *American Brewer* magazine identified Pacific Hop Exchange in Novato, California, as the smallest commercial brewery in the United States. To most microbrewers, some notoriety is better than none, but to the guys at Pacific Hop Exchange, this is a title they would rather do without.

They were celebrating their one-year anniversary at the time the article was published. Their first year was highlighted by growing product sales and distribution of their beers. The handcrafted ales have been well received by beer aficionados in Marin, Sonoma, and San Francisco — the extent of their distribution at the time. Since then, brewery representatives have been actively promoting their product line at a variety of beer festivals including the KQED event in San Francisco and the Great American Beer Festival, where a national audience has been treated to their fine brews. They are also happy to be working with the Pacific Stock Exchange in providing their beer for customers and executives of the Exchange at a series of California events.

The current beer lineup includes: '06 Stout, a creamy, roasty stout described by some as "chewy"; Grain Trader Wheat Ale, a crisp, dry-hopped ale made from 50 percent wheat malt (it's light, not "lite"); and their seasonal Christmas beer, Holly Hops Spiced Ale, which is subtlely spiced with cloves, nutmeg, cinnamon, and hints of chocolate and orange. The demand for this beer far exceeded the available supply in the last holiday season. Last but not least is the silver medal winner in the 1992 Great American Beer Festival, Gaslite Pale Ale. This aromatic brew is dry-hopped in the traditional English method of adding fresh hops directly into the fermentation vessel. All of these beers are unfiltered, bottle-conditioned, and handcrafted from quality grains and fresh, whole leaf hops.

Pacific Hop Exchange has plans underway to expand their brewing operations. A new facility, targeted for an area north of San Francisco, is expected to open in 1995. The new 25-barrel brewing system will be housed in a combination brewery and brewpub. With the ability to brew in larger batches, expansion of the beer distribution network will go well beyond the current geographic base. The demand is there, according to the people at Pacific Hop Exchange. They just need to build the facility to meet it. In the near future Pacific Hop Exchange will also be acting as a contract brewer for a company in Menlo Park.

Pike Place Brewery

Already America's most impressive importer of specialty beers, distributor Merchant Du Vin has now taken its place among the highly respected brewers that they have long represented. The idea for Seattle's Pike Place Brewery was conceived by Charles Finkel, the founder of Merchant Du Vin. This a natural extension for a company that is the sole United States agent for a complete range of authentic beers representing each of the classic brewing styles. Since the October 1989 debut of their Pike Place Ale, the brewery has developed a strong following for their top-fermented, handcrafted beers that include Pike Place Pale Ale, XXXXX Stout, and Old Bawdy Barleywine.

The brewing facility is located in the Pike Place Market, Seattle's largest tourist attraction, which draws millions of food and beer enthusiasts from across the country. The demand for Pike Place beers in Seattle, where it is featured at most of the finest hotels and restaurants, has exceeded current supply. Such demand makes it nearly impossible to introduce these beers to other American markets. With that in mind, Pike Place Brewery has contracted with two other American microbreweries in strategic locations to duplicate their Pike Place Ale for that region. The Catamount Brewing Company in White River Junction, Vermont, and the Indianapolis Brewing Company in

Drawing Pints and Blanks

Armed with bare necessities as I begin to write my epistle —
a quill, a scroll, some Indian ink . . . and an ale to wet my whistle.

A scribble here, an erasure there — a sip of ale 'fore and aft —
'tisn't but a little while, I'm into a second draught!

The blackness of the inkwell inspires me to a porter,
quatrains and pentameters are soon found out of order.

The candle is growing shorter, my mind is wavering about:
shall I light another candle, or pour myself a stout?

The room is growing darker, my pen can write no wrong;
pint glass is fully empty and begs for ale that is strong.

Still, mind and parchment, equally blank; of inspiration I am in need.
Pint glass is traded for Mazer filled with a honey-mead.

Staring into an empty cup, I fear a prompt dismissal —
I'd hoped to write, perhaps to teach — and now I can't even whistle!

—Marty Nachel

Indianapolis, Indiana, were chosen to brew the Pike Place ales for the eastern and midwestern regions, respectively. Both of these breweries have demonstrated their devotion to quality beers and appreciate the challenge of brewing with the special malt, hops, and yeast supplied by the Seattle brewery. Algernon "Fal" Allen, the original brewmaster, has brewed at both locations, learning about the brewing systems and teaming up with the other brewers to reproduce the distinctive taste of Pike Place Pale Ale.

According to Mr. Finkel, creating the Pike Place Brewery and developing the Pike Place ales was a great learning experience. As experimental batches were brewed in the development of the pale ale recipe, subtle taste differences were recognized with each variation in malt, hop, and yeast type used. Since the malt is considered the soul of the beer, the finest malt available had to be procured. Crisp Malting Ltd. of Norwich, England, specializes in a variety called Marris Otter — considered the Cabernet Sauvignon of the malt world. The hop supply comes from England, Canada, and the American Northwest and includes clusters, fuggles, and the noble East Kent goldings for the aromatics in their ales.

The Pike Place ales have received high praise. Noted beer authority Michael Jackson hands out three stars apiece to Pike Place Pale Ale and the quintuple X Stout. Bill Owens, editor of the *American Brewer* magazine, calls the Pike Place beers "the finest ales in the Northwest." And in Chicago 40 journalists, restauranteurs, and beer enthusiasts chose Pike Place Pale Ale as the top beer among the 12 tasted, giving it top points for color, aroma, flavor, and character.

Portland Brewing Company

Portland Brewing Company began in 1983 as the dream of two friends — Fred Bowman and Art Larrance — who cultivated an interest in beer flavors through their numerous travel, college, and work experiences. This led them to homebrewing, and, ultimately, to the startup of a microbrewery. Brewing commenced in January, 1986. By 1992, brewery output had exceeded 9,000 barrels. Because capacity was 9,600 barrels, and demand seemed to be growing faster than supply, a new, larger brewery was constructed and was producing by the spring of 1993. The brewery expanded into an adjacent warehouse for additional fermentation space, storage, and bottling operations.

The Portland Brewing Company is an English-style pub: small, quiet, dark, homey, and quaint, with a brick and stucco exterior and an Honduran mahogany interior. There are large windows separating the brewhouse from the pub, so patrons can see the brewers work their magic. The pub seats only 35 people, but what it lacks in size it makes up for with gustatory treats: all the food is homemade. You can choose from a selection that includes meat loaf, chili, stew, veggies, ham and cheese sandwiches, turkey, and pizza. The big attraction, however, is the line-up of beers available for your tasting pleasure. The brewery produces a total of eight different brews, six of which are regular production beers: Portland Porter, Portland Stout, McTarnahan's Ale, Timberline Ale, and Mt. Hood Beer. Two are seasonal favorites: Oregon Dry Beer, a summer thirst quencher; and Winter Ale, a festive holiday libation. Winter Ale is a special treat when served in the medieval tradition of mulled ale — warm, with honey and spices added to celebrate the season.

All of the beers produced at the Portland Brewing Company are brewed according to the famous German Beer Purity Law (see page 23). The barley is grown locally, as are the Oregon and Washington state hops. The water is charcoal-filtered to remove residual chlorine and other minerals. The yeast culture comes from a strain isolated by Bert Grant of Yakima Brewing and is very important to the distinctive flavor of their beers.

One of the most popular selections from Portland Brewing is McTarnahan's Ale, a complex, copper-colored, Scottish-style ale (see Beer Styles, pages 2–17) of great character, made with pale and caramel malts and Cascade hops. Scottish ales are generally stronger and heavier than their English counterparts, and this beer fits that profile. A couple of these and you'll be wanting to try on that old kilt in the attic!

Tours of the brewery are given, but it's wise to reserve three weeks in advance.

Rogue Brewery and Tasting Room Oregon Brewing

Many West Coast microbrewers have gained national prominence and have grown to be among the largest craft brewers in the country. Oregon has long been on the cutting edge of the microbrewing movement. One Oregonian brew-

Beer Legend

The history and tradition of beer are solidly rooted in Europe during the Middle Ages, and many legends abound. There was the mythical figure of King Gambrinus, who was to beer what Bacchus was to wine. Actually, there may indeed have been a real Gambrinus. The rotund Belgian blueblood of French extraction bore the title of Duke Jean the First of Brabant. In the Flemish-speaking regions he was known as Duke Jan Primus, and over time this may have been corrupted to Gambrinus. A popular tale tells of the portly aristocrat's fondness for beer leading to seemingly endless beer-drinking marathons. In one instance it is said that Gambrinus consumed 388 glasses of beer in one sitting. For this dubious distinction he has been immortalized as the King of Beer.

Another story told is of Arnoldus the Strong, who, in the midst of an eleventh century battle in Flanders, beseeched God for beer to slake the thirst of his parched combatants. For his ability to procure beer at the utterance of a prayer, he is now venerated as St. Arnold, patron saint of beer.

er has been there since the early days and has gained widespread notoriety, but continues to operate on an intimate scale. As of 1993, the company, known simply as Rogue Ales, was the forty-fifth largest brewery in the United States. In fact, the 52,000 kegs brewed by Rogue last year were produced at three separate locations.

After several successful years of operation at the Ashland facility in southern Oregon, the owners of Rogue Ales decided to open a second facility on the coast at Newport, Oregon. The Bayfront Brewery and Public House opened in 1989, with 1988 Homebrewer of the Year, John Maier, taking over as brewmaster. Most recently, the third facility, Rogue Ale Brewery in South Beach, just across Yaquina Bay from Newport, began its operation.

The Rogue Ales company vision is to be the preeminent Northwest creator of varietal ales through innovative creation and aggressive marketing. This focus on quality delivers to the consumer the character, depth, and value expected from an established microbrewer.

Rogue Ales produces a wide variety of full-bodied ales handcrafted from quality grain, hops, and proprietary yeast. According to wording on the bottles, there are "No additives. No preservatives. No kidding." If variety is the spice of life, then Rogue Ales make life worth living. Here is a partial listing of their products: St. Rogue Red, NewPorter, Mogul Madness, Mexicali Rogue (with chili peppers), Rogue 'N Berry (a fruit beer), Rogue Smoke (using malts smoked with alder and cherry wood), Old Crustacean Barleywine, Maierbock, and Rogue Ale.

Rogue Ales is no stranger to award winning. Their smoked beer won a gold medal in 1990 and three successive silver medals at the Great American Beer Festival; Old Crustacean Barleywine took a silver in 1992 and garnered the gold in

1993, and Mogul Madness took home a bronze in 1994. The smoked beer, like many of the other specialties, is bottled and sold only in September and October. The barleywine, on the other hand, is available all year long — but there is a catch: it is a "draught only" product, except for a small number of bottles sold during the Thanksgiving, Christmas, and New Year's holidays. If you wish to sample these impressive brews, a trip to Oregon is recommended.

The Bayfront Brewery and Public House, "Home of the Rogue Ales," has much to offer the visitor to Newport. Sweet barley–crusted pizzas, Cornish pastries, ale bread, and beer-soaked sausages are on the menu, along with pasta dishes, soups and salads, sandwiches, and seasonal fish dinners. Also featured are recipes from *Mama Ross' Book on Beer Cooking:* ale shrimp, beer chili, and beercheese soup.

In true pub tradition, minors are welcome to dine until 8:00 P.M. There are no pool or gaming tables, but table games like cribbage or backgammon are encouraged. Equipment is supplied, or you can bring your own.

Tours of the brewery are available upon request.

SLO Brewing

In San Luis Obispo, California, the Spanish *padres* set out to spread the word of God and to convert the unconverted by building a religious mission. A couple of hundred years later there is another mission in town — but it is drawing converts of another kind.

The SLO Brewing Company, in the heart of downtown San Luis Obispo, is reviving a tradition. It is the first brewery-restaurant since Prohibition, and is located in the historic Hanna Hardware Building, just across from the Mission Plaza. The Hanna Hardware Building, with its red-bricked walls, beamed ceiling and oak floors, dates back to 1902. The SLO Brewing Company took up residence in 1988. Lunch and dinner is served, the food is prepared fresh, and is modestly priced. There are a variety of appetizers and entrees to please every taste and every pocketbook. Dinner specials are offered nightly, except Thursdays and Saturdays.

Recently, a new turn-of-the-century Classic Billiard Parlor was opened downstairs. Along with this, their Garden

Alley Amber ale was released for the first time in 22-ounce, "fat boy" bottles. Garden Alley Amber, with its deep, reddish color, medium body, and fragrant hop aroma is achieved with the use of a blend of several high quality grains and hops which sets it apart from ordinary amber ales on the market. Garden Alley Amber is rarely surpassed by other brews in the regular "drinkability polls" conducted at the brewery.

The new, large bottles bear a striking four-color label with an illustration of the historic Hanna Building. The bottled product will be available wherever fine beers are sold and in restaurants where gourmet beers are appreciated. According to brewmaster and SLO president, Michael Hoffman, "We have had so many requests by area restaurants and retailers for our beer in bottles that we finally had to give our fans the brew they demanded." The retail outlets were stunned by the response to the introduction of the SLO beer in bottles. Some stores sold over 100 cases in less than a week. The second batch of beer was completed just in time to refill all the orders.

Michael Hoffman spent 11 years as an international award-winning winemaker before venturing into the beer brewing business. In addition to the Garden Alley Amber, Hoffman's brewing repertoire includes two other basic recipes — Brickhouse Pale Ale and Cole Porter, along with intriguing specialty brews occupying space at the fourth tap.

Beer tastings and tours of the brewery, conducted by the brewmaster himself, can be arranged by calling in advance.

Other special events include the Monday through Friday "Happy Hour-and-a-Half" and live reggae and rock bands that perform Thursday through Saturday evenings at 9:30 P.M. There is also a free Irish happy hour from 5:30 to 7:00 P.M. every second Wednesday of the month.

Look for the beer bottle and tankard on display from the old McCaffrey Brothers Brewery. They were unearthed during excavations for the new brewery.

Sierra Nevada Brewery

Beer lovers are crazy about the Sierra Nevada line of beers. Calling them beers, or even ales, just doesn't do them justice. What we're talking about here is liquid lunch.

The Sierra Nevada Brewery in Chico, California, has been called the "Chateau Latour among American microbreweries" by beer writer Michael Jackson. Author James Robertson calls their brews "handmade gems" and "big and gutsy." Still others have been moved to utter superlative adjectives about the Sierra Nevada products.

The company was started in 1978 by the two principal owners and managers, Ken Grossman and Paul Camusi, who learned the trade by brewing at home and by extensive research and reading. The design and construction of the first brewery was done entirely by Ken and Paul. It took over a year and a half while they worked at other, full time jobs. Construction of the brewing facility was completed in 1981 inside the empty 3,000 square foot shell at 2539 Gilman Way.

The original brewing equipment was made from adapted dairy equipment or converted from other equipment purchased in scrap yards. A used bottling line was purchased from a soft drink bottler and converted for filling beer. For the first year, all engineering, production, and administrative work was done by the two partners. Ken's responsibilities included daily brewing as well as plant development and maintenance. Paul handled the fermentation and aging of the beer as well as microbiological control. His other duties included bookkeeping, financial management, and product distribution.

The Right Glass

With the proliferation of brewpubs and their preponderance of brewing styles comes the return of interesting beer glassware. The range of glassware styles is almost as extensive as the number of beer styles being produced. Many beer styles traditionally have a glass style dedicated to them. A stout served in anything but a pint glass, preferably an Imperial pint, just doesn't taste the same. A Pilsner beer belongs in a tall, hourglass-shaped Pilsner-style glass. English ales and bitters are at home in a dimpled pint mug, while Scottish ales call for a thistle glass (a flourish attributed to the Belgians). German altbiers and Kölschbiers have their own styles; both are smaller versions of the cylindrical Tom Collins type glass. Aromatic Trappist ales and Belgian fruit beers are served in stemmed glasses; the more tulip-shaped, the better. A Berliner weisse demands the wide-rimmed accessibility of a bowl-shaped goblet, while its Bavarian brethren enjoy the deep recesses of a towering weizenbier glass. Rich and spirituous barleywines deserve nothing less than to be served in brandy snifters at room temperature.

Europeans, in general, are more observant and compliant of the unwritten etiquette associated with serving beer. Germans and Belgians can be downright fastidious about it. In some instances, Belgian and German brewers have commissioned world famous glassmakers to design unique glasses for their brews. In contrast, most Americans would seem to have no qualms about drinking from mason jars. (Come to think of it, pouring a national brand beer into a mason jar would be a touch of class.) It's unfortunate that far too many American beer drinkers are still in the habit of drinking straight from the bottle. The use of style-specific glassware is meant to be a product enhancement. Specialized beer glassware is also meant to enhance the aromatics of the beer.

Since the first year, the brewery has experienced steady sales growth and almost continual plant expansion. Currently the largest of the new quality brewers on the West Coast, Sierra Nevada Brewery has been growing at an annual rate of 40 percent, and the prospects for the future are good.

In 1989, in order to meet the demand created by this steady increase in sales, Ken and Paul completed their brand new brewing facility at 1075 East 20th Street. They are extremely proud of this brewery and consider it a fitting showcase for their business. It is capable of a capacity of over 80,000 barrels annually and is equipped to produce lager beers as well as ales. In October, 1989, they opened their new brewpub — the Sierra Nevada Taproom & Restaurant. Like the beers produced there, it has proven to be a great success.

The Sierra Nevada product line offers seven excellent choices: Pale Ale, Porter, Stout, Summerfest Beer, Pale Bock, Bigfoot Barleywine Style Ale, and Celebration Ale 1992 — the bottle labels indicate the year because of the limited annual run of this beer, which is only available throughout the year and holiday season. Celebration Ale is big, zesty, and robust — ideally suited to be a sipping beer. This incredible brew can be equally savored with the Thanksgiving turkey (give thanks for great microbrewed beer), the Christmas ham (ask Santa to leave a case of Sierra Nevada under the tree), or as the perfect beverage to help ring in the New Year (resolve to drink nothing but great beer).

Yakima Brewing & Malting Company

One cannot easily write about the successes of the Yakima Brewing & Malting Company without first mentioning its founding father and brewmaster, Bert Grant. Herbert L. Grant, an expatriate Scotsman, is not just the force behind the brewery, he *is* the brewery. Grant comes by this claim rightfully — he has spent two-thirds of his life devoted to the brewing industry; if not directly, then by allied industry. Mr. Grant's career in brewing extends back to 1945 and includes positions as a chemist with a major Canadian brewer, a research director for a large American brewer, and a technical director for the world's second largest hop grower. It's no small wonder that his own homebrewed beers won such rave reviews that the tasters decided to finance a small brewery with Bert Grant at the helm.

The fledgling Yakima Brewing & Malting Company, originally built in 1982 in a turn-of-the-century opera house, became the first modern American pub brewery. After spilling into an adjacent room out of necessity, the oak-paneled, non-smoking pub gained in popularity and additional expansion was sorely needed. Eventually, the brewery had to be relocated to larger quarters, so Grant's Brewery Pub was opened across the street in the old railway depot.

One of the benefits of the expanded facility was a wide variety of gourmet, pub-style food available for both lunch and dinner, seven days a week. Standard items include fish and chips, British bangers, Scotch eggs, homemade soups, and a wide variety of daily specials. Continuing the tradition of the old opera house, the new pub also has regular musical events, as well as special events.

The demand for Grant's ales from the far reaches of the United States necessitated the installation of a bottling line in 1987. Space within the old brewery was limited and the increasing number of trucks pulling in and out of the brewery was becoming a problem in the historic and tourist-oriented section of Yakima. New orders for Grant's ales were being turned down. Another move for the brewery was imminent.

In 1990, with the aid of a federal Small Business Administration loan, Bert Grant oversaw the construction of the new two-million-dollar Yakima Brewing & Malting Company on the outskirts of town. Grant's environmentally friendly company now employs 40 people, and Grant's Ales can be found in 23 states, as well as British Columbia. The annual output exceeded 7,500 barrels in 1992 and monthly increases are not uncommon.

In addition to the trademark Scottish Ale, the Yakima Brewing & Malting Company produces a weiss beer, an Imperial stout, India pale ale, a spiced ale, apple honey ale, and the low-alcohol, low-calorie Grant's Celtic Ale. Touted as the "world's best light beer," Celtic Ale is not a diluted beer but a special brew, mashed for low calories but retaining the flavor and body of an Irish mild ale.

Pairing Beer with Food

Until recently, beer's place in the American dining experience has been largely inconsequential, and the pairing of a certain beer with a certain food has occurred mostly by coincidence. While even novice wine drinkers have a simple "red meat, red wine" axiom to follow, no such guideline exists for beer drinkers, novice or otherwise. The first and favorite rule of pairing beer and food is based on the subjective nature of the human palate: disregard all the rules! This works well for those who have some familiarity with beer styles and flavor profiles; for those who have none, decision-making can be a daunting experience. Today, it is conceivable that for every food there is an appropriate beer choice, necessitating the most fundamental of guidelines.

To fully enjoy any beer and food combination, time and place must be factored into the equation. Grilled chicken on a hot August afternoon begs for something cold, light, and refreshing like a wheat beer or a Pilsner. At the opposite extreme, steak and kidney pie on a frosty winter evening deserves the complement of a rich porter or stout, served at cellar temperature (see glossary). Certain well-hopped beers such as steam beers and India pale ales make excellent aperitifs, while a post-prandial beer list might include a brown ale or a bitter. As the day winds down, nothing can match the malty excesses of barleywine, doppelbock or Imperial Russian stout — served at slightly above room temperature, of course!

Pacific Brewer Profiles

"Buffalo Bill" Owens

Buffalo Bill's brewpub in Hayward, California, was opened in 1983 by a professional photojournalist and homebrewer named Bill Owens. Small brewing operations were largely unheard of in those days, and there were no manufacturers around to produce small-scale brewing equipment. It took nine months and $90,000 to start, and Owens estimates that the same start-up today would cost as much as $600,000.

Bill Owens's passion for beer goes far beyond that of the common man, and it pervades all areas of his life. Relying on his journalistic talents and his intimate knowledge of small-scale brewing, he published a book entitled, *How to Build a Small Brewery*, written about the same time that Buffalo Bill's opened. Owens, still needing a creative outlet for his journalistic bent, also publishes two magazines: *American Brewer* is written for the homebrewer who aspires to become a microbrewer, and *BeeR: the magazine*, takes a much broader approach to beer — not just as a beverage, but as a lifestyle. The first issue of *BeeR: the magazine* sold all 10,000 copies and has since sold an additional press run of 20,000. Owens also founded BrewPAC, a lobbying group to encourage the legalization of brewpubs in all 50 states. All of these ventures originate from the same 40" x 60" space in the back of the brewpub — believed to be the smallest corporate office in the world.

Did I mention that Bill Owens also brews beer? His products are primarily of the ale variety and have been pretty much unheralded since the boom in the microbrewing industry. They are known but to a few. In order for Bill's beer to reach the masses, he has had to turn to contract brewing (see page 201). Pumpkin Ale is just one example of Bill's unorthodox approach to brewing. Another of Bill's beers (and one can only imagine the inspiration for this one) is called Alimony Ale, "the bitterest beer in America."

In time, Owens would like to open a microbrewery, complete with bottling facilities, where he could continue to produce an eclectic array of beers such as rauchbiers and fruit beers. Until then, Buffalo Bill Owens continues to dabble with other beer-related ideas including an electronic bulletin board for computer users and E-mail on Internet and Compuserve. Call his toll-free number for details: 1-800-646-2701.

Bert Grant

Bert Grant's career began with Canadian Breweries, Ltd. at the tender age of 16. After a number of years experimenting with beer recipes and yeast varieties, Bert crossed the river into Detroit where he became director of brewing research at Stroh's. Dealing with "bottom line" people who insisted on producing a lighter, cheaper product, Grant became increasingly disenchanted with the corporate brewing industry and struck out on his own as a private brewing consultant. Relying on his vast experience in this field, Grant traveled the world, trouble shooting for other breweries.

In the late 1960s, Grant was lured to the lush Yakima Valley in Washington State to become technical director for S.S. Steiner, the world's second largest hop grower. In this capacity, Bert did pioneering work in laboratory analysis of hops and the manufacturing of hop extracts, as well as hop pelleting, and a number of patents were taken out on these processes.

Still missing the "old way" of brewing, Grant began brewing beer in his basement using a hybrid yeast strain he had developed back in the 1950s. In 1981, he served some of his Scottish ale to members of a local enological society (fancy term for wine club). Impressed with his beer, a handful of members decided to

pool their financial resources to finance a small hobby brewery from which Grant could sell his draught product to accounts in the Yakima Valley. The end result has been a very popular and successful Yakima area brewpub and brewery.

According to Grant: "Great beer, like fine wine, should reflect the character and opinions of the brewer." From the start, he has kept complete control of the brewery, so Grant's Ales are faithful to his strong opinions about beer and brewing. Says Grant: "When you buy a Grant's Scottish ale, Imperial stout, or any one of our other beers, you can be sure you are buying a drink with personality — MY personality! I think that's the way brewing should be."

Fritz Maytag

Fritz. Not exactly a household name. Maytag. Definitely a household name. Now, put them both together and you've got a soon-to-be household name.

Fritz Maytag is credited with rescuing the now legendary Anchor Brewing Company in California from financial ruin and its eventual demise. For this, he can be rightly called the godfather of the American microbrewing industry.

Fritz Maytag grew up in Newton, Iowa, heir to the Maytag family's washing machine business. His move to the West Coast was a result of going to college at Stanford University. While pursuing a master's degree, Fritz was working on a project with friends involving business in South America. At the time, rumors were circulating about a local brewery about to

Complementing Tex-Mex and Asian Cuisines

The range of styles from light to dark, dry to sweet, mild to robust, make for an unlimited number of culinary combinations. Here are two worth considering:

Most people's first inclination upon ingesting a heaping helping of five-alarm chili is to reach for something cold and wet in an effort to wash away the lingering heat. This may work sufficiently, but why not enjoy both the hot spiciness and the beer? Try a medium- to full-bodied lager, such as a bock beer or a Märzenbier. These choices are substantially malty and have a creamy mouthfeel. Rather than rinsing the mouth, they will coat the mouth and tongue, and the sweetness will help to extinguish the flames — enjoyably.

On the other side of the coin, a premium lager beer such as a Munich helles pairs nicely with Indian and other Asian cuisines. These foods occasionally are spicy and are prepared with subtle finesse. Lightly hopped and mildly sweet beers are recommended so as not to overpower the food's subtleties.

---

go bankrupt. Intrigued enough to investigate, Maytag eventually bought the majority ownership. In order to do so, it was necessary to relinquish some of his share of the family company. By doing this, Fritz took a huge risk in a business and an industry, the future of which was tenuous at best. Today, the Anchor Brewing Company, with its gleaming brewhouse and untarnished reputation as a producer of high quality ales, serves as an inspiration for the rest of the microbrewing industry, even though Anchor itself is not considered a microbrewery.

The Anchor Brewery's flagship Steam Beer (now a registered trademark) and the steam beer style, was rescued from the brink of extinction and redefined by Fritz and his new brewery. The style has been called the only indigenous American brewing style.

Despite his status among lovers of handcrafted beer, Fritz Maytag is also a lover and advocate of fine wine. He also has an interest in vineyards in the Napa and Sonoma valleys. There are 125 acres of grapes outside St. Helena known to wine aficionados as York Creek Vineyards.

Don't let this viticulturist avocation dim your view of Fritz Maytag. He is on the board of directors for the Brewers Association of America, as well as a director for the United States Brewers' Association. Just to fill in the empty hours in his life, Fritz serves as a member of several civic and educational boards, and is chairman of the board of Iowa's Grinnell College.

Pacific Region Beer Festivals

Northwest Microbrew Expo
Eugene, OR
February (second week)
(800) 284-6529

This festival is held at the Lane County Convention Center, and an estimated 60 brews from 30 breweries are available. The focus is on Pacific Northwest beers, but others are welcomed. There is live entertainment, a food court, and 15-minute "Beer Tours," hosted by brewers, which explain brewing processes.

California Festival of Beers
San Luis Obispo, CA
May (4th week)
(800) 549-1538

The eighth annual California Festival of Beer will be held in May 1995. Tickets must be ordered in advance.

KQED Beer & Food Fest
San Francisco, CA
July
(415) 553-2200

This is the Rolls Royce of American Beer Festivals. Multinational in flavor, the KQED event showcases more than 200 beers from over 30 countries. Part beer-tasting, part fundraiser for public radio broadcasting, this event raises more than $100,000 annually. There is an eclectic collection of live entertainment with beer and food. The KQED Beer & Food Fest is well-attended and advance ticket purchase is strongly recommended.

Oregon Brewer's Festival
Portland, OR
July
(503) 222-7150

America's premier beer city is host to more than 60 breweries from 17 states, serving over 200 different brews. The scenic Riverside Park in downtown Portland provides the perfect backdrop for the event, which attracts 70,000 people over the course of one midsummer weekend. A hop head's nirvana.

California Small Brewer's Festival
Mountain View, CA
July
(408) 243-5861

Small refers to the brewers, not the festival; this is a huge outdoor beer party complete with marching bands! As the marquee suggests, it is a celebration of the California microbrewing industry and is held in Mountain View, at the southern end of San Francisco Bay.

Northwest Ale Festival
Seattle, WA
September (first week)
(206) 527-7331

More than just a beer festival, this is the country's biggest pub crawl. The ninth annual Northwest Ale Festival commences after Labor Day and lasts one week. Twenty-five to 30 Seattle area ale houses participate by featuring or spotlighting the beers of specific breweries. There is no entrance fee; just pay as you go. Sponsored by the Pint Post/Micro Appreciation Society.

Great Northwest Microbrewery Invitational
Seattle, WA
September (third week)
(206) 232-2982

The festival is held at the Seattle Center Exhibition Hall and is dedicated to microbrewers in the Pacific Northwest.

Pacific Region Listings

Alaskan Brewing & Bottling

Anchor Brewing

Anderson Valley Brewery

Alaska

Alaskan Brewing & Bottling
5429 Shaune Dr.
Juneau, AK 99801
(907) 780-5866
Microbrewery
Brews: Alaskan Amber, Pale
Ale. *Seasonals:* Arctic Ale,
Alaskan Smoked Porter, Spring
Wheat, Winter Stock Ale,
Autumn Ale, Breakup Bock
Tours: May–Sept., Tues.–Sat.,
11AM–4:30PM, on the hour and
half hour; Oct.–April,
Thurs.–Sat., 11AM–5PM.
Groups of 6 or more, advance
notice requested.

Bird Creek Brewery
310 E. 76th
Anchorage, AK 99518
(907) 344-2473
Microbrewery
Brews: Old 55, Anchorage,
Denali Style Ale
Tours: By appointment

**Raven Ridge
Brewing Company**
Fairbanks, AK
No further information avail-
able at press time.

California

American River Brewing
100 Borland Ave.
Auburn, CA 95603
(916) 889-0841
Microbrewery
Brews: American River Gold
Lager, amber lager
Tours: Sat., 9AM–5PM

Anchor Brewing
1705 Mariposa St.
San Francisco, CA 94107
(415) 863-8350
Microbrewery
Brews: Anchor Steam Beer,
Anchor Porter, Liberty Ale,
Anchor Wheat Beer, Old
Foghorn. *Seasonal:* Our
Special Ale
Tours: By appointment with at
least 2 weeks notice required.

**Anderson Valley Brewery
(Buckhorn Saloon)**
14081 Hwy. 128
Boonville, CA 95415
(707) 895-BEER
Brewpub
Brews: Boont Amber, Poleeko
Gold, High Rollers Wheat
Beer, Deep Enders Dark,

Barney Flats Oatmeal Stout.
Seasonals: Whamber, Winter
Solstice, Oktoberfest, ESB

Hours: Sun., Mon., & Thurs.,
11AM–9PM; Fri.–Sat.,
11AM–11PM; closed Tues. and
Wed. during off-season

Angeles Brewing
10009 Conoga Ave.
Chatsworth, CA 91311
(818) 407-0340
Microbrewery
Brews: Angeles Amber Ale,
Shams
Tours: By appointment

Belmont Brewing
25 39th Pl.
Long Beach, CA 90803
(213) 433-3891
Brewpub
Brews: Marathon Ale, Top Sail
Ale, Long Beach Crude.
Seasonals: Strawberry Blonde,
McWheat
Hours: Mon.–Fri., 11:30AM–
midnight; Sat.–Sun., 9AM–
midnight

Bison Brewing
2598 Telegraph Ave.
Berkeley, CA 94704
(510) 841-7734
Brewpub
Brews: Honey-Basil Ale,
Chocolate Porter, Peach Sunset
Red Ale, Nut Brown Ale, Black
Shadow Bock, and others on
rotation
Hours: Daily, 11AM–1AM

Blind Pig Brewing
42387 Avenida Alvarito #108
Temecula, CA 92390
(909) 569-4646

Microbrewery
Brews: Bootleg Bitter, Blind
Pig Pale Ale, Butterfield
Amber, stout, barleywine
Tours: Call for information

Blue Water Brewing
850 N. Lake Blvd.
Tahoe City, CA 96145
(916) 581-2583
Brewpub
Brews: Palisades Extra Pale,
Arrowhead Red Ale, Misty
Mountain Oatmeal Stout.
Seasonals: Brown Ale, Eagle
Rock Raspberry Ale,
Sabertooth India Pale Ale
Hours: Daily, 11AM–1:30AM

Bootleggers Brewing
3401 Chester Ave. #H
Bakersfield, CA 93301
(805) 323-2739
Brewpub
Brews: Bootleggers American
Ale, Voluptuous Blonde Ale,
Big Red Ale, Snake Bite
Amber, 34th Street Porter.
Seasonal: Summer Wheat
Hours: Sun.–Thurs.,
11AM–11PM; Fri.–Sat.,
11AM–midnight

**Boulder Creek Brewing
(Boulder Creek
Grill & Cafe)**
13040 Hwy. 9
Boulder Creek, CA 95006
(408) 338-7882
Brewpub
Brews: Ghost Rail Pale Ale,
P.O.F. ESB, Red Wood Ale,
Danish Holiday Cheer, St.
Severin's Kölsch, O'Meal Stout,
Pilsner Vaclar, Old MacLunk's
Scottish Ale, and seasonals

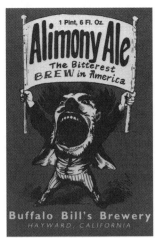

Buffalo Bill's Brewery

Hours: Mon.–Thurs., noon–11PM; Fri.–Sat., noon–midnight; Sun., noon–10PM

Brewery at Lake Tahoe
3542 Lake Tahoe Blvd.
South Lake Tahoe, CA 96150
(916) 544-BREW
Brewpub

Brews: Paramount Porter, Washoe Wheat, Alpine Amber, Needle Peak Ale. *Seasonals:* fruit beers, strong ales, stouts

Hours: Daily, 11AM–closing

Brewmeisters of Palm Springs
369 N. Palm Canyon Dr.
Palm Springs, CA 92262
(619) 327-2739
Brewpub

Brews: Desert Mist Pale Ale, Moonlight Amber Ale. *Seasonals:* Wilson's Wheat, Dark Roasted Chocolate Porter

Hours: Daily, 11:00AM–1:00AM

Brewski's GasLamp Pub, Bistro & Brewery
310 Fifth Ave.
San Diego, CA 92101
(619) 231-7700
Brewpub

Brews: Whale's Tale Pale Ale, Aztec Amber, Red Sails Ale, Pioneer Porter, Stingaree Stout, raspberry ale, weizen beer

Hours: Mon.–Fri., 11:30AM–2AM; Sat., 10AM–2AM; Sun., 10AM–11PM

Buffalo Bill's Brewpub
1082 B St.
Hayward, CA 94541
(510) 886-9823

Brewpub

Brews: Buffalo Brew, amber, stout. *Seasonals:* Alimony Ale, Pumpkin Ale, Rauch Smoked Porter

Hours: Mon.–Thurs., 11:30AM–11:30PM; Fri., 11:30AM–midnight; Sat., 10:30AM–midnight; Sun., 10:30AM–9PM

Butterfield Brewing, Bar & Grill
777 E. Olive Ave.
Fresno, CA 93728
(209) 264-5521
Brewpub

Brews: San Joaquin Golden Ale, Bridalveil Ale, Tower Dark Ale. *Seasonals:* Oktoberfest, Sierra Spring Ale, Mt. Whitney Ale, raspberry wheat ale

Hours: Mon.–Thurs., 10:45AM–11PM; Fri., 10:45AM–1:45AM; Sat., 10:45AM–1AM; Sun., 10AM–9PM

Cafe Pacifica/Sankt Gallen Brewery
333 Bush St.
San Francisco, CA 94104
(415) 296-8203
Brewpub

Brews: pale, amber, dark ale

Hours: Mon.–Fri., 11AM–10PM; Sat.–Sun., 11AM–9PM

Callahan's Pub & Brewery
8280-A Mira Mesa Blvd.
San Diego, CA 92126
(619) 578-7892
Brewpub

Brews: Blueberry Wheat, Mesa Pale Ale, Callahan Red, Black Mountain Porter, Bernard Bitter, Nameless Nut Brown

Seasonals: Anniversary Ale, Christmas Ale

Hours: Mon.–Thurs., 11AM–midnight; Fri.–Sat., 11AM–1AM; Sun., 10AM–10PM

Covany Brewing
359 Grand Ave.
Grover Beach, CA 93433
(805) 489-4042

Brewpub

Brews: Copper Penny Amber, Grover Gold Pale Ale, Sandy Wheat, Pismo Porter, and seasonals

Hours: Mon.–Wed., noon–midnight; Thurs.–Sat., noon–2AM; closed Sun.

Crown City Brewery
300 S. Raymond Ave.
Pasadena, CA 91105
(818) 577-5548

Brewpub

Brews: Mt. Wilson Wheat, Arroyo Amber Ale, Black Cloud Oatmeal Stout, Yorkshire Porter. *Seasonals:* Father Christmas Wassail, Irish Red Ale, and others

Hours: Mon.–Thurs., 11AM–midnight; Fri.–Sat., 11AM–1AM; Sun., 11AM–10PM

Dempsey's Sonoma Brewing
50 E. Washington St.
Petaluma, CA 94952
(707) 765-9694

Brewpub

Brews: Golden Eagle Ale, Red Rooster, Bad Brown Bear Ale, Ugly Dog Stout. *Seasonals:* Bock, Irish Ale, Petaluma Strong Ale, and others

Hours: Daily, 11:30AM–10PM

Devil Mountain/Bay Brewing
2283 Camel Road
Benicia, CA 94510
(707) 747-6961

Microbrewery

Brews: Railroad Ale, Devil's Brew. *Seasonals:* ESB, Diablo Gold, IPA, Devil Mountain Wheat

Tours: Call at least one day in advance.

Downtown Joe's Brewery & Restaurant
902 Main St.
Napa, CA 94559
(707) 258-2337

Brewpub

Brews: Lickity Split Lager, Ace High Cream Ale, Tail Waggin' Ale, Past Due Dark Ale, Golden Thistle Bitter Ale, and seasonals

Hours: Daily, 8AM–midnight

El Toro Brewing
17370 Hill Road
Morgan Hill, CA 95037
(408) 778-BREW

Microbrewery

Brews: El Toro Oro, Poppy Jasper Amber Ale. *Seasonals:* Apricot, William Jone's Wheat, and others

Tours: Daily, 11AM–5PM

Etna Brewery
131 Callahan St.
Etna, CA 96027
(916) 467-5277

Microbrewery

Brews: ale, Export lager, dark lager, weizen

Tours: Sat., 1PM–5PM, or by appointment

Fremont Brewing
3350 Stevenson Blvd.
Fremont, CA 94538
(510) 651-5510
Brewpub
Brews: California Amber,
Mission Peak Porter, Mission
Wheat, Black Cow Stout, and
seasonals
Hours: Daily, 11AM–midnight
(9AM on Sat. during football
season)

Fullerton Hofbrau
323 N. State College Blvd.
Fullerton, CA 92631
(714) 870-7400
Brewpub
Brews: King's Lager, Prince's
Pilsner. *Seasonals:* Duke's
Bock, Earl's Ale, Baron's
Wheat
Hours: Mon.–Sat.,
11:00AM–1AM

Golden Pacific Brewing
5515 Doyle St.
Emeryville, CA 94608
(510) 547-8270
Microbrewery
Brews: Golden Pacific
Bittersweet Ale, Golden Beer
Lager, Black Bear Dark, Cable
Car Classic Lager, Golden Gate
Malt Liquor, Golden Pacific
Pale Ale
Tours: By appointment

Gordon Biersch Brewing
640 Emerson St.
Palo Alto, CA 94301
(415) 323-7723
Brewery Restaurant
Brews: Export, Märzen, dun-
kles, hefe-weizen, doppelbock
Hours: Sun.–Wed.,

11AM–11PM; Thurs. 11AM–midnight; Fri.–Sat., 11AM–1AM

Gordon Biersch Brewing
41 Hugus Alley
Pasadena, CA 91103
(818) 449-0052
Brewery Restaurant
Brews: Export, Märzen, dun-
kles, bock, hefe-weizen
Hours: Sun.–Thurs.,
11AM–11PM; Fri.–Sat.,
11AM–midnight

Gordon Biersch Brewing
2 Harrison St.
San Francisco, CA 94120
(415) 243-8246
Brewery Restaurant
Brews: export, Märzen, dun-
kles, doppelbock
Hours: Sun.–Wed., 11AM–11PM;
Thurs.–Sat., 11AM–1AM

Gordon Biersch Brewing
33 E. San Fernando St.
San Jose, CA 94301
(408) 294-6785
Brewery Restaurant
Brews: export, Märzen, dun-
kles, hefe-weizen, doppelbock
Hours: Sun.–Wed., 11AM–11PM;
Thurs. 11AM–midnight;
Fri.–Sat., 11AM–1AM

Hangtown Brewery
560A Placerville Dr.
Placerville, CA 95667
(916) 621-3999
Microbrewery
Brews: Placerville Pale Ale,
Boysenberry Ale, Mad Dog
Brown
Tours: Mon.–Thurs., noon–7PM;
Fri.–Sat., 11AM–8PM;
Sun., noon–5PM

Heritage Brewing
24921 Dana Point Harbor Dr.
Dana Point, CA 92629
(714) 240-2060

Brewpub

Brews: Lantern Bay Blonde,
Sail Ale, Dana Porter.
Seasonals: IPA, No Doubt
Stout, N.B.A., Christmas Ale,
High Seas Oatmeal Stout

Hours: Sun.–Thurs.,
11:30AM–midnight;
Fri.–Sat., 11:30AM–2AM

Hogshead Brewpub
114 J St.
Sacramento, CA 95814
(916) 443-BREW

Brewpub

Brews: Hogshead Lager,
McSchlueter, Hogshead Pale
Ale

Hours: Sun.–Thurs.,
11:30AM–11PM; Fri.–Sat.,
11:30AM–2AM

Hops Bistro & Brewery
4353 La Jolla Village Dr. H-29
San Diego, CA 92122-1212
(619) 587-6677

Brewpub

Brews: Pilsner, hefe-weizen,
raspberry lager, ESB, oatmeal
stout. *Seasonals:* Oktoberfest,
bock, barleywine, export lager,
spiced ale, doppelbock

Hours: Sun.–Thurs.,
11:30AM–11:30PM; Fri.–Sat.,
11:30AM–midnight

Humboldt Brewery
856 Tenth St.
Arcata, CA 95521
(707) 826-BREW

Brewpub

Brews: Gold Rush Pale Ale,

Red Nectar Ale, oatmeal stout.
Seasonals: wheat beer,
Humboldt Honey, Holidaze
Ale, Cheshire Cat Barleywine

Hours: Mon.–Thurs.,
noon–11PM; Fri.–Sat.,
noon–2AM; Sun., noon–10PM

Humes Brewing
2775 Cavedale Road
Glen Ellen, CA 95442
(707) 935-0723

Microbrewery

Brews: Deep Canyon Stout,
Whitwan Honey Wheat, India
pale ale, Virgin Ginger Brew,
seasonals

Tours: Call for information

**Huntington Beach
Beer Company**
201 Main St. #E
Huntington Beach, CA 92648
(714) 960-5343

Brewpub

Brews: Huntington Beach
Blonde, Pier Pale Ale, Main
Street Wheat, Bohemian
Pilsner, Bolsa Chica Bitter,
Brickshot Red, Dextrous Ale,
and others

Hours: Sun.–Thurs.,
11:30AM–midnight; Fri.–Sat.,
11:30AM–2AM

**Karl Strauss
Brewery Gardens**
9675 Scranton Road
San Diego, CA 92121
(619) 587-BREW

Brewpub

Brews: Red Trolley Ale, Karl
Strauss Light, America's Finest
Pilsner, Karl Strauss Amber
Lager, and others on rotation

Hours: Mon.–Fri., 7AM–10PM;

Humboldt Brewery

Lost Coast Brewery & Cafe

Mad River Brewing

Sun. 11:30AM–sunset; closed Sat. for weddings and private functions

Karl Strauss' Old Columbia Brewery & Grill
1157 Columbia St.
San Diego, CA 92101
(619) 234-BREW
Brewpub
Brews: Red Trolley Ale, Karl Strauss Light, America's Finest Pilsner, Karl Strauss Amber Lager, and more on rotation
Hours: Mon.–Thurs., 11:30AM–midnight; Fri.–Sat., 11:30AM–1AM; Sun., 11:30AM–10PM

La Jolla Brewing
7536 Fay Ave.
San Diego, CA 92037
(619) 456-2739
Brewpub
Brews: Little Point Ale, Sea Lane Amber, Red Roost Ale, Big Rock Bock, Pumphouse Porter. *Seasonals:* Windansea Wheat, Blitzen Ale, and others
Hours: Sun.–Thurs., 11AM–11PM; Fri.–Sat., 11AM–1AM

Lind Brewing
1933 Davis
San Leandro, CA 94577
(510) 562-0866
Microbrewery
Brews: Drake's Gold, Drake's Ale, Sir Francis Stout, Drake's Pale Ale. *Seasonals:* Drake's IPA, Lind Bock, Lind Wheat, Jolly Roger's Holiday Ale, Drake's Nog, and others
Tours: Fri., 4PM–6PM, parties of 10 or more should call in advance

Live Soup Brewery Cafe
1602 Ocean St.
Santa Cruz, CA 95060
(408) 458-3461
Brewpub
Brews: Lemming Ale; rotating: special bitter, wheat beer, porter, Kölsch, dark wheat
Hours: Mon.–Sat., 11:30AM–1AM; Sun., 11:30AM–10PM

Los Gatos Brewing
130G N. Santa Cruz
Los Gatos, CA 95030
(408) 395-9929
Brewpub
Brews: lager, Oktoberfest, Märzen, dunkel. *Seasonals:* bock, doppelbock, pale ale, nut brown, hefe-weizen
Hours: Sun.–Thurs., 11AM–11PM; Fri.–Sat., 11AM–2AM

Lost Coast Brewery & Cafe
617 4th St.
Eureka, CA 95501
(707) 445-4480
Brewpub
Brews: amber, harvest wheat, Downtown Brown. *Seasonals:* chocolate porter, hefe dunkel-weizen, Summerfest, Oktoberfest
Hours: Mon.–Thurs., 11AM–midnight; Fri.–Sat., 11AM–1AM; Sun., 11AM–11PM

Mad River Brewing
195 Taylor Way
Blue Lake, CA 95525
(707) 668-4151
Microbrewery
Brews: Steelhead Extra Pale Ale, Extra Stout

Tours: Sat., or by reservation Mon. through Fri.

Manhattan Beach Brewing
124 Manhattan Beach Blvd.
Manhattan Beach, CA 90266
(310) 798-2744
Brewpub

Brews: Dominator Wheat, Rat Beach Red, Manhattan Beach Blonde. *Seasonals:* Strand Amber, Pacifica Pale Ale, Pier Pale Ale, Buccaneer Black, and others

Hours: Sun.–Thurs., 11AM–midnight; Fri.–Sat., 11AM–1AM

Marin Brewing
1809 Larkspur Landing Circle
Larkspur, CA 94939
(415) 461-HOPS
Brewpub

Brews: Mount Tam Pale Ale. *Seasonals:* Albion Amber Ale, Marin Weiss, Marin Hefe Weiss, St. Brendan Irish Red Ale, blueberry ale, Raspberry Trail Ale, and others

Hours: Sun.–Thurs., 11:30AM–midnight; Fri.–Sat., 11:30AM–1AM

Mendocino Brewing (Hopland Brewery Restaurant)
13351 S. Hwy. 101 S
Hopland, CA 95449
(707) 744-1361
Brewpub

Brews: Red Tail Ale, Blue Heron Pale Ale, Black Hawk Stout, Peregrine Pale Ale. *Seasonals:* Yuletide Porter, Springtide Ale, Eye of the Hawk

Hours: Sun.–Thurs.,

11AM–10PM; Fri., 11AM–11PM; Sat., 11AM–1:30AM

Monterey Brewing
511 Tyler St.
Monterey, CA 93940
(408) 375-3634
Brewpub

Brews: Save the Ale Pale Ale, Killer Whale Amber Ale, Sea Lion Stout. *Seasonals:* Great White Lite, Cheery Whale Cherry Ale

Hours: Sun.–Fri., 8PM–2AM; Sat., 4PM–2AM

Moonlight Brewing
P.O. Box 316
Santa Rosa, CA 95401
Microbrewery

Brews: Moonlight Pale Ale, Twist of Fate Bitter, Death & Taxes Black Beer, Full Moon Light Ale, Bombay by Boat IPA. *Seasonal:* Santa's Tipple

Tours: By appointment. Call for directions.

Murphys Creek Brewing
Murphys Grade Road
Murphys, CA 95247
(209) 736-BREW
Microbrewery

Brews: golden wheat, Murphys Red, Black Gold Stout. *Seasonals:* raspberry wheat, Oktoberfest, bock, Jule

Tours: Sat.–Sun., 11AM–5PM

Napa Valley Brewing (Calistoga Inn)
1250 Lincoln Ave.
Calistoga, CA 94515
(707) 942-4101
Brewpub

Brews: Wheat Ale, Red Ale,

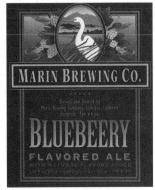

Marin Brewing

Mendocino Brewing

Golden Lager, Calistoga.
Seasonals: IPA, Porter,
Barleywine, Stout, Oktoberfest,
ESB

Hours: Daily, 11:30AM–closing

Nevada City Brewing
75 Bost Ave.
Nevada City, CA 95959
(916) 265-2446
Microbrewery

Brews: Nevada City Brew,
California Gold Lager, Nevada
City Brew, California Dark
Lager. *Seasonal:* California
Stout Lager

Tours: Sat., 1PM–5PM

North Coast Brewing
444 N. Main
Ft. Bragg, CA 95437
(707) 964-2739
Brewpub

Brews: Ruedrich's Red Seal
Ale, Old Number 38,
Scrimshaw. *Seasonals:*
Centennial Ale, Oktoberfest
Ale, Christmas Ale, Traditional
Bock, and others

Hours: Tues.–Sat., 2PM–11PM;
closed Sun.–Mon.

Pacific Beach Brewhouse
4475 Mission Blvd.
San Diego, CA 92109
(619) 274-ALES
Brewpub

Brews: Pacific Beach Blonde,
Crystal Pier Pale, Sunset Red,
Over-The-Line Stout.
Seasonals: IPA, brown ale,
Scotch ale, Belgian strong ale,
and others

Hours: Daily, 11:30AM–closing

Pacific Coast Brewing
906 Washington St.
Oakland, CA 94607
(510) 836-BREW
Brewpub

Brews: Gray Whale Ale, Blue
Whale Ale, Imperial Stout.
Seasonals: Acorn Ale, Emerald
Ale, Amethyst Ale, Holiday
Ale, and others

Hours: Mon.–Thurs.,
11:30AM–midnight; Fri.–Sat.,
11:30AM–1AM; Sun.,
11:30AM–11PM

Pacific Hop Exchange Brewing
158 Hamilton Dr. #A1
Novato, CA 94949
(415) 884-2820
Microbrewery

Brews: Gaslight Pale Ale, 06
Stout, Graintader Wheat Ale.
Seasonal: Holly Hops

Tours: Annually on Feb. 30

Pacific Tap & Grill
812 4th St.
San Rafael, CA 94901
(415) 457-9711

Brews: Mission Gold, Bootjack
Amber; and specialties in
rotation

Hours: Mon.–Thurs.,
11:30AM–10PM; Fri.–Sat.,
11:30AM–11PM; Sun.,
12:30PM–9:30PM

Pizza Port Solana Beach Brewery
135 N. Hwy. 101
Solana Beach, CA 92075
(619) 481-7332
Brewpub

Brews: Pillbox Pale Ale,
Solana Beach, Sharkbite Red,

Swami's IPA, Port's Porter, and seasonals

Hours: Sun.–Wed., 11AM–11PM; Thurs.–Sat., 11AM–midnight

Red, White & Blue
2181 Hill Top Dr.
Redding, CA 96002
(916) 222-5891
Brewpub
Brews: Kölsch, light amber, medium amber, and seasonals
Hours: Daily, 11AM–11PM

Redondo Beach Brewing
1814 S. Catalina Ave.
Redondo Beach, CA 90277
(310) 316-8477
Brewpub
Brews: Redondo Beach Blonde, Pier Pale Ale, South Bay Bitter, Rat Beach Red
Hours: Daily, 11:30AM–1AM

River City Brewing
545 Downtown Plaza #1115
Sacramento, CA 95814
(916) 447-BREW
Brewpub
Brews: River City Lager, hefeweizen, pale ale, Vienna, porter, and seasonals
Hours: Sun.–Wed., 11:30AM–11PM; Thurs., 11:30AM–midnight; Fri.–Sat., 11:30AM–1:30AM

Riverside Brewing
3397 7th St.
Riverside, CA 92501
(909) 784-BREW
Brewpub
Brews: Golden Spike Pilsner, Rain Cross Wheat, Pullman

Pale Ale, Victoria Avenue Amber Ale, No. 119, 77th Street Stout
Hours: Sun.–Thurs., 11:30AM–11PM; Fri.–Sat., 11:30AM–1AM

Rubicon Brewing
2004 Capitol Ave.
Sacramento, CA 95814
(916) 448-7032
Brewpub
Brews: Summer Wheat, India Pale Ale, Amber, Stout. *Seasonals:* Ol' Moe, Rosemary Porter, Winter Wheat Wine, Irish Red Ale, and others
Hours: Mon.–Thurs., 11:30AM–11:30PM; Fri., 11:30AM–12:30AM; Sat., 9AM–12:30AM; Sun., 9AM–10PM

San Andreas Brewing
737 San Benito St.
Hollister, CA 95023
(408) 637-7074
Brewpub
Brews: Earthquake Pale, Seismic Ale, Kit Fox Amber, Earthquake Porter, Survivor Stout. *Seasonals:* apricot ale, cherry ale, woodruff, and others
Hours: Sun., Tues.–Thurs., 11AM–10PM; Fri.–Sat., 11AM–11PM

San Diego Brewing
10450 Friars Road
San Diego, CA 92120
(619) 284-BREW
Brewpub
Brews: Grantville Gold, San Diego Amber, Mission Gorge Porter, Admiral Baker Bitter, Old Town Nut Brown, Old 395 Barleywine; over 40 guest beers on tap

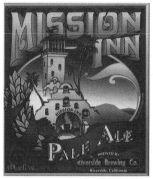

Riverside Brewing

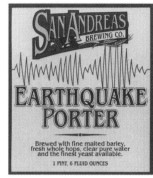

San Andreas Brewing

Hours: Mon.–Thurs., 11AM–midnight; Fri.–Sat., 11AM–1AM; Sun., 10AM–midnight

San Francisco Brewing
155 Columbus Ave.
San Francisco, CA 94133
(415) 434-3344
Brewpub
Brews: Albatross Lager, Emperor Norton Lager, Gripman's Porter, Serpent Stout. *Seasonals:* Grace Darling Bock, Andromeda

Wheat Beer, Oofty Goofty Barleywine

Hours: Mon.–Thurs., 11:30AM–12:30AM; Fri., 11:30AM–1:30AM; Sat., noon–1:30AM; Sun., noon–midnight

San Marcos
Brewery & Grill
1080 San Marcos Blvd.
San Marcos, CA 92069
(619) 471-0050
Brewpub
Brews: Pier Pale Ale, Premium

The Name Game

From early on, beer brands were recognized easily and differentiated by the breweries which produced them. They often bore the name of the brewery's owner. This was never more evident than in the late 1800s when a large number of Germans emigrated to America. Where Germans settled, breweries opened and prospered. Schlitz, Heileman, Coors, Stroh, and Anheuser and Busch have become household words, thanks to the popularity of the beers that bear their names. As new breweries opened and existing ones expanded, quality alone was not enough to attract the beer consumer. Product awareness and name recognition became the key factor in the high stakes game of beer advertising. Somewhere along the line, there was a break from traditional appellations, as marketing strategies dictated a need for a fresher approach. In the wake of this Madison Avenue method of selling beer, the brewing industry has left a legacy of colorful, interesting, and often irreverent monikers for us to ponder over a cold glass of beer.

Microbrewers have taken this game to a new level. While product recognition is still a worthy goal of any business, craft brewers

seem to take a more light-hearted approach to the idea. Generally an irreverent and creative lot, the microbrewers manage to conceive beer sobriquets that run the gamut from pious to pitiful. Like proud parents presenting a newborn child to the world, craft brewers take time and care to christen the new beer with a name befitting the offspring. (Fortunately, beers don't have to suffer indignities and humiliation at the hands of taunting friends and classmates.)

Many brewers name beers for local points of interest or geographic and topographic features, such as Seismic Ale from the San Andreas Brewing Company. Others relate to the brewing company's name more directly, such as Tut Brown Ale from the Oasis Brewing Company, or Honkers Ale from Goose Island Brewery. The majority make a go of it with puns, double entendre, and tongue-in-cheek humor based on beer styles or seasonal varieties, among which you will find Voluptuous Blonde Ale and Weisenheimer Wheat Beer. Originality may be in short supply, though; there are enough Coal Porters out there to score Broadway shows into the next millenium.

Amber, winterfest, oatmeal stout, raspberry ale, Oktoberfest, weizen

Hours: Daily, 11:30AM–closing

San Rafael Brewery (TJ's Bar & Grill)
7110 Redwood Blvd.
Novato, CA 94947
(415) 892-3474

Brewpub

Brews: San Rafael Amber Ale, San Rafael Golden Ale, San Rafael Diamond Ale

Hours: Mon.–Fri., 11AM–2AM; Sat., noon–2AM; Sun., 2PM–2AM

Santa Clarita Brewing
20655 Soledad Canyon Road
Santa Clarita, CA 91351
(805) 298-5676

Brewpub

Brews: VanLeeuwen Lager, Desert Stream Lager, Tumble Weed Wheat, Golden Oak Ale, Beeles Bitter, Railroad Porter, Wild Blackberry Ale, and seasonals

Hours: Sun.–Thurs., 11AM–midnight; Fri.–Sat., 11AM–1AM

Santa Cruz Brewing (Front Street Pub)
516 Front St.
Santa Cruz, CA 95060
(408) 429-8838

Brewpub

Brews: Lighthouse Lager, Lighthouse Amber, Pacific Porter. *Seasonals:* Hoppy Holidays, Barleywine, Pacific Stout, Pacific Beacon Bock, Lighthouse Dark Lager, and others

Hours: Sun.–Thurs., 11:30AM–midnight; Fri.–Sat., 11:30AM–12:30AM

Santa Rosa Brewing
458 B St.
Santa Rosa, CA 95401
(707) 544-HOPS

Brewpub

Brews: pale ale, Two Rock Amber, Santa Rosa Red Ale, Cascades IPA, chocolate stout, and more

Hours: Sun.–Wed., 11:30AM–midnight; Thurs.–Sat., 11:30AM–1AM

Seabright Brewery
519 Seabright Ave. #107
Santa Cruz, CA 95062
(408) 426-2739

Brewpub

Brews: Pelican Pale, Seabright Amber. *Seasonals:* Red Nose Ale, Honey-Wheat Beer, Banty Rooster India pale ale, oatmeal stout, and others

Hours: Sun.–Thurs., 11:30AM–midnight; Fri.–Sat., 11:30AM–12:30AM

Shields Brewing
24 E. Santa Clara St.
Downtown Ventura, CA 93001
(805) 643-1807

Brewpub

Brews: Gold Coast Beer, Channel Islands Ale, Shields Stout. *Seasonals:* West Coast Wheat, Winter Storm, Oktoberfest, Bobby's Bock

Hours: Sun., Tues.–Thurs., 11:30AM–9PM; Fri.–Sat., 11:30AM–10PM; closed Mon.

Sierra Nevada Taproom & Restaurant
1075 E. 20th St.
Chico, CA 95928
(916) 345-2739

Brewpub

Sierra Nevada
Taproom & Restaurant

SLO Brewing

St. Stan's Brewery & Restaurant

Sudwerk
Privatbrauerei Hubsch

Brews: pale ale, porter, stout, draught. *Seasonals:* Pale Bock, Celebration Ale, Bigfoot Barleywine Style Ale, Summerfest Beer

Hours: Tues.–Sat., 11AM–11PM; Sun., 10AM–2PM; closed Mon.

Tours: Tues.–Fri., 2:30PM; Sat., 12:30PM–3:30PM

SLO Brewing
1119 Garden St.
San Juis Obispo, CA 93401
(805) 543-1843
Brewpub

Brews: amber ale, pale ale, porter. *Seasonals:* wheat beer, Summer Dry, ESB, Nut Brown Ale, Holidaze Ale, Cherry Bomb Ale

Hours: Mon.–Wed., 10:30AM–10PM; Thurs.–Sat., 10:30AM–12:30AM; Sun., 10:30AM–8PM

Southern California Brewing (Alpine Inn)
833 W. Torrance Blvd.
Torrance, CA 90502
(310) 329-8881
Brewpub

Brews: Hofbrau Lager, Hofbrau Pilsner, Premium Light. *Seasonals:* Winter Bock, Red Ale, Honey Wheat, and others

Hours: Daily, 11AM–midnight

Stoddard's Brewhouse & Eatery (Benchmark Brewery)
111 S. Muphy Ave.
Sunnyvale, CA 94086
(408) 733-7824
Brewpub

Brews: kölsch, pale ale, porter, kristall weizen, ESB

Hours: Mon.–Fri., 11:30AM–1AM; Sat.–Sun., noon–1AM

St. Stan's Brewery & Restaurant
821 L St.
Modesto, CA 95354
(209) 524-4PUB
Brewpub

Brews: Amber, Dark, Wheat, Light, Pale Ale, Barleywine. *Seasonals:* Fest, Graffiti, pumpkin ale, fruit beers, Red Sky Ale, Angel Tears

Hours: Mon.–Thurs., 11AM–11PM; Fri.–Sat., 11AM–midnight; Sun., 11AM–9PM

Sudwerk Privatbrauerei Hubsch
2001 Second St.
Davis, CA 95616
(916) 756-2739
Brewpub

Brews: Lager, Pilsner, Hefe-Weizen, Dark, Märzen. *Seasonals:* Christmas Bock Dark, Maibock

Hours: Mon.–Wed., 11:30AM–midnight; Thurs., 11:30AM–12:30AM; Fri.–Sat., 11AM–1AM; Sun., 11AM–midnight

Tied House Cafe & Brewery
954 Villa St.
Mountain View, CA 94042
(415) 965-BREW
Brewpub

Brews: Alpine Gold, Cascade Amer, Ironwood Dark, New World Wheat, and seasonals

Hours: Daily, 11:30AM–midnight

Tied House Cafe & Brewery
65 N. San Pedro
San Jose, CA 95110
(408) 295-BREW
Brewpub
Brews: Alpine Gold, Cascade
Amber, Ironwood Dark, New
World Wheat, and seasonals
Hours: Daily, 11:30AM–
midnight

Tied House Pub & Pool
8 Pacific Marina
Alameda, CA 94501
(510) 521-4321
Brewpub
Brews: Alpine Gold, Cascade
Amber, Ironwood Dark, New
World Wheat, and seasonals
Hours: Daily, 11:30AM–
midnight

Triple Rock Brewing
1920 Shattuck Ave.
Berkeley, CA 94704
(510) 843-2739
Brewpub
Brews: Pinnacle Pale Ale, Red
Rock Ale, Stove Hinge Porter.
Seasonals: Century Ale,
Lodestone Stout, Hop of the
Rock IPA, Ruby Rock Strong
Ale, and others
Hours: Sun.–Wed.,
11AM–12:30AM; Thurs.–Sat.,
11AM–1:30AM

Truckee Brewing
(Pizza Junction)
11401 Donner Pass Road
Truckee, CA 95734
(916) 587-5406
Brewpub
Brews: Truckee Amber,
Truckee Dark
Hours: Daily, 11AM–11PM

Tuscan Brewing
25009 Kauffman Ave.
Red Bluff, CA 96080
(916) 527-7048
Microbrewery
Brews: pale ale, amber, porter
Tours: By appointment

Twenty Tank Brewing
316 11th St.
San Francisco, CA 94103
(415) 255-9455
Brewpub
Brews: Mellow Glow Pale Ale,
Moody's High Top Ale, Red
Top, Kinnikinick Club Ale,
Kinnikinick Old Scout Stout.
Seasonals: Heifer-Weizen,
King Tut Golden
Hours: Daily, 11:30AM–1:30AM

Hawaii

Gordon Biersch Brewing
101 Ala Moana Blvd. #1123
(at Aloha Tower Marketplace)
Honolulu, HI 96813
(808) 599-4877
Brewery Restaurant
Brews: export, Märzen, dun-
kles, dopplebock.
Hours: Sun.–Wed.,
11AM–11PM; Thurs.,
11am–midnight; Fri.–Sat.,
11AM–1AM

Kona Brewing
74-5617 Pawai Place
P.O. Box 181
Kailua-Kona, HI 96740
(808) 334-1133

Bridgeport Brewing
& Public House

Nevada

Carson Depot Brewing
111 E. Telegraph
Carson City, NV 89701
(702) 884-4546
Brewpub
Brews: Griz Ale, Kati Porter, Wabuska Wheat, Roundhouse Red
Hours: Daily, 11AM–11PM

Great Basin Brewing
846 Victorian Ave.
Sparks, NV 89431
(702) 355-7711
Brewpub
Brews: Nevada Gold, Wild Horse Ale, Ichthyosaur Pale Ale, Jack Pot Porter, and seasonals
Hours: Sun.–Thurs., 11:30AM–10PM; Fri.–Sat., 11:30AM–11PM

HOLY COW!
Casino Cafe Brewery
2423 Las Vegas Blvd.
Las Vegas, NV 89104
(702) 732-2697
Brewpub
Brews: pale ale, dark ale, weiss beer, brewmaster's special
Hours: Daily, 24 hours

Union Brewery
28 North C St.
Virginia City, NV 89440
(702) 847-0328
Brewpub
Brews: Union Amber Lager, Union Black Lager
Hours: Museum & Brewery:
Mon.–Sun., 11AM–4PM; Saloon: Tues.–Sun., 3PM–5AM; closed Mon.

Oregon

Blue Pine Brewing
422 SW 5th St.
Grants Pass, OR 97526
(503) 476-0760
Brewpub
Brews: pale ale, Rip Roarin' Red, Midnight Stout. *Seasonal:* Oktoberfest
Hours: Daily, noon–11PM

Bridgeport Brewing & Public House
1313 N.W. Marshall
Portland, OR 97209
(503) 241-7179
Brewpub
Brews: Bridgeport Original Ale, Blue Heron Pale Ale, Coho Pacific Light Ale. *Seasonals:* Pintail ESB, XX Stout, Freemont Porter, Old Knucklehead, and others
Hours: Mon.–Thurs., 2PM–11PM; Fri., 2PM–midnight; Sat., noon–midnight; Sun., 1PM–9PM

Cornelius Pass Roadhouse & Brewery
Route 5 Box 340
Hillsboro, OR 97124
(503) 640-6174
Brewpub
Brews: Cascade Head, Ruby, Crystal, Hammerhead, Terminator. *Seasonals:* Purple Haze, wheat, and others
Hours: Sun.–Thurs., 11AM–midnight; Fri.–Sat., 11AM–1AM; winter hours vary

Deschutes Brewery
901 SW Simpson
Bend, OR 97702
(503) 385-8606
Microbrewery

Brews: Cascade Golden Ale,
Bachelor Bitter, Black Butte
Porter, Obsidian Stout, Mirror
Pond Pale Ale, Bond Street
Brown Ale, and seasonals

Tours: Call for information

**Deschutes Brewery &
Public House**
1044 Bond St. NW
Bend, OR 97701
(503) 382-9242
Brewpub

Brews: Cascade Golden Ale,
Bachelor Bitter, Black Butte
Porter, Obsidian Stout, Mirror
Pond Pale Ale, Bond Street
Brown Ale, and seasonals

Hours: Mon.–Thurs.,
11AM–11:30PM; Fri.–Sat.,
11AM–12:30AM; Sun.,
noon–10PM

Edgefield Brewery
2126 SW Halsey St.
Troutdale, OR 97060
(503) 669-8610
Brewpub

Brews: IPA, Edgefield Extra,
Transformer, Black Rabbit
Porter, wheat beer. *Seasonals:*
raspberry stout, Edgefield
Golden, Troutdale Pale Ale,
Edgefield Mild

Hours: Daily, 7AM–1AM

**Full Sail Brewery
at the River Place
(The Pilsner Room)**
0307 SW Montgomery
Portland, OR 97201

(503) 222-5343
Brewpub

Brews: McCormick & Schmick
Pilsner, golden ale, amber ale,
brown ale. *Seasonals:* Maibock,
Main Sail Stout, and others

Hours: Mon.–Fri.,
11:30AM–midnight; Sat.–Sun.,
11:30AM–1AM

Fulton Pub & Brewery
0618 SW Nebraska St.
Portland, OR 97201
(503) 246-9530
Brewpub

Brews: Cascade Head, Crystal
Ale, Hammerhead, Terminator
Stout, Ruby, Nebraska Bitter.
Seasonals: Nut Brown,
Raspberry Stout, Summer
Wheat

Hours: Mon.–Sat., 11AM–1AM;
Sun., noon–midnight

**Golden Valley
Brewery & Pub**
980 E. 4th St.
McMinnville, OR 97128
(503) 472-BREW
Brewpub

Brews: golden ale, amber ale,
porter, Red Thistle Ale, and
seasonals

Hours: Sun.–Thurs.,
11:30AM–11:30PM; Fri.–Sat.,
11:30AM–12:30AM

Hair of the Dog Brewing
4509 SE 23rd Ave.
Portland, OR 97202
(503) 232-6585
Microbrewery

Brews: Adambier, Belgian
Trippel

Tours: By appointment, weekdays only

Deschutes Brewery

High Street Pub
1243 High St.
Eugene, OR 97401
(503) 345-4905
Brewpub

Brews: Cascade Head, Ruby, Crystal, Hammerhead, Terminator. *Seasonals:* wheat beer, bock beer, Kris Kringle, Hobbits Habit

Hours: Mon.–Sat., 11AM–1AM; Sun., noon–midnight

Highland Pub & Brewery
4225 SE 182nd Ave.
Gresham, OR 97030
(503) 665-3015
Brewpub

Brews: Cascade Head, Ruby, Crystal, Hammerhead, Terminator. *Seasonals:* wheat beer, bock beer, Kris Kringle, ESB, Dunkelweizen

Hours: Mon.–Sat., 11AM–1AM; Sun., noon–midnight

**Hillsdale Brewery
& Public House**
1505 SW Sunset Blvd.
Portland, OR 97201
(503) 246-3938
Brewpub

Brews: Cascade Head, Crystal Ale, Ruby, Hammerhead, Terminator Stout. *Seasonals:* Bock, Nebraska Bitter, Summer Wheat, and more

Hours: Mon.–Sat., 11AM–1AM; Sun., noon–midnight

Lighthouse Brewpub
4157 N. Hwy. 101
Lincoln City, OR 97367
(503) 994-7238
Brewpub

Brews: Cascade Head, Ruby,

Crystal, Hammerhead, Terminator, and seasonals

Hours: Mon.–Sat., 11AM–1AM; Sun., noon–midnight; Daily in winter, 11AM–11PM

Lucky Labrador Brewpub
915 SE Hawthorne
Portland, OR 97214
(503) 236-3555
Brewpub

Brews: Kölsch, Brown Ale, IPA, Oatmeal Porter, Stout

Hours: Daily, 11AM–11PM

McMenamin's
6179 SW Murray Blvd.
Beaverton, OR 97005
(503) 644-4562
Brewpub

Brews: Cascade Head, Crystal Ale, Ruby, Hammerhead, Terminator. *Seasonals:* nut brown ale, Stella Blue

Hours: Mon.–Sat., 11AM–midnight; Sun., noon–midnight

McMenamin's
2090 SW 8th Ave.
West Linn, OR 97005
(503) 656-2970
Brewpub

Brews: Cascade Head, Crystal Ale, Ruby, Hammerhead, Terminator. *Seasonal:* Willamette River Bitter

Hours: Mon.–Thurs., 11AM–midnight; Fri.–Sat., 11AM–1AM; Sun., noon–midnight

Mt. Hood Brewpub
87304 Government Camp Loop
Government Camp, OR 97028
(503) 272-3724

Brewpub

Brews: Southside Light Session Ale, Cloudcap Amber Ale, Ice Axe IPA, Gypsy Ale, and others

Hours: Mon.–Thurs., noon–9PM; Fri.–Sun., noon–11PM

Multnomah Brewing
1603 SE Pardee St.
Portland, OR 97202
(503) 236-3106
Microbrewery

Brews: Figure Head, and seasonals

Tours: Call for appointment

Nor' Wester Willamette Valley Brewing
66 SE Morrison St.
Portland, OR 97214
(503) 222-9771
Brewpub

Brews: Best Bitter, weizen, porter. *Seasonals:* dunkel weizen, hefe-weizen, Smith's Black, raspberry weizen

Hours: Mon.–Thurs., 11AM–11PM; Fri.–Sat., 11AM–1AM; Sun., 1PM–8PM

Northwestern Brewpub
711 SW Ankeny
Portland,OR 97205
(503) 226-2508
Brewpub

Brews: Czech Bitter, Vienna, Alt, strong ale, rye beer, others on rotation

Hours: Mon.–Fri., 11AM–midnight; Sat., 11AM–1AM; closed Sun.

Oak Hills Brewpub
14740 NW Cornell Road
Portland, OR 97229
(503) 645-0286

Brewpub

Brews: Cascade Head, Crystal Ale, Ruby, Hammerhead, Terminator. *Seasonals:* Apollo Pale Ale, dunkel weizen, nut brown, Golden Oak, Kris Kringles

Hours: Mon.–Sat., 11AM–1AM; Sun., noon–midnight

Oregon Trader Brewing
140 Hill St.
Albany, OR 97321
(503) 928-1931
Microbrewery

Brews: hefe-weizen, amber lager, Scottish ale, nut brown, Russian Imperial Oatmeal Stout, Green Chili Beer, and seasonals

Tours: By appointment only

Oregon Trail Brewing (Old World Deli)
341 SW 2nd St.
Corvallis, OR 97333
(503) 758-3527
Brewpub

Brews: Oregon Trail Ale, white ale, brown ale, stout, and seasonals

Hours: Daily, 8AM–10PM

Portland Brewing
1339 NW Flanders St.
Portland, OR 97209
(503) 222-7150
Brewpub

Brews: Portland Ale, Portland Porter, Timerline Classic Ale, Oregon Honey Beer, Mt. Hood Beer, McTarnahan's Ale, Portland Stout. *Seasonal:* winter ale

Hours: Mon.–Thurs., 11AM–11PM; Fri., 11AM–1AM; Sat., noon–1AM; closed Sun.

Nor' Wester Willamette Valley Brewing

Portland Brewing

Rogue Brewery
& Public House

**Portland Brewing
(The Brewhouse
Taproom & Grill)**
2730 NW 31st St.
Portland, OR 97210
(503) 226-7623
Brewpub
Brews: Portland Ale, Portland
Porter, Timberline Classic Ale,
Oregon Honey Beer, Mt. Hood
Beer, McTarnahan's Ale,
Portland Stout. *Seasonal:* winter
ale
Hours: Mon.–Thurs.,
11AM–10:30PM; Fri., 11AM–
midnight; Sat., noon–midnight;
Sun., noon–7:30PM

**Rogue Ale Brewery
& Tasting Room
(Oregon Brewing)**
2320 O.S.U. Dr.
Newport, OR 97365
(503) 867-3660
Brewpub
Brews: Ashland amber,
Golden, New Porter. *Seasonals:*
Rogue-N-Berry, Shakespeare
Stout, St. Rogue Red,
Welkommen, Waterfront, Old
Crustacean, Mexicali Stout, and
others
Hours: Daily, 11AM–7PM;
Summer: Daily, 10AM–9PM

**Rogue Brewery
& Public House**
31-B Water St.
Ashland, OR 97520
(503) 488-5061
Brewpub
Brews: golden, new porter.
Seasonals: Rogue-N-Berry,
Oatmeal Stout, Welkommen,
Waterfront, St. Rogue Red,
Mexicali Stout, Mogul Madness,

Old Crustacean, and others
Hours: Sun.–Thurs.,
11AM–11PM; Fri.–Sat.,
11AM–midnight

Saxer Brewing
5875 SW Lakeview Sr.
Lake Oswego, OR 97035
(503) 699-9524
Microbrewery
Brews: Amber Lager, Three
Finger Jack Stout, Saxer
Pilsner, Lemon Lager, Hefe
Dunkel
Tours: Tasting room and view-
ing area open to public during
business hours.

Star Brewing
5231 NE Martin Luther King
Jr. Blvd.
Portland, OR 97211
(503) 282-6003
Microbrewery
Brews: India pale ale, nut brown
ale, hop gold, altbier, and others
Tours: Call for information

Steelhead Brewery & Cafe
199 E. 5th Ave.
Eugene, OR 97401
(503) 686-BREW
Brewpub
Brews: McKenzie Light, amber
ale, Station Square Stout,
Bombay Bomber, IPA.
Seasonals: Ginger Bell's, Time
Warp Weizenbock, Steelhead
Cream Ale, oatmeal stout,
French Pete's Porter
Hours: Sun.–Thurs.,
11:30AM–midnight; Fri.–Sat.,
11:30AM–1AM

**Thompson Brewery
& Public House**
3575 Liberty Road
Salem, OR 97302
(503) 363-7286
Brewpub
Brews: Cascade Head Ale,
Crystal Ale, Ruby, Fruit Beer,
Hammerhead, Terminator.
Seasonals: Thompson Kriek,
wheat beer, and others
Hours: Mon.–Sat., 11AM–1AM;
Sun., noon–midnight

Umpqua Brewing
328 SE Jackson
Roseburg, OR 97470
(503) 672-0452
Brewpub
Brews: summer wheat, Douglas
Draft, Umpqua Gold, Roseburg
Red, Downtown Brown,
No Doubt Stout. *Seasonal:*
Festive Ale
Hours: Wed.–Thurs.,
5PM–11PM; Fri.–Sat., 5PM–1AM;
closed Sun.–Tues.

**West Bros. Bar B-Q
(Eugene City Brewing)**
844 Olive St.
Eugene, OR 97401
(503) 345-8489
Brewpub
Brews: honey orange wheat,
Orca Pale Ale, hefe-weizen,
IPA, Red Tape Ale, bitter,
Ponderosa Porter, Black Hole
Stout, and seasonals
Hours: Sun., 11AM–9:30PM;
Fri.–Sat., 11AM–10PM

**Whitecap Brewpub
(Full Sail Brewery)**
506 Columbia St.
Hood River, OR 97031
(503) 386-2247
Brewpub
Brews: golden ale, amber ale,
brown ale, Main Sail Stout,
Pilsner. *Seasonals:* Best Bitter,
Maibock, Wassail Winter Ale,
Old Boardhead Barleywine
Hours: Summer: Daily,
noon–8PM; Winter: Wed.–Fri.,
4PM–8PM; Sat.–Sun., 2PM–8PM;
closed Mon.–Tues.

Widmer Brewing
929 N. Russell St.
Portland, OR 97227
(503) 281-2437
Microbrewery
Brews: alt, weizen, hefe-
weizen. *Seasonals:* bock, fest-
bier, Oktoberfest, Märzen, sum-
merbrau, doppelbock
Tours: Sat., noon and 1PM

**Widmer Brewing
(The Heathmen
Bakery & Pub)**
901 SW Salmon
Portland, OR 97205
(503) 227-5700
Brewpub
Brews: alt, Widmer Weizen,
hefe-weizen, Kölsch, dunkel
weizen. *Seasonals:* bock, fest-
bier, Oktoberfest, doppelbock
Hours: Daily, 7AM–11PM

Wild River Brewery
249 N. Redwood Hwy.
Cave Junction, OR 97523
(503) 592-3556
Brewpub

Big Time Brewing

Brews: nut brown ale, Harbor Lights, hefe-weizen, ESB, Double Eagle Imperial Stout, and seasonals

Hours: Mon.–Sat., 10AM–10PM; Sun., noon–9:30PM

Wild River Brewing & Pizza
595 NE East St.
Grants Pass, OR 97526
(503) 471-RIVR
Brewpub

Brews: nut brown ale, Harbor Lights, hefe-weizen, ESB, Double Eagle Imperial Stout, many seasonals

Hours: Daily, 7AM–midnight

Willamette Brew Pub
120 Commercial St. NE
Salem, OR 97301
(503) 363-8779
Brewpub

Brews: Capitol Rush Light, Willamette Wheat, Millrace Amber Ale, Santiam Porter, Marion Berry. *Seasonal:* Helles Bock

Hours: Mon.–Thurs., 11AM–11PM; Fri., 11AM–1AM; Sat., noon–midnight; closed Sun.

Washington

Big Time Brewing
4133 University Way NE
Seattle, WA 98105
(206) 545-4509
Brewpub

Brews: Prime Time Pale Ale, Atlas Amber Ale, Coal Creek Porter. *Seasonals:* Bhagwans Best, Rainfest ESB, Slam Dunkel, Old Woolly, and others

Hours: Sun.–Thurs., 11:30AM–12:30PM; Fri.–Sat., 11:30AM–1AM

California & Alaska Street Brewery
4720 California Ave. SW
Seattle, WA 98116
(206) 938-2476
Brewpub

Brews: Junction Gold, Alki Ale, Honey Brown, Fauntleroy Stout, Admiral ES Bitter, Vashon Old Stock. *Seasonals:* Irish Porter, West Seattle Weiss, and others

Hours: Tues.–Thurs., 3PM–11PM; Fri.–Sat., 2PM–midnight; Sun., 4PM–9PM; closed Mon.

Fish Brewing (The Fish Bowl)
515 Jefferson St. SE
Olympia, WA 98501
(206) 943-6480
Brewpub

Brews: Flying Fish Golden, Fishtale Pale Ale, Fish Eye IPA, Trout Stout, Mudshark Porter; and seasonals on rotation

Hours: Mon.–Sat., 11AM–midnight; closed Sun.

Fort Spokane Brewery
West 401 Spokane Falls Blvd.
Spokane, WA 99201
(509 838-3809
Brewpub

Brews: blonde alt, Border Run Ale, red alt, Bulldog Stout. *Seasonals:* Godzilla Holiday Ale, and others

Hours: Mon., 11AM–1:30AM; Tues.–Thurs., 11AM–midnight; Fri.–Sat., 11AM–2AM; Sun., 11AM–10PM

**Front Street Ale House
(Friday Harbor Brewing)**
1 Front St.
Friday Harbor, OR 98250
(206) 378-BEER
Brewpub

Brews: Lime Kiln Lager, Eichenberger Hefe-Weizen, Pickett's Pale Ale, Pig War Stout, and seasonals

Hours: Sun.–Thurs., 7AM–midnight; Fri.–Sat., 7AM–1AM

Grant's Brewery Pub
32 N. Front St.
Yakima, WA 98901
(509) 575-2922
Brewpub

Brews: Scottish ale, Imperial stout, India pale ale, apple honey ale, wheat beer, Celtic ale, Perfect Porter. *Seasonal:* spiced ale

Hours: Mon.–Sat., 11:30AM–10PM; Sun., 11:30AM–8:30PM

Grant's Yakima Brewing
1803 Presson Pl.
Yakima, WA 98902
(509) 575-1900
Microbrewery

Brews: Scottish ale, Imperial stout, India pale ale, apple honey ale, wheat beer, Celtic ale, Perfect Porter. *Seasonal:* spiced ale

Tours: Call for information

Hale's Ales
East 5634 Commerce St.
Spokane, OR 99212-1307
(509) 534-7553
Microbrewery

Brews: Hale's Pale American Ale, Hale's Special Bitter,

Hale's Celebration Porter, Moss Bay Amber Ale, Moss Bay Extra Ale, Moss Bay Stout, and seasonals

Tours: By appointment

Hart Brewing
110 W. Marine Dr.
Kalama, WA 98625
(206) 673-2962
Microbrewery

Brews: pale ale, Wheaton Ale, Best Brown Ale, amber wheat beer, hefe-weizen, apricot ale, Hart's Espresso Stout

Tours: Mon.–Fri., 10AM–4PM (year-round); Sat., 10AM–4PM (April 1–Sept. 30)

Hazel Dell Brewpub
8513 NE Hwy. 99
Vancouver, WA 98665
(206) 576-0996
Brewpub

Brews: Hazel Dell Golden, Red Zone Bitter, hefe-weizen, Black Cannon Porter, Capt. Moran's Irish Stout, and seasonals

Hours: Mon.–Thurs., 11AM–midnight; Fri.–Sat., 11AM–1AM; Sun., 11AM–11PM

Kirkland Roaster & Ale House (Hale's Ale)
109 Central Way
Kirkland, WA 98033
(206) 827-4359
Brewpub

Brews: Hale's Pale American Ale, Special Bitter, Celebration Porter, Moss Bay Amber Ale, Moss Bay Extra Ale, and seasonals

Hours: Daily, 11AM–2AM

Hart Brewing

Leavenworth Brewing
636 Front St.
Leavenworth, WA 98826
(509) 548-4545
Brewpub
Brews: Escape
Altbier,Whistling Pig Wheat,
Bull's Tooth Porter, Friesian
Pilsner. *Seasonals:*
Oktoberfest, Christmas bock,
and more
Hours: Winter: Sun.–Thurs.,
11AM–10PM; Fri.–Sat.,
11AM–midnight; Summer:
Mon.–Thurs., 11AM–11PM;
Fri.–Sat., 11AM–1AM; Sun.,
11AM–midnight

**Maritime Pacific
Brewing Company**
1514 NW Leary Way
Seattle, WA 98107
(206) 782-6181
Microbrewery
Brews: Flagship Red Ale,
Clipper Gold Wheat Ale,
Islander Pale Ale, Nightwatch
Ale. *Seasonals:* Windjammer
Dark Wheat Ale, Windfest, and
others
Tours: Sat., call in advance

Northern Light Brewing
1701 S. Lawson
Airway Heights, WA 99001
(509) 244-4909
Microbrewery
Brews: cream ale, crystal bitter
ale, chocolate ale
Tours: By appointment

Onalaska Brewing
248 Burchett Road
Onalaska, WA 98570
(206) 978-4253
Microbrewery

Brews: Onalaska Ale, Red
Dawg Ale, Howlin' Stout
Tours: By appointment

Pacific Northwest Brewing
322 Occidental Ave. South
Seattle, WA 98104
(206) 621-7002
Brewpub
Brews: Blonde Ale, Gold Ale,
Bitter, amber, stout, Cream
Porter. *Seasonals:* Christmas
Gold, Christmas Mild
Hours: Tues., 11:30AM–11PM;
Wed.–Thurs., 11:30AM–mid-
night; Fri.–Sat., 11:30AM–1AM;
Sun., 12:30PM–9PM; closed Mon.

Pike Place Brewery
1432 Western Ave.
Seattle, WA 98101
(206) 622-1880
Microbrewery
Brews: Pike Place Pale Ale,
XXXXX Stout, East India Pale
Ale. *Seasonals:* Cerveza
Rosanna Red Chili Ale, Pike
Place Porter, Old Bawdy
Barleywine, A. A. Spiced
Christmas Ale
Tours: By appointment

**Redhook Ale Brewery
(Trolleyman Pub)**
3400 Phinney Ave. North
Seattle, WA 98103
(206) 548-8000
Brewpub
Brews: Ballard Bitter, Redhook
ESB, Blackhook Porter, Wheat
Hook Ale. *Seasonals:*
Winterhook, Redhook Ale,
Scotch ale, honey stout
Hours: Mon.–Fri.,
8:30AM–11PM; Sat., 11AM–mid-
night; Sun., noon–7PM

Tours: Mon.–Fri., 3PM;
Sat.–Sun., 1:30PM, 2:30PM,
3:30PM, 4:30PM

**Redhook Ale Brewery
(Forecasters Public
House & Taproom)**
14300 NE 145th St.
Woodinville, WA 98072
(206) 483-3232

Brewpub

Brews: Ballard Bitter, Redhook
ESB, Blackhook Porter, Wheat
Hook Ale. *Seasonals:*
Winterhook, Redhook Ale,
Scotch ale, honey stout

Hours: Mon.–Thurs.,
8:30AM–10PM; Fri.,
8:30AM–midnight; Sat.,
10AM–midnight; Sun.,
10AM–7PM

Tours: Call information line
(206) 548-8000

Roslyn Brewing
208 Pennsylvania Ave.
Roslyn, WA 98941
(509) 649-2232

Brewpub

Brews: Roslyn Beer, Brookside
Beer

Hours: Sat.–Sun., noon–5PM

Seattle Brewers
530 S. Holden
Seattle, WA 98108
(206) 762-7421

Microbrewery

Brews: Bay Bitter, Seattle
Stout, Beaches Brew

Tours: Call for information

Thomas Kemper Brewing
22381 Foss Road
Poulsbo, WA 98370
(206) 697-1446

Brewpub

Brews: pale lager, Pilsner,
hefe-weizen, Integralé, weizen
berry. *Seasonals:* Rolling Bay
Bock, Helles Blueberry Lager,
Oktoberfest, Winterbrau

Hours: Sun.–Thurs.,
11AM–6PM; Fri., 11AM–10PM;
Sat., 11AM–7PM

Winthrop Brewing
155 Riverside Dr.
Winthrop, WA 98862
(509) 996-3183

Brewpub

Brews: Outlaw Pale Ale,
Schoolhouse Red, Black
Canyon Porter

Hours: Sun.–Thurs.,
11AM–10PM; Fri.–Sat.,
11AM–midnight

Thomas Kemper Brewing

Part III

MOUNTAIN/ HIGH PLAINS REGIONS

Mountain/High Plains Brewery Profiles

Celis Brewery, Inc.

Belgian beer brewed in Texas? Pierre Celis thought so. A genial man, Celis once made a comfortable living as a milk distributor in his hometown of Hoegaarden, Belgium. Hoegaarden had long ago established itself as a respected brewing city, and one style in particular had become synonymous with Hoegaarden. Witbier, Flemish for "white beer," (see Beer Styles, pages 16–17) was very popular in the region, and several breweries brewed this style exclusively. Unfortunately, as the ubiquitous Pilsner beers' popularity grew in Europe, production of witbier declined steadily until 1955, when the last of the Hoegaarden breweries ceased to exist. Not to be denied his favorite beer, Pierre Celis began brewing in his home. Combining his experience in the milk industry with lessons learned while working at a brewery in his youth, Pierre set out to revive the famed witbier.

With the help of a former brewer and researchers at the nearby University in Leuven, Mr. Celis built a reputation as the style's premier brewer. His brewery, the DeKluis Brewery, employed more than 90 people. Beer drinkers from as far away as Paris were choosing the "new beer" over other, more popular European brews. By 1984, Pierre began exporting his beer to the United States. During the course of his many visits here, three things happened. First, he took note of the growing popularity of microbrewed beer. Second, he realized that these small breweries would have significant advantages over importers. And, finally, Pierre fell in love with the United States — especially the state of Texas.

By 1987, several more Belgian breweries were producing witbiers modeled after Celis's beer. The giant Belgian brewing firm, Interbrew, wanted a piece of the action and offered to buy the DeKluis Brewery. Pierre saw this as an opportunity to fulfill his lifelong dreams. He could live in the United States and open a new brewery. The decision to sell the old brewery was not easy, but finding a location for his new brewery was. Austin, Texas was the ideal spot, centrally located for distribution and supply. Celis also liked the clean environment and the friendly people he met there. Construction of the new brewery began in the spring of 1991, and brewing commenced in March of the following year.

The new Celis Brewery is a marvelous combination of the best of old and new brewing art and technology. The brewhouse contains three large copper vessels that were handmade in Belgium more than 60 years ago. As in those days, much of what goes into them is weighed and pitched into the brewkettle by hand.

The brewery's flagship style is the original witbier developed by Pierre back in Hoegaarden. Another Belgian specialty beer, Celis Grand Cru, was originally crafted by the Trappist monks in Belgium and contains about 7.5 percent alcohol by weight. There is also a Celis Golden and a Celis Pale Bock beer. Ironically, the bock beer is not a bock beer at all. The Celis Brewing Company only produces ales. Unfortunately, the Texas Alcohol Beverage Commission Board uses antiquated laws restricting beer designations: by law, Celis must call this pale ale a bock beer. The

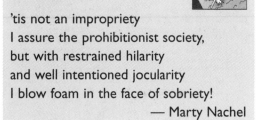

The Volstead Act 1, scene 2

'tis not an impropriety
I assure the prohibitionist society,
but with restrained hilarity
and well intentioned jocularity
I blow foam in the face of sobriety!
— Marty Nachel

newest brew, Celis Raspberry, was introduced at the 1994 Great American Beer Festival, where it was well received — but not quite as well as its stable-mate: Celis Witbier won a silver medal.

Celis's current production is approximately 12,000 barrels per year, and the brewery has the capacity to brew as many as 45,000 barrels. The distribution of the Celis brand beers is soon to be nationwide, following the purchase of a controlling interest in the Austin brewery by the Miller Brewing Company. The agreement allows Celis to take advantage of Miller's established marketing and distribution network. Brewery tours are offered occasionally throughout the week and tours and tastings are complimentary. Reservations are needed for groups larger than ten. Available breweriana includes T-shirts, caps, keychains, and coaster holders with coasters.

Coeur D'Alene Brewing Co.

Good beer, good people, good times. What could be more inviting than that? That's what's promised at T. W. Fisher's Brewpub in Coeur D' Alene,

Idaho. T. W. Fisher's is the first brewpub in Idaho and the largest in the Pacific Northwest. Fisher's opened its doors on July 22, 1987 — just three weeks after it became legal to operate a brewpub in Idaho. The first batch of beer was tapped on November 6th of that year. By the time the brewpub was six-months-old, the brewing capacity had to be doubled just to keep up with the demand for their beer. Since then, three additional expansions and a bottling line have been added to stay current with the market. Now that T. W. Fisher's beers are bottled, the brewpub is also recognized as the Coeur D' Alene Brewing Company and distribution of their bottled and kegged product expands over a territory covering Idaho, Montana, Oregon, Washington, and Wyoming. There are now more than 800 locations serving their bottled and draught accounts.

T. W. Fisher's is the culmination of the efforts of the brewery's founder and name-sake, Tom Fisher. Tom is a Coeur D' Alene native, and was employed by a corporate newspaper chain for 14 years. His father, Don Fisher, also was enlisted in the brewery project when he retired. He has the enviable position of brewery supervisor. Brad McQuhae, a former brewmaster and a present brewery consultant, was hired to assist in the brewing processes.

The beers produced by Coeur D'Alene Brewing include T. W. Fisher's Centennial Pale Ale, awarded a gold medal for pale ale in 1988 at the Great American Beer Festival; Fisher's Festival Dark; Fisher's refreshing Weizen Light; and Fisher's Full Moon Stout (technically an oatmeal stout with the inclusion of raw rolled oats). All of these beers are made from different combinations of two-row pale malt, caramel malt, black malt, and roasted barley. Willamette, cascade, and bullion hops are added in varying measures to give the beers their distinctive flavor and aroma.

The brewpub is for the most part a neighborhood-type sports bar. There are lots of windows providing unobstructed views of the brewery. The bar also showcases a great collection of breweriana: beer bottles, trays, and coasters, among other items. Open seven days a week, the brewpub offers a simple menu of standard pub fare and a few Italian dishes. There are also brewery souvenirs available for purchase: T-shirts, hats, pins, and beer glasses. For entertainment the brewpub offers cribbage, videogames, five televisions, darts, and an "attitude adjustment" period (happy hour) from 4 to 6 P.M.

Crested Butte

"Thar's gold up in them thar hills!" Well, there is in a sense. It's of the liquid variety, even though the discovery of precious metals is not unheard of in these parts. "These parts" are in central Colorado, and Crested Butte is halfway to the clouds.

The town's origins as a mining camp began in the early 1880s when gold and coal were extracted from its foundations. Certain architectural relics remain from that era. In addition to City Hall, the Protestant Church, and the Elk Mountain House, there is a two-story outhouse in the alley behind the company store. Thankfully, its creators had the foresight to offset the upper level from the lower, so as to minimize the danger to simultaneous users.

More recently, the picturesque little mountain town, at an altitude of 8,867 feet and with a population of 900, has become a favorite winter destination of the downhill ski crowd. For the rest of the year, Crested Butte lures tourists to its hideaway location with many attractions. To go along with 360 degrees of scenery, Elk Avenue, the main street in town, offers bars, boutiques, restaurants, and rental stores. As you stroll westward along the Avenue, shopping, taking pictures, and working up a thirst, try to hold out until you reach the post office. Right across the street — Eureka! — is liquid gold.

The Crested Butte Brewery and Pub, also known as The Idlespur, has all the gold, amber, and black beer a prospector can drink. Opened in February, 1991, this 5,300 square foot honkytonk offers a

Choosing Beer for Recipes

The two major flavor components found in beer are the sweetness of the malt and the bitterness of the hops. Sour/tangy flavors manifest themselves regularly in certain beer styles, such as a German weissbier (see page 16), and saltiness, although very rare, still surprises beer drinkers now and again.

The overriding taste that beer imparts to recipes, however, is its sweet grain flavor. Choose beer by its color and level of sweetness. Avoid bitter beers, as bitterness tends to be accentuated by cooking processes. Unless one is well versed in beer styles and knows what to expect, the Munich helles style is best suited for cross-culinary beer usage. Don't worry about the alcohol content in beer, as it has a lower boiling point than water and evaporates quickly in the presence of heat.

The human tongue has four distinct taste regions: sweet, sour, salty, and bitter. These regions not only identify what we are tasting, but also control when in the tasting process we experience the different flavors. Sweetness is sensed at the tip of the tongue and is thus the first sensation, while bitterness and astringencies are experienced at the back of the tongue. Since this is an area of lasting impression, a little bitterness goes a long way.

Here's a tip: Combinations of different foods and beer that include most, if not all, of the four taste components make for a more interesting meal. More important, however, is not allowing one flavor to dominate a meal, or not allowing its complete absence.

half dozen handcrafted beers. Take a seat at the bar where the brewhouse is in full view, and watch the brewmaster put the equipment through its paces. Choose from among a wheat beer, three ales, a stout, and a light beer, or four other bottled selections to slake your thirst.

Make yourself comfortable amidst the mountain lodge decor. Notice the mountain lion prowling atop the fireplace mantle. The food menu at the Crested Butte Brewery and Pub features salads, seafood, chicken, steaks, and ribs. The house specialty is anything done on the open wood barbeque grill. There is restaurant seating for 170 and a front porch that is perfect for enjoying your favorite summertime libation. Live music and a large dance floor make for a good time.

Crested Butte is an easy and scenic half-hour drive north of Gunnison, Colorado, and certainly worth the trip.

Kessler

"What a beautiful world it was once . . . you could leave beer to cool in the river . . . a beer made in the next town if the town were ten thousand or over. So it was either Kessler Beer made in Helena or Highlander Beer made in Missoula that we left to cool in the Blackfoot River. What a wonderful world it was once when all the beer was not made in Milwaukee, Minneapolis, or St. Louis."

— *A River Runs Through It*
by Norman McLean, 1976

The Kessler Brewery mentioned in this excerpt is not the same brewery that presently makes beer by the same name, but it is the predecessor to the little brewery located in Helena today. The original brewery was founded by Charles Beehrer in 1864 and purchased by Nicholas Kessler, an immigrant from Luxembourg, in 1866. Mr. Kessler turned the enterprise into Montana's finest brewery. His was the first in Montana to use refrigeration and the first brewery in the United States to use a carbonic acid machine. The brewery managed to stay open through two world wars, the Great Depression, and even Prohibition, only to fall victim, in 1957, to the dominance of the American beer market by big breweries in Milwaukee, Minneapolis, and St. Louis.

Today's Kessler Brewery got its start in 1984, thanks to Richard Bourke and Bruce DeRosier. For nostalgic reasons they used the Kessler name to evoke the memory of the once great Montana beer. This reincarnation of the brewery almost bit the dust a few years ago. The Chapter 11 status taken on by the brewery instead, proved to be a catalyst for change. A reorganization of management, coupled with the dedication of the employees, helped to turn the operation around. Most important, however, the support of loyal Kessler customers has kept the doors open. It's no small wonder, either. The beers made there are award winners.

Brewmaster Steve Schellhardt is producing seven consistent, high quality brews. The two standards, Centennial Beer and Lorelei Extra Pale Ale, are available all year long. Additionally, four seasonal favorites are produced: bock beer, wheat beer, Oktoberfest beer, and holiday beer. The seventh beer, called Kessler Ale #7, is considered a "temporary standard," brewed to fill in the lag time between the production of the seasonal beers. One perennial Kessler favorite is the Oktoberfest beer, made with pale, Munich, and caramel malts, along with a generous amount of Czechoslovakian saaz hops.

In keeping with traditional Bavarian customs, the Oktoberfest beer should be served at an optimum temperature of 48°F (8°C). It goes particularly well with a hearty meal on a brisk autumn evening. According to a staff report in a popular consumer beer magazine, Kessler Oktoberfest is "a pleasant surprise . . . a rich, amber brew that is malty, yet has a restrained tartness that stops things from getting too cloying . . . it would make a

The Drink of Our Founding Fathers

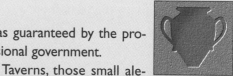

Craft brewing in America began with the colonization of the New World. From the diary of a passenger aboard the Mayflower came this information about the landing of the Pilgrim ship at Plymouth Rock: "We could not now take time for further search . . . our victuals being much spent, especially our beer." Beer was an important provision for ships at sail for long periods of time. Large amounts of liquid refreshment were needed for the ship's passengers, and beer was far more healthful than the impure water sources available to them. Breweries in the New World were among the first businesses established. It can be said truthfully that American breweries preceded American government, and some of the breweries' staunchest supporters were also the leaders of our new nation. Our first president, George Washington, was a brewer, as was fellow patriot Samuel Adams. They were joined in their love of beer by Patrick Henry, Benjamin Franklin, and James Madison. It was Franklin who proposed the idea of a government-run brewery. Thomas Jefferson is said to have written the first draft of the Declaration of Independence over a draught of ale at his favorite tavern in Philadelphia. The revolution that followed was fought and won by soldiers whose daily rations included one quart of beer, which was guaranteed by the provisional government.

Taverns, those small alehouses, played an important role in colonial America. In addition to being the place where a brewer plied his trade, the tavern also served as the unofficial town hall, the focal point of every town — churches notwithstanding. It was here that the townsfolk gathered to deliberate and debate, to socialize, and to share news and information with the community. As early as 1768, the Sons of Liberty were holding meetings at the Liberty Tree in Providence. The Green Dragon Inn in Boston was called the headquarters for the Revolution. George Washington made his headquarters at Fraunces Tavern in New York, which still stands today, in the heart of the financial district.

With the founding of a new country and the establishment of a democratic government, the United States became an instant magnet for immigrants. Breweries sprang up as each ethnic neighborhood was settled, and the trend continued with each subsequent wave of arrivals. Throughout the 1800s, most of these immigrants came from the "beer belt" countries of northern Europe. With them came great knowledge of brewing and thirsts equaling the task.

good compromise between a heavyweight sipper and a session brew." That about says it all.

Rockies Brewing Company

Rockies Brewing of Boulder, Colorado, used to be called Boulder Brewing and was originally located in Longmont. If this sounds strange, wait until you hear about the goat shed.

It all started in the mid-1960s when astrophysicist David Hummer was working on his Ph.D. in London, England. Like most Americans abroad, Hummer's palate became acclimated to the full-bodied English ales, and he had even tried dabbling at brewing his own at home. When he returned to the United States in the 1970s, Hummer invited fellow Colorado physics professor Randolph Ware to join him in his homebrewing activities. The pair's mutual interest in, and appreciation for, a well-crafted ale led them to obtain their federal brewery license in 1979. Here's where the goats come in. Al Nelson, a "freelance engineer and professional scrounger," was a friend of Hummer's. He was willing to construct the new brewery — adjacent to the goat-raising facilities on his property! Nelson's construction assistant was Otto Zavarone, the erstwhile brewmaster whose sole qualifying factor was his great love of beer.

Since the early days, a number of major changes have taken place in location, equipment, personnel, and ownership. The first major change came in 1982, when the brewery was incorporated and shares were

sold to the public. Stockbroker Jerry Smart became president of the first publicly held microbrewery in the country. Over $1.5 million was raised, and plans for the new brewery were launched. Construction was completed in 1985, the year that Boulder Brewing became the nation's fastest growing brewery, posting a 290 percent production increase.

The new structure has been described as a cross between a cathedral and a neo-medieval castle. Whatever your perspective, the three-story building is reminiscent of the tall, gravity-feed brewhouses of Europe. The expansive areas of glass give visitors complete visual access to the brewing and bottling processes.

The tasting room is a popular community gathering spot, much like those of America's early breweries. Although completely modern, it harks back to the recent past, when every town in the West had its own brewery and served distinctive beers on the premises. Creative deli selections make up the menu, which changes regularly. Lunch and dinner are served in the taproom and the patio/beer garden, where views of the Flatiron Mountains are surpassed only by the local brew.

The original Boulder beers were the extra pale ale and the porter. Because these brews were bottle-conditioned, there was a light layer of yeast sedimentation at the bottom of every bottle. In the early days of microbrewing, hazy, yeasty beers were quite contrary to the crystal-clear products that Americans were used to drinking. Boulder Brewing used that to their advantage by marketing the beer as "The Ugly Brew," showing a bottle of Boulder beer partially covered by a brown paper bag and sunglasses. The accompanying slogan said, "There is more to good taste than good looks." In addition, there is also Boulder Amber Ale, Rockies Premium Ale, Wrigley Red,

Beer Nutrition

Of all the alcoholic beverages on the market, beer is the most nutritious. It became even more so with the introduction of craft brewing. While the industrial breweries are allowed by law to use any and all of 57 different ingredients, adjuncts, additives, and preservatives (see page 24), microbrewers who adhere to the German Purity Law (see page 23), produce the closest thing to healthy beer.

The United States Department of Agriculture provides the following nutritional values for a 12-ounce serving of a typical American lager:

    92 percent water
    151 calories (⅔ of which are from
      the alcohol)
    1.1 grams protein
    0 grams of fat
    13.7 grams carbohydrate
    25 mg. sodium

There are also traces of calcium, potassium, phosphorus, and many of the B-vitamins. These quantities tend to improve commensurate to the quality of the beer. For the sake of comparison, here are similar numbers for the respected Grant's Scottish Ale, presented in the same standard FDA format:

    Serving size: 12 oz.
      (355 ml.)
    Ingredients: refiltered pure water, barley
      malt, Yakima Valley hops, and pure cul-
      tured yeast.
    145 Calories (⅔ from the alcohol)
    2.24 grams protein
    0 grams of fat
    12.7 grams carbohydrate
    75 mg. sodium
    0 grams cholesterol
    195 milligrams potassium

There are also measurable amounts of riboflavin (B_2), niacin, folacin, pyroxin (B_6), and almost twice the recommended daily allowance of vitamin B_{12}.

Unfortunately, the Bureau of Alcohol, Tobacco, and Firearms, the federal regulatory agency overseeing the brewing industry, has prohibited listing nutritional content and any other information suggesting "curative and therapeutic claims" on beer packaging. Go figure.

The Profitability of Style

A new brewpub owner revealed the results of an unplanned study: all of his house beers initially were served in generic, straight-sided glasses. As the pub's budget would allow, additional styles of beer glassware were added, until each brew could be served in its own style of glassware. Not only did overall beer sales increase, but the average customer was also more willing to try new and different beers.

and seasonals such as Boulder Stout, Summer Ale, Fall Festival, and a lightly spiced Igloo Ale. The porter garnered a gold medal at the 1992 Great American Beer Festival, and the amber took home a silver medal in 1993.

The ownership of the brewery, as well as the name, changed a while back, but the brewery still holds the title of America's oldest operating microbrewery (not to mention one of the largest). No beer trekker's list can be considered complete without a visit here.

San Juan Brewing Company

What first caught my attention, as I read through their promotional material, was the truly unique location described in the San Juan Brewing brochure. Yes, it is in Telluride, Colorado, and yes, it is set in an old railroad depot, but how many brewpubs can say they are located between chairlifts 7 and 8? It's one of the advantages of operating a brewpub in a skiing mecca, I guess.

The building now occupied by the San Juan Brewing Company was once the Telluride railroad depot, part of the Rio Grande Southern Line that arrived here in 1891. In its heyday, hundreds of people came through the old depot, hoping to cash in on the area's mining boom. When the mining operations went bust, the trains stopped chugging into Telluride, and the old depot eventually fell into disrepair. Exactly 100 years later, the San Juan Brewing Company celebrated the centennial by opening its doors on December 26, 1991.

This brewpub in the mountains is the realization of James Loo's dream. Once Mr. Loo decided on the location, he hired local artisans to build the massive mahogany bar with etched and stained glass accents. Then he asked an old college buddy, homebrewer Archie Byers, to become San Juan's brewmaster. Byers says homebrewing was just a hobby-level activity until James Loo asked him if he would be interested in brewing full time in Telluride. Byers enrolled in an intensive ten-week course in the brewing sciences at the famed Siebel Institute in Chicago, before setting up shop in Colorado, where, according to Byers, "like a couple of mad scientists, we started making beer."

Like most microbrewers, the San Juan Brewing Company is respectful of the Reinheitsgebot, or German Purity Law (see page 23) and brews beer with nothing but four natural ingredients — barley, hops, yeast, and pure mountain water. All of the beers brewed by Byers are of the ale variety. After a two-week primary fermentation period, the beer is filtered and transferred to the bright beer tanks, in the refrigeration room located in the basement of the brew-pub. All of the beers are naturally carbonated and drawn directly from the bright beer tanks to the taps at the bar.

The three regular handcrafted brews include Galloping Goose Golden Ale, Little Rose Amber Ale, and Black Bear Porter. The brewer's specials may include Suzzane's Cream Ale, India Pale Ale, Tomboy Bitter, Boomerang Brown Ale, Palisade Peach, Winter Ale, and Willy's Wheat. The original goal was to keep a golden beer, a middle-of-the-road beer, and a porter on tap at all times, but they had to be flexible to accommodate tastes. They recently added a stout and a pale ale. Brewmaster Byers says the key to a successful brewery is having a product with a high level of drinkability in a decent variety of beer styles. At San Juan, he brews a full spectrum of beers with a full slate of different tastes.

Don't forget that the San Juan Brewing Company also serves lunch and dinner seven days a week: fine cuisine, home-baked breads, and seasonal surprises. Patrons can dine on great food at reasonable prices in the bar, the upstairs dining room, or on the patio. The summertime patio, nestled alongside the banks of the San Miguel River, is a favorite place for

locals to escape the hustle and bustle of the downtown area.

Be sure not to miss the San Juan Brewing Company Mercantile, located in the bar area. There are T-shirts, hats, and beer glasses, as well as an assortment of beer-related gourmet food items and books.

Sante Fe Brewing Company

Santa Fe, New Mexico, is well-known and internationally regarded for its highbrow, artsy-craftsy culture and lifestyle. While the town maintains a strong link with its historical and architectural past, it is also a mecca for the New Age crystal and cappucino crowd. Tourists flock here from all over the world to browse the myriad art galleries, dine at the preponderance of world-class restaurants, or just to enjoy the dry heat and sun-soaked skies that dominate the region. It is only fitting then that Santa Fe should have a beer to call its own.

The Santa Fe Brewing Company was established in 1988, the dreamchild of horse rancher Mike Levis, who also was part owner in a Phoenix diversified packaging company when he first contemplated brewing beer in the mid-1980s. He yearned to

SANTA FE PALE ALE

create a beer with personality to supplant the bland and lifeless beers made by mass market producers and served at area bars and restaurants. While he would have preferred to open his brewery in the heart of downtown, real estate had become outrageously expensive. The idea of finding a cheaper and less desirable location on the outskirts of town — away from the action and attention — left Levis with one logical alternative: building the brewery on his ranch gave him 24-hour, seven-day a week control of the operation, as well as a rent free location.

The Flying M Ranch, a mere 20 minutes from Santa Fe, became the first microbrewery in the state of New Mexico and one of the first in the American Southwest. It is located just one mile north of Galisteo, situated among the scrubby, Pinon pine-studded foothills of northern New Mexico. It was later discovered that the ranch had access to an underground water source that was well-suited to brewing beer. Experts from the Siebel Brewing Institute, hired by Levis to test the water,

declared it the best they had seen outside of Burton-on-Trent, England.

The equipment for the new brewery was purchased from the recently refurbished Boulder Brewing Company in Colorado. After inspecting the equipment, Levis submitted an offer that was quickly accepted. According to the agreement, a representative from Boulder Brewing would come down to the Flying M and help Levis to install the brewhouse. First, however, the old quarter horse barn on the ranch was remodeled to accommodate the used brew system.

The first batch of Santa Fe Pale Ale was produced in June 1988, and the local brew was quickly placed in more than 100 "high end" accounts in New Mexico and Arizona. Current availability has extended to select markets in Indiana, Colorado, and Washington, DC. The brewery has continued to expand its lineup of beers, as well. Today, along with the pale ale, one can find Santa Fe Nut Brown Ale, Old Pojoaque Porter, and specialties Chicken Killer Barleywine, Galisteo Weiss, and a fruit beer, Sangre de Frambuesa (blood of the raspberry). All of the Santa Fe products are naturally carbonated, all-malt beers that are handmade, hand-bottled and hand-labeled. The bottles are capped with crowns bearing the "Zia" symbol, which has strong Native American ties and is featured prominently throughout New Mexico.

Schirf Brewing

Utah. When this state becomes the topic of conversation, two things come to mind: spectacular geography and

Mormons. One of the last things one thinks of is beer.

With regard to spectacular geography, Utah certainly has its share. Millions of years of wind and water have wrought fascinating natural sculptures in this land. There are five national parks and six national monuments in the state, as well as thousands of acres of pristine forests. Canoeing, whitewater rafting, skiing, rock climbing, four-wheeling — it's all here, taking full advantage of Mother Nature's generous endowment.

The land we know as Utah was first explored by Europeans in the late 1700s. The capital, Salt Lake City, was founded and settled in 1847 by the followers of Brigham Young, who traveled westward seeking refuge from persecution for their religious beliefs. The region was acquired in the Treaty of Guadalupe Hidalgo and gained statehood in 1896. Since the Mormons had so much to do with settling the region, it is only logical that these people and their religious practices still hold sway in the state. Because of the restrictive laws regarding the production and consumption of beer, "half of the people in Utah don't drink beer, so it's incumbent upon the rest of us to make up for it," says Gregory Schirf.

Greg Schirf is the president and founder of the Schirf Brewing Company in Park City, Utah, a town southeast of Salt Lake City known for its prime skiing facilities. Undaunted by the existing laws then in force, Schirf opened his brewing company in 1986, making it the first brewery in the state since the old Becker Brewery in Ogden closed in

1965. In 1989, Schirf challenged the state legislature to pass a brewpub law. Through his efforts, a law supporting the existence of brewpubs was passed, paving the way for the six breweries now operating in the state. One of these six is Schirf's own Wasatch Brew Pub, which was added on to the extant brewery in 1989. The new three-story structure, named for the surrounding mountain range, features three separate areas including the all copper and glass brewhouse located behind the first floor bar. The 1,000-gallon, stainless steel fermentation tanks were custom-made in Portland, and the filtration equipment came from Germany. The contemporary design is such that patrons have an interesting vantage point of all the different brewing functions.

Since the brewpub's production was running at near capacity, a second and larger production facility was established in Salt Lake City. Total output in 1993 was 7,500 barrels but is expected to reach 18,000 in 1995.

There are four regular bottled products marketed under the Wasatch name, and they are sold only in Utah: premium ale, slickrock, weizenbier, and stout. There are additional specialty brews such as a bock beer, a raspberry wheat beer, and a Christmas ale. Because of the aforementioned beer production laws, all of these products contain a maximum alcohol content of 3.2 percent by weight (4.0 percent by volume). Whatever the case, Wasatch's naturally brewed products fit well with Utah's desert and mountain recreational opportunities.

Wynkoop Brewery

Visiting Denver today, it's hard to imagine what it must have been like in the 1850s when it was just a frontier outpost. One of the founders of the city was Edward Wanshear Wynkoop, and the Wynkoop name is, therefore, one of the oldest and most famous in Denver's history. Wynkoop was a devoted husband and father of eight children. He also was Denver's first sheriff. At the outbreak of the Civil War, Wynkoop joined the Union army and was given command of Fort Lyon. The army's official directive to Wynkoop and his men was to kill all renegade Indians on sight, which went against Wynkoop's beliefs. When he tried to broker a peace with the Indians, the army promptly relieved him of his command. Shortly after he left the fort, a massacre of 125 Indians took place. Outraged by the army's actions, Wynkoop led the investigation against his fellow officers and was disparaged openly by the press and the public. In less than a year, Edward Wynkoop had gone from proud founding father to one of the most hated men on the frontier. For all his troubles, the city of Denver named a street after him.

The Wynkoop name is now better known and more highly respected than ever, with the 1988 opening of the Wynkoop Brewery in Denver. Occupying a red brick building in the old warehouse district, complete with maple floors and stamped tin ceilings, the brewpub has made its home in a structure listed in the National Register of Historic Buildings. Since its inception, Wynkoop Brewery has been among the most successful brewpubs in the country and is now the largest producing one, with an annual output of approximately 5,000 barrels.

There are several reasons for this success, starting with its good location. The brewery is in the gentrified, lower downtown district, just down the street from the bustling Union Station. Furthermore, it is in a building that lends itself easily to expansion. There is an extremely well-thought-out presentation and a menu teeming with food choices. From appetizers to desserts, there are almost 60 items from which to choose, including a section called "Hop Healthy Fare." These foods are prepared in accordance with strict nutritional guidelines. Last, but certainly not least, is the beer. Customers faced with the difficult decision of choosing among the many beers may order a sampler of six four-ounce glasses called a "flight of beer." The glasses are served on a paper placemat which identifies each type, as well as a step-by-step description of the beermaking process. A typical

Beers to Complement French Haute Cuisine

Defined by pungent cheeses, fine meats, and rich sauces, French haute cuisine is no place for timid beers. The rich, earthy Trappist beers are a natural with aged and herbed cheeses. Belgian brown and red ales complement most red meats nicely. For rich sauces, a mildly malty but sharply refreshing Kölschbier is just what the gourmand ordered.

"flight" might include Wilderness Wheat Beer, Classic Amber, India Pale Ale, St. Charles E.S.B., Quinn's Scottish Ale, and Sagebrush Stout. There are additional choices such as Jedfest, Splatz Porter, Mark's Mild, and other specialties, depending on the holiday, the season, or the whim of the brewmaster.

Upstairs from the brewery is Wynkoop Billiards, an elegant turn-of-the-century pool hall and one of the city's most popular attractions. Downstairs there is live entertainment, including Comedy Sports. The Wynkoop is always busy and festive; the atmosphere fun and casual.

Take time to peruse the *Wynkoop Brewer's Gazette,* the brewery newspaper/menu which features small articles and explanations about the brewery. There are also columns for the chef and the brewmaster to speak their piece. One quote reads, "You're a stranger here but once."

Mountain/High Plains Brewer Profiles

Charlie Papazian

Though it may no longer be the case, early in the microbrewing revolution you would have been hard-pressed to find someone who *didn't* know Charlie Papazian. And there was good reason — Charlie was one of the first Americans to take advantage of the new law passed in 1978 that made homebrewing legal (though it is rumored that he began brewing his own beer long before then). In that year, Charlie founded the American Homebrewers Association in Boulder, Colorado, to promote public awareness and appreciation of the quality and variety of beer. From the AHA came many outgrowths including Brewers Publications, the Institute for Brewing Studies, and the hallowed Great American Beer Festival, all of which came under the aegis of the Association of Brewers. Charlie Papazian is both president and treasurer of the organization. The association publishes two of the foremost publications of their kind: *Zymurgy* and *The New Brewer* magazines.

Papazian began teaching homebrewing courses through the Boulder Free School in the early 1980s. This spawned a great deal of interest in the craft. Several of his students/apostles became fervent homebrewers and helped to spread the good word about homebrewing. It has been well documented that modern American homebrewing sowed the seeds of the beer renaissance that was to follow. A fair number of microbrewers trace their roots to homebrewing and many are quick to acknowledge Papazian's guidance and contribution. Many of these pioneering homebrewers-turned-microbrewers could readily produce a tattered and dog-eared copy of Papazian's *The Complete Joy of Homebrewing* — long considered the homebrewer's bible. Over 350,000 copies of this tome and the all-new *Home Brewers Companion* have been sold.

Charlie has traveled much in his research of good beer, appearing at tastings, festivals, competitions, and conferences all over the United States and elsewhere in the world. In addition, he continues to write for several beer and brewing magazines, remains an active member of the American Society of Brewing Chemists, and is an allied member of the Master Brewers Association of the Americas.

Russell Schehrer

Among the hundreds of brewmasters who create the vast number of outstanding microbrewed beers across the nation, a good many of them credit a homebrewing background for their success. One such person is Russell Schehrer of Colorado. His first exposure to homebrew took place in Charlie Papazian's kitchen when Charlie was teaching a homebrewing course through the Boulder Free School. Either Charlie was a great teacher or Russell was a quick study (or both!), because Schehrer soon began entering his homebrewed beers in local competitions and steadily winning awards!

Russell's real emergence on the beer scene occurred in 1984 at the National Homebrew Competition sponsored by the American Homebrewers Association. That year, 694 entries from 42 states and several Canadian provinces were attracted to the event. Schehrer's brews garnered second place ribbons in the pale ale and Oktoberfest categories, and first place ribbons in both the porter and the British pale ale categories. Russell's British ale then went on to win the British Bitter Champion Trophy. Combined awards totaled enough points to make Russell Schehrer the 1985 Homebrewer of the Year. Almost as impressive as his winnings was the fact that his brews, made from extract, scored better than others made from all grain.

In the wake of these accomplishments, there was no doubt in which direction Russell would be heading. By 1987, he had joined forces with a couple of unemployed geologists who shared his dream of opening a brewpub. In 1988 their dreams were realized when the Wynkoop Brewing Company in Denver became the first brewpub in the state of Colorado.

Schehrer now divides his time between the successful brewpub operation and his private consulting business. He has designed brewpubs in Vail and Ft. Collins, and he also provides training assistance to CooperSmith's in Ft. Collins and Lazlo's, Nebraska's first brewpub, in Lincoln.

Eric Warner

Born and raised in Denver, Colorado, Eric Warner successfully completed his degree in German studies at Lewis and Clark College in Portland, Oregon. This was accomplished in preparation for his pursuits of a formal education in the brewing sciences in Germany. Eric was awarded the degree *Diplom-Braumeister* after three years of extensive brewery, laboratory, and course work at the prestigious Technical University of Munich at Weihenstephan. The Weihenstephan Institut is widely regarded as the finest brewing school in the world.

Since receiving his degree, Eric has worked in and visited breweries both in the United States and Europe. Most notably, he worked at Brauerei Widmann and Hofbrauhaus Moy, both in the Munich area. Warner also brewed at the Wynkoop Brewery in his hometown.

A big fan of traditional German weissbier, Eric entered his homebrewed version in the 1992 National Homebrew Competition and took first place in the wheat beer category. Warner also has authored a comprehensive book on the subject titled *German Wheat Beer*. According to one reviewer, it is ". . . packed with information, both technical and anecdotal, Warner educates and entertains in a compendium that's hard to put down."

Working as an independent consultant in the microbrewing industry, Eric Warner is president and head consultant for Blue River Brewing Consultants. More recently, Eric and three partners pooled their knowledge and resources in order to open one of Colorado's newest microbreweries. The Tabernash Brewing Company is named for a small town in the mountains; a crossroads in the days when the West was being settled. The brewery's creations represent a union of the great brewing traditions of Germany with the innovations of the American West. To Eric and his partners' credit, two of the Tabernash brews took bronze medals at the 1994 Great American Beer Festival, and one of them brought home the gold — Tabernash weiss!

In his spare time, Eric enjoys hiking, fly fishing, reading, tennis, and — of course — homebrewing.

Mountain/High Plains Beer Festivals

Colorado Brewers Festival

Ft. Collins, CO
June
(303) 498-9070

More than 10,000 thirsty people pack Ft. Collins' Pioneer Square each June in anticipation of sampling beer from each of Colorado's breweries. Only one product from each of the home state's brewers — including Coors and Anheuser-Busch — can be showcased at this event. Brewers, food booths, local musicians, and assorted merchants all vie for your attention.

Great Rocky Mountain Beer Festival

Copper Mountain, CO
August (third week)
(303) 968-2318, ext. 6505

The Great Rocky Mountain Beer Festival features the best of the Rocky Mountain brewers. This festival is part microbrew-tasting, part homebrew competition.

Great American Beer Festival

Denver, CO
October (second week)
(303) 447-0816

The grandaddy of American beer festivals, the Great American Beer Festival will be celebrating its fourteenth year in 1995. It has outgrown the cavernous Currigan Hall and will be celebrating in a new location, to be announced. The Great American Beer Festival is well known for the coveted medals awarded to brewers each year. It is also the single largest conglomeration of beers and brewers in America. One weekend every October is dedicated to this beer orgy, which consists of more than 1,200 beers from approximately 260 breweries across the nation. Join the 30,000 people who know where the real action is! Meet the brewers, taste the award-winning brews, learn how to brew beer, buy a beer book, and have it autographed by the author — all this and more at the biggest and the best.

Mountain/High Plains Region Listings

Arizona

Bandersnatch Brewpub
125 E. 5th Ave.
Tempe, AZ   85281
(602) 966-4438
Brewpub
Brews: Cardinal Pale Ale,
Bighorn Premium Ale,
Bandersnatch Milk Stout, and
seasonals
Hours: Mon.–Sat.,
11AM–1:15AM; Sun.,
noon–1:15AM

**Beaver Street Brewery &
Whistle Stop Cafe**
11 S. Beaver St.
Flagstaff, AZ 86001
(602) 779-0079
Brewpub
Brews: Detail Pale Ale, Beaver
Street Bitter, red ale, raspberry
ale, porter, oatmeal stout.
Seasonals: American wheat
ale, Märzen
Hours: Daily, 11:30AM–
midnight

**Coyote Spring
Brewing & Cafe**
4883 N. 20th Street
Phoenix, AZ 85016
(602) 468-0403

Brewpub
Brews: Trick Pale Ale, Fair
Dinkum Ale, Toby Stout, Nuts
to You Nut Brown Ale, Koyote
Kölsch
Hours: Daily, 11AM–1AM

**Crazy Ed's Black
Mountain Brewery**
6245 E. Cave Creek Road
Cave Creek, AZ 85331
(602) 253-6293
Brewpub
Brews: Black Mountain Gold,
Frog light, Crazy Ed's Arizona
Pilsner, Ed's Original Cave
Creek Beer, Ed's Original Cave
Creek Chili Beer
Hours: Mon.–Thurs.,
11AM–11PM; Fri.–Sat.,
11AM–1AM; Sun., 9AM–10PM

Flagstaff Brewing
16 E. Highway 66
Flagstaff, AZ 86004
(602) 773-1442
Brewpub
Brews: Agassi Amber,
Ponderosa Pale, Dibindorf Dark
Hours: Daily, 11AM–1AM

Gentle Ben's Brewing
841 N. Tyndall
Tucson, AZ 85719
(602) 624-4177
Brewpub
Brews: Tucson Blonde, Red
Cat Amber, Copperhead Pale
Ale, Taylor Jayne's Raspberry,
Nolan Porter, and others
Hours: Daily, 11AM–1AM

Hops! Bistro & Brewery
2584 E. Camelback Road
Phoenix, AZ 85016
(602) 468-0500
Brewpub
Brews: Pilsner, hefe-weizen,
amber ale, raspberry, Peter's
Porter. *Seasonals:* Oktoberfest,
nut brown ale, barleywine,
stout, Dictator's Little Sister
Bock
Hours: Daily, 11:30AM–1AM

Hops! Bistro & Brewery
7000 E. Camelback Road
Scottsdale, AZ 85251
(602)423-5557 or 945-HOPS
Brewpub
Brews: Pilsner, hefe-weizen,
amber ale, raspberry, Peter's
Porter. *Seasonals:* Oktoberfest,
nut brown ale, barleywine,
stout, Dictator's Little Sister
Bock
Hours: Daily, 11:30AM–1AM

Prescott Brewing
130 W. Gurley St.
Prescott, AZ 96301
(602) 771-2795
Brewpub
Brews: Lodgepole Light,
Prescott Pale Ale, Liquid
Amber, Petrified Porter, Scotch
Whisky, and seasonals

Hours: Sun.–Wed., 11AM–midnight; Thurs.–Sat., 11AM–1AM

Colorado

Avery Brewing
5763 E. Arapahoe
Boulder, CO 80301
(303) 440-4324
Microbrewery
Brews: Redpoint Ale, Elle's
Brown Ale, Out of Bounds
Stout, Razzy Wheat Ale
Tours: By appointment

**Baked & Brewed
in Telluride**
127 S. Fir
Telluride, CO 81435
(970) 728-4705
Brewpub
Brews: Kady's Irish Ale,
Stormy Stout, Runner's High,
Pandora Porter, Snow Wheat
Hefe-Weizen. *Seasonal:*
Oktoberfest
Hours: Mon.–Sat.,
noon–9:30PM; Sun., noon–8PM

Breckenridge Brewery
2220 Blake St.
Denver, CO 80205
(303) 297-3644
Brewpub
Brews: Avalanche, Mountain
wheat, oatmeal stout, Ballpark
Brown, and others
Hours: Daily, 11AM–2AM

Bristol Brewing
4740 Forge Road
Colorado Springs, CO 80907
(719) 535-2824
Microbrewery
Brews: Red Rocket Pale Ale,

Breckenridge Brewery

Laughing Lab Scottish Ale
Tours: Sat., 10AM–4PM
Growlers to go.

Broadway Brewing
2441 Broadway
Denver, CO 80205
(303) 292-5027
Brewpub
Brews: Railyard Ale, Doggie Style Ale, Red Lady Ale, and others
Hours: Mon.–Fri., 10:30AM–closing; Sat., 5PM–closing

Carver's Bakery Cafe Brewery
1022 Main Ave.
Durango, CO 81301
(970) 259-2545
Brewpub
Brews: Golden Wheat & Honey Old Oak Amber Ale, Iron Horse Stout, Carver IPA. *Seasonals:* raspberry wheat ale, barleywine, English mild, and monthly specials
Hours: Mon.–Sat., 6:30AM–10PM; Sun., 6:30AM–1PM

Casa De Colorado Brewery
320 Link Lane
Fort Collins, CO 80524
(970) 493-2739
Brewpub
Brews: Fort Collins Pride, Poudre Porter. *Seasonals:* Oktoberfest, stout, bitter, golden, brown, Pilsner
Hours: Mon.–Sat., 11AM–2AM; closed Sun.

Champion Brewing
1442 Larimer Square
Denver, CO 80202
(303) 534-5444
Brewpub
Brews: Buck Wheat Beer, Home Run Ale, Coal Porter, Larimer Lager, Red Light, Stout Street Stout, Norm Clark's Sport Beer, Irish Red Ale, and seasonals
Hours: Daily, 11AM–2AM

CooperSmith's Pub & Brewing
No. 5 Old Town Square
Fort Collins, CO 80524
(970) 498-0483
Brewpub
Brews: Pedestrian Light Ale, Poudre Pale Ale, Albert Damm Bitter, Not Brown Ale, Horsetooth Stout, Punjabi Pale Ale, Sigda's Green Chili Beer, dunkelweizen, Dunvaven Ale, and seasonals
Hours: Mon.–Sat., 11AM–1:30AM; Sun., 11AM–midnight

Crested Butte Brewery (The Idlespur)
226 Elk Ave.
Crested Butte, CO 81224
(970) 349-5026
Brewpub
Brews: India pale ale, Red Lady Ale, Rodeo Stout, White Buffalo Peace Ale, Southwest Light, Bucks Wheat, 3-Pin Grin Porter
Hours: Daily, 2PM–2AM; Happy hour: Daily, 2PM–6PM

Durango Brewing
3000 Main St.
Durango, CO 81301
(970) 247-3396
Microbrewery
Brews: Durango Dark Lager.
Seasonals: Winter Ale,
Colorfest, Anasazi Wheat
Tours: By appointment

Estes Park Brewery
470 Prospect Village Dr.
Estes Park, CO 80517
(303) 586-5421
Brewpub
Brews: Miners Pale Ale,
Renegade Red, Estes Park
Porter; rotating specialties
Hours: Daily, noon–closing

**Flying Dog
Brewpub & Grille**
424 E. Cooper
Aspen, CO 81611
(970) 925-7464
Brewpub
Brews: Ol' Yeller, Doggie Style
Amber Ale. *Seasonals:* Hair of
the Dog, Rin Tin Tan, Dog
House Wheat, Bull Dog
Imperial Stout, and others
Hours: Daily 11:30AM–
midnight

Golden City Brewery
920 12th St.
Golden, CO 80401
(303) 279-8092
Microbrewery
Brews: Golden Cream Ale,
Golden City Red
Tours: Tues.–Sat., noon–5PM

Great Divide Brewing
Denver, CO 80205

Microbrewery
No further information available at press time

H. C. Berger Brewing
1900 E. Lincoln Ave.
Fort Collins, CO 80524
(970) 493-9044
Microbrewery
Brews: Indego Pale Ale,
Whistlepin Wheat Ale, Red
Banshee Ale, and seasonals
Tours: Call in advance

**Heavenly Daze
Brewery & Grill**
1860 Ski Time Square Dr.
Steamboat Springs, CO
80479
(970) 879-8080
Brewpub
Brews: raspberry wheat, rye
beer, Porcupine Pale Ale, Dog's
Breath Brown Ale, Woodchuck
Porter, Cows Creek Cream Ale,
Heavenly Hefe-Weizen
Hours: Daily, 11AM–10PM

Hubcap Brewery & Kitchen
143 E. Meadow Dr.
Vail, CO 81657
(970) 476-5757
Brewpub
Brews: White River Wheat,
Camp Hale Golden Ale, Ace
amber Ale, Beaver Tail Brown
Ale, Rainbow Trout Stout, Rock
N' Roll Solstice Ale, and
seasonals
Hours: Daily, 11AM–2AM

Irons Brewing
12354 W. Alameda Parkway
Lakewood, CO 80228
(303) 985-BEER
Microbrewery

Irons Brewing

Left Hand Brewing

New Belgium Brewing

Brews: Hellbender, Manatee, Condor American Iron, Ironheart, and others

Tours: By appointment

Judge Baldwin's Brewing
4 S. Cascade
Colorado Springs, CO 80903
(719) 473-5600
Brewpub
Brews: pale ale, amber ale, nut brown ale, wheat beer, raspberry, and specialties
Hours: Mon.–Thurs., 11AM–midnight; Fri.–Sat., 11AM–1AM

Left Hand Brewing
1265 Boston Ave.
Longmont, CO 80501
(303) 772-0258
Microbrewery
Brews: Motherlode Golden Ale, Sawtooth Ale, Juju Ginger, porter
Tours: Whenever you can get there (but call first to make sure they are open)

Lone Wolfe Brewing
0898 Highway 133
Carbondale, CO 81623
(970) 963-8777
Microbrewery
Brews: standard lager, and seasonals
Tours: By appointment

Mountain Sun Pub & Brewery
1535 Pearl St.
Boulder, CO 80302
(303) 546-0886
Brewpub

Brews: Quinn's Golden Ale, Colorado Kind Ale, Thunderhead Stout, Raspberry Wheat. *Seasonals:* Oktoberfest, bock, wheat, nut brown ale
Hours: Mon.–Thurs., 11AM–1AM; Fri.–Sat., 11AM–2AM; Sun., 11AM–midnight

New Belgium Brewing
350 Linden St.
Fort Collins, CO 80524
(970) 221-0524
Microbrewery
Brews: Abbey, Fat Tire, Sunshine Wheat, Old Cherry Beer, trippel, and seasonals
Tours: Sat., 1PM–5PM, and by appointment

Oasis Brewery & Restaurant
1095 Canyon Blvd.
Boulder, CO 80302
(303) 449-0363
Brewpub
Brews: Oasis Pale Ale, Tut Brown Ale, Capstone ESB, Scarab Red, Zoser Oatmeal Stout. *Seasonals:* Christmas Spiced Ale, doppelbock, blueberry ale, and others
Hours: Mon.–Sat., 11:30AM–2AM; Sun., 10AM–midnight

Odell Brewing
800 E. Lincoln Ave.
Fort Collins, CO 80524
(970) 498-9070
Microbrewery
Brews: 90 Shilling, Old Town Ale, Cut Throat Porter, Easy Street Wheat. *Seasonals:* Riley's Red, Christmas Shilling

Tours: Fri.–Sat., 2PM–5PM, or by appointment

Phantom Canyon Brewing
2 E. Pike Peak Ave.
Colorado Springs, CO 80903
(719) 635-2800
Brewpub
Brews: porter, blond ale, cascade amber, IPA, and seasonals
Hours: Sun.–Thurs., 11AM–10PM; Fri.–Sat., 11AM–11PM

Pike's Peak Brewery
2547 Weston Road
Colorado Springs, CO 80910
(719) 391-8866
Microbrewery
Brews: Jack Rabbit, Red Granite, Moonlight
Tours: Sat., 1PM–5PM

Rock Bottom Brewery
1001 16th St.
Denver, CO 80265
(303) 534-7616
Brewpub
Brews: Rocky Premium Ale, Falcon Pale Ale, Molly's Titanic Brown Ale, Red Rocks Red, Black Diamond Stout. *Seasonals:* Old Thumper, Jingle Bells Rock, Jazzberry
Hours: Mon.–Sat., 11AM–2AM; Sun., 11AM–midnight

Rockies Brewing (Wilderness Pub)
2880 Wilderness Pl.
Boulder, CO 80301
(303) 444-8448
Brewpub
Brews: Boulder Extra Ale, Boulder Porter, Boulder Amber Ale, Rockies Premium Ale,

Buffalo Gold Premium Ale, Wrigley Red. *Seasonals:* Boulder Stout, and others
Hours: Mon.–Thurs., 11AM–midnight; Fri.–Sat., 11AM–2AM; closed Sun.

San Juan Brewing
300 S. Townsend
Telluride, CO 81435
(970) 728-4587
Brewpub
Brews: Galloping Goose Golden Ale, Black Bear Porter, Little Rose Amber Ale. *Seasonals:* IPA, Brown Boomerang, Tomboy Bitter
Hours: Daily, 11:30AM–2AM

Silver Plume Brewing Company
Silver Plume, CO
Microbrewery
No further information available at press time

Steamboat Brewery & Tavern
435 Lincoln Ave.
Steamboat Springs, CO 80477
(970) 879-2233
Brewpub
Brews: Hahn's Peak Golden Ale, Pinnacle Pale Ale, Jane's Brown Ale, Powder Keg Porter, Skull Creek Stout, and seasonals
Hours: Daily, 11:30AM–1AM

Tabernash Brewing
205 Denargo Market
Denver, CO 80216
(303) 293-2337
Microbrewery
Brews: Tabernash Weiss,

Rockies Brewing

Silver Plume Brewing Company

Golden Spike Lager, Denargo Lager. *Seasonals:* Derailer, doppelbock, Tabernash O-Fest

Tours: Sat., 10AM–4PM

II Vicino-Salida Inc.
Salida, CO

Brewpub

No further information available at press time

Walnut Brewery
1123 Walnut
Boulder, CO 80302
(303) 447-1345

Brewpub

Brews: Indian Peaks Pale Ale, Buffalo Gold Premium Ale, Old Elk Brown Ale, Jazzberry Ale, Bighorn Bitter, James Irish Red, Devil's Thumb Stout, Sub-Zero, and others

Hours: Mon.–Sat., 11AM–2AM; Sun., 11AM–11PM

Wild Wild West Gambling Hall & Brewery
443 E. Bennett Ave.
Cripple Creek, CO 80813
(719) 689-3736

Brewpub

Brews: Vindicator Pale, Full Moon Lager, Cripple Creek Beer, Mine Shaft Stout. *Seasonals:* Womach Wheat, West Fest

Hours: Daily, 8AM–2AM

Wynkoop Brewing
1534 18th St.
Denver, CO 80202
(303) 297-2700

Brewpub

Brews: Sagebrush Stout, Holiday Ale, St. Charles ESB. *Seasonals:* Wilderness Wheat,

Jed Fest, IPA, Quinn's Scottish Ale, Splatz Porter, Elvis Brau, Irish Cream Stout, and others

Hours: Mon.–Thurs., 11AM–1AM; Fri.–Sat., 11AM–2AM; Sun., 11AM–midnight

Idaho

Beier Brewing
Boise, ID

Microbrewery

No further information available at press time.

Coeur D'Alene Brewing (T.W. Fisher's Brewpub)
204 N. 2nd St.
Coeur D'Alene, ID 83814
(208) 664-BREW

Brewpub

Brews: Light Wheat, Centennial Pale Ale, Festival Dark, Full Moon Stout. *Seasonals:* winter warmer, bock, summerfest, Red Oktober, nut brown ale, cream ale

Hours: Mon.–Thurs., 7AM–11PM; Fri., 7AM–1AM; Sat., 11AM–1AM; Sun., 11AM–midnight

Harrison Hollow Brewhouse
2455 Harrison Hollow Blvd.
Boise, ID 83702
(208) 343-6820

Brewpub

Brews: Ginger Wheat, Fiegwirth, Western Ale, rotating seasonals

Hours: Daily, 11AM–1AM

McCall Brewing
807 N. 3rd St.
McCall, ID 83638
(208) 726-1832

Brewpub

Brews: Whitewater Wheat, Jughandle Amber, Mackinaw Red Ale, Cut Throat Porter, and seasonals

Hours: Daily, 11:30AM–midnight

Sun Valley Brewing
202 N. Main St.
Hailey, ID 83333
(208) 788-6319

Brewpub

Brews: Sawtooth Gold Lager, Sun Valley Blonde, White Cloud Ale. *Seasonal:* Our Holiday Ale

Hours: Mon.–Fri., 8AM–11PM; Sat., 2:30PM–11PM; closed Sun.

Tablerock Brewpub & Grill
705 Fulton
Boise, CO 83702
(208) 342-0944

Brewpub

Brews: Depot Gold, Tablerock Red, T. D.'s Nut Brown Ale, Brewer's Whim. *Seasonals:* harvest ale, IPA, wheat, stout, and others

Hours: Mon.–Thurs., 11:30AM–11PM; Fri.–Sat., 11:30AM–11:30PM; Sun., noon–10PM

Thunder Mountain Brewing
591 4th St. East
Ketchum, ID 83340
(208) 726-1832

Brewpub

Brews: High Thunder Pale Ale, amber ale, dark ale

Hours: Daily, 11AM–8PM

Treaty Grounds Brewing
W. 2124 3rd St.
Moscow, ID 83843
(208) 883-4253

Brewpub

Brews: Moscow Gold, Pullman Red

Hours: Sun.–Mon., 11AM–9PM; Tues.–Thurs., 11AM–10PM; Fri.–Sat., 11AM–11PM

Kansas

Free State Brewing
636 Massachusetts
Lawrence, KS 66044
(913) 843-4555

Brewpub

Brews: Ad Astra Ale, Wheat State Golden, Copperhead Pale Ale, oatmeal stout, and seasonals

Hours: Mon.–Sat., 11AM–midnight; Sun., noon–11PM

Little Apple Brewing
1110 W. Loop Center
Manhattan, KS 66502
(913) 539-5500

Brewpub

Brews: Aggie Wheat, Big Red Ale, Boston Bitter, Black Squirrel Stout. *Seasonals:* Pillsbury Porter, Golden Wheat

Hours: Mon.–Thurs., 7AM–midnight; Fri.–Sat., 11AM–2AM; Sun., 11AM–midnight

Miracle Brewing
311 S. Emporia
Wichita, KS 67202
(316) 265-7256

Microbrewery

Brews: Red Devil Ale, Ark Angel, Purgatory Porter,

Screamin' Demon Imperial Stout

Tours: By appointment

River City Brewing
150 N. Mosley
Wichita, KS 76202
(316) 263-BREW
Brewpub
Brews: Harvester Wheat,
Hockaday Pale Ale, Railyard
Amber Ale, 4 Horsemen Stout,
2 Rivers Bitter. *Seasonals:* fest,
cherry
Hours: Mon.–Thurs.,
11AM–midnight; Fri.–Sat.,
11AM–2AM

Montana

**Bayern Brewing
(Iron Horse Brewpub)**
North Higgens Ave.
Missoula, MT 59807-8043
(406) 721-8705
Brewpub
Brews: amber, premium
Pilsner, bock, dopplebock,
wheat. *Seasonals:* Killarney,
Oktoberfest, traditional dark
Hours: Mon.–Fri., 11AM–2AM;
Sat., 1PM–2AM; Sun., 3PM–2AM

Lang Creek Brewery
655 Lang Creek Road
Marion, MT 59925
(406) 858-2200
Microbrewery
Brews: Tri Motor Amber,
Windsock Ale, Scud Runner
Dark
Tours: By appointment

**Miles Town Brewing
(Golden Spur)**
1014 S. Haynes
Miles City, MT 59301
(406)232-3898
Brewpub
Brews: Old Milestown, Coal
Porter. *Seasonals:* Paul's Lemon
Grass, Buckinghorse Bock, Prof.
Bock, Celebrator, and others
Hours: Daily, 10AM–2AM

**Montana Beverages
(Kessler Brewery)**
1439 Harris St.
Helena, MT 59601
(406) 449-6214
Microbrewery
Brews: lorelei, centennial.
Seasonals: wheat, bock,
Oktoberfest
Tours: Mon.–Fri., 2PM and 4PM,
reservations suggested

**Spanish Peaks Brewing
& Italian Cafe**
120 N. 19th Ave.
Bozeman, MT 59715
(406) 585-2296
Brewpub
Brews: Yellowstone Pale Ale,
Blackdog Bitter, Spanish Peaks
Porter, Eye of the Rockies
Wheat. *Seasonals:* oatmeal
stout, Irish Red, spring rye ale,
and others
Hours: Daily, 11:30AM–11PM

Whitefish Brewing
P.O. Box 1949
Whitefish, MT 59937
(406) 862-2684
Microbrewery
Brews: Melikian Ale, Pale Ale,
Porter

Tours: Call for information and directions.

Nebraska

Crane River Brewpub & Cafe
200 N. 11th St.
Lincoln, NE 68508
(402) 476-7766
Brewpub
Brews: Platte Valley ESB, Zlate Pivo, Sod House Altbier, Homestead Pale Ale, Good Life Stout, Whooping Wheat.
Seasonals: Solstice Spice and others
Hours: Mon.–Sat., 11AM–1AM; Sun., noon–midnight

Jaipur Brewing
10922 Elm St.
Omaha, NE 68144
(402) 392-7331
Brewpub
Brews: Royal Golden Pale Ale, Huntsman Brown Ale, Tusk Dark Ale, Black Stripe Stout, Pink City Weizen Beer.
Seasonal: cherry ale
Hours: Mon.–Sat., 11:30AM–10PM; Sun., 5:30PM–10PM

Johnny's Brewing
4150 144th St.
Omaha, NE 68137
(402) 895-1122
Brewpub
Brews: Pilsner, amber lager.
Seasonals: pale ale, wheat, and others
Hours: Daily, 11:30AM–1AM

Jones Street Brewery
1316 Jones St.
Omaha, NE 68102
(402) 344-3858
Brewpub
Brews: Harvester Wheat, Patch Pale Ale, Ryan's Irish Stout, Bolt, Nut & Screw Golden Ale.
Seasonals: Holiday Ale, Dunkelweizen, Slapshot Winter Ale, and others
Hours: Daily, 11:30AM–1AM

Lazlo's Brewery & Grill
710 P St.
Lincoln, NE 68508
(402) 474-2337
Brewpub
Brews: Lougale's Gold, Reckless Red's Special Amber, Black Jack Stout. *Seasonals:* porter, dark wheat, lambic style ale, Christmas ale
Hours: Mon.–Sat., 11AM–1AM; Sun., 11AM–10PM

Sharkey's Brewery
7777 Cass
Omaha, NE 68114
(402) 390-0777
Brewpub
Brews: Great Red Shark Ale, Great White Shark Ale, Hammerhead Ale. *Seasonals:* Wahoo Wheat Ale, Honest Don's Irish Stout, and others
Hours: Mon.–Fri., 11AM–1AM; Sat.–Sun., noon–1AM

New Mexico

Assets Grille & Brewing
6910 Montgomery N.E.
Albuquerque, NM 87109
(505) 889-6400
Brewpub

Brews: Duke City Amber, Rio Grande Wheat, Roadrunner Golden Ale. *Seasonals:* hefeweizen, sandia, black cherry stout

Hours: Mon.–Tues., 11:30AM–midnight; Wed.–Sat., 11:30AM–2AM; Sun., noon–midnight

Organ Mountain Brewing (O'Ryan's Tavern)
700 S. Telshor Blvd.
Las Cruces, NM 88001
(505) 522-8191
Brewpub

Brews: Organ Mountain Gold, Red Dog Pale Ale, Dark Spit Stout, O'Ryan's Stout, Rio Grande Porter, and seasonals

Hours: Mon.–Sat., 11AM–1AM

Preston Brewery (Embudo Station Restaurant)
P.O. Box 154
Embudo, NM 87531
(505) 852-4707
Brewpub

Brews: Railroaders Stout, Rio Grande Green Chili Beer, Rio Grande Ristra-Red Chili Ale, Narrow Gauge Ale, Brewmasters Reserve

Hours: Summer: Tues.–Sun., noon–9PM; Fall and Spring: Tues.–Thurs., noon–4PM; Fri.–Sun., noon–9PM; Winter (Nov.18–mid-Feb.) closed

Rio Bravo Restaurant & Brewery
515 Central Ave. NW
Albuquerque, NM 87102
(505) 242-6800

Brewpub

Brews: Coronado Gold, High Desert Pale Ale, Esteban Dark, and frequent seasonals

Hours: Mon.–Sat., 11:30AM–midnight; closed Sun.

Rio Grande Brewing
3760 Hawkins N.E.
Albuquerque, NM 87109
(505) 343-0903
Microbrewery

Brews: Outlaw Lager

Tours: By appointment

Russell Brewery
1242 Siler Road
Santa Fe, NM 87501
(505) 438-3138
Microbrewery

Brews: Light Ale, Pale Ale, Porter

Tours:: By appointment

Sangre de Cristo Brewery (Eske's Embudo Station)
106 Des Georges Lane
Taos, NM 87571
(505) 758-1517
Brewpub

Brews: 26 rotating beers including Wanda's Wicket Wheat, El Jefe Weizen, Peach Naked Ale, Berry Beer, Cherry Delight, Cheer Beer, Rio Refresco, Ol' 43 Blonde Ale, and more

Hours: Daily, noon–closing

Santa Fe Brewing
Flying M Ranch
Galisteo, NM 87540
(505) 466-3333
Microbrewery

Brews: Santa Fe Pale Ale, nut brown ale, Old Pojoaque Porter.

Seasonals: Chicken Killer Barleywine, Sangre de Frambuesa, Galisteo Weiss

Tours: Sat., call for information

Il Vincino
Wood Oven Pizza
3403 Central Ave. East
Albuquerque, NM 87106
(505) 266-7855
Brewpub
Brews: Three unnamed ales
Hours: Mon.–Thurs.,
11:30AM–11PM; Fri.–Sat.,
11:30AM–midnight; Sun.,
11:30AM–10PM

North Dakota

No microbreweries at press time

Oklahoma

Bricktown Brewery
One N. Oklahoma Ave.
Oklahoma City, OK 73104-
2413
(405) 232-2739
Brewpub
Brews: Bison Weizen, Land
Run Lager, Santa Fe Rail Ale,
Copperhead amber Ale, Red
Brick Ale

Hours: Mon.–Thurs.,
11AM–11PM; Fri.–Sat.,
11AM–1AM; Sun., 11AM–10PM

Cherry Street Brewing
1516 S. Quaker
Tulsa, OK 74123
(918) 582-2739
Brewpub
Brews: Weoka, Prairie,
Blackboard Bitter, Redbud,

Good Gus, Lincoln Lager
Hours: Daily, 11AM–midnight

Interurban Brewing
105 W. Main St.
Norman, OK 73069
(405) 364-7942
Brewpub
Brews: Honey Blonde Light
Pale Ale, Route 66 amber Ale,
Tornado Alley Porter, Osage
Golden Wheat, and seasonals
Hours: Daily, 11AM–2AM

Norman Brewing
102 W. Main St.
Norman, OK 73069
(405)360-5726
Brewpub
Brews: Harvester Wheat,
Golden Blonde, Railyard Amber,
Downtown Brown, Roughneck
Porter, and seasonals
Hours: Sun.–Thurs.,
11AM–midnight; Fri.–Sat.,
11AM–1:30AM

Royal Bavaria Brewing
3401 S. Sooner Road
Moore, OK 73160
(405) 799-7666
Brewpub
Brews: lager, wheat
Hours: Tues.–Thurs.,
5PM–10PM; Fri., 5PM–11PM;
Sat.–Sun., 12:30PM–11PM

Tulsa Brewing
7227 S. Memorial Dr.
Tulsa, OK 74133
(918) 459-BREW
Brewpub
Brews: Honey Blonde Light
Pale Ale, Route 66 Amber Ale,
Osage Golden Wheat Ale, IPA,

Celis Brewery

Legendary Lager, and seasonals

Hours: Mon.–Thurs., 11AM–midnight; Fri.–Sat., 11AM–2AM; Sun., 11AM–10PM

South Dakota

Fire House Brewing
610 Main St.
Rapid City, SD 57701
(605) 348-1915
Brewpub

Brews: Wilderness Wheat, Eagle Pale Ale, Buffalo Bitter, Brown Cow Ale, Rushmore Stout, Firehouse Red, Rough Rider Barleywine

Hours: Mon.–Thurs., 11AM–midnight; Fri.–Sat., 11AM–2AM; Sun., 4PM–10PM

Texas

Armadillo Brewing
419 E. 6th St.
Austin, TX 78701
(512) 322-0039
Brewpub

Brews: 6th Street Wheat, Road Kill Red, Axe's Pale Ale, River City Raspberry Ale. *Seasonals:* oatmeal stout, Bohemian Pilsner, blonde, Dillo ESB, and others

Hours: Mon.–Sat., 11AM–2AM; Sun., noon–11PM

Bitter End Brewing
311 Colorado
Austin, TX 78701
(512) 478-2337
Brewpub

Brews: Bitter End Bitter, Austin Pale, EZ Wheat, Sledgehammer Stout, Downtown Brown, and seasonals

Hours: Mon.–Thurs., 11:30AM–1AM; Fri., 11:30AM–2AM; Sat., 2PM–2AM; Sun., 5PM–midnight

Boardwalk Bistro
4011 Broadway
San Antonio, TX 78209
(210) 824-0100
Brewpub

Brews: Barblager, Windsors Ale, Bistro Bock, Smithson Stout. *Seasonals:* Peach Weizen, Steve's London Ale, and others

Hours: Mon.–Thurs., 11AM–10:30PM; Fri.–Sat., 11AM–11:30PM; closed Sun.

Celis Brewery
2431 Forbes Dr.
Austin, TX 78754
(512) 835-0884
Microbrewery

Brews: white, golden, pale bock, grand cru, raspberry

Tours: Tues.–Sat., 2PM–4PM; retail shop

Coppertank Brewing
504 Trinity St.
Austin, TX 78701
(512) 478-8444
Brewpub

Brews: Copper Light, White Tail Ale, Big Dog Brown Ale, Firehouse Stout, Coppertank Red Raspberry, and future seasonals

Hours: Daily, 4PM–2AM

Fredericksburg Brewing
245 W. Main St.
Fredericksburg, TX 78624
(210) 997-1646
Brewpub

Brews: lager, bock, stout, weizen, and future seasonals

Hours: Mon., Tues. and Thurs., 11AM–9PM; Fri.–Sat., 11AM-10PM; Sun., 11AM-6PM; closed Wed.

Hill Country Brewing & Bottling
730 Shady Lane
Austin, TX 78702
(512) 385-9111
Microbrewery
Brews: Balcones Fault Red Granite Ale, Pale Malt
Tours: Call for information

Hubcap Brewery & Kitchen
1701 N. Market #130
Dallas, TX 75202
(214) 651-0808
Brewpub
Brews: West End Wheat, Alley Cat Ale, Ranger Red, Downtown Brown, Rainbow Trout Stout, and seasonals
Hours: Daily, 11AM–2AM

Rock Bottom Brewery
6111 Richmond Ave.
Houston, TX 77057
(713 974-2739
Brewpub
Brews: Palomino Pale Ale, Cryin' Coyote Wheat Ale, Aspen Leaf Golden Ale, Rocket Red Ale, Big Horn Brown Ale, Black Gold Stout
Hours: Daily, 11AM–2AM

Saint Arnolds Brewing
2522 Fairway Park Dr.
Houston, TX 77092
(713) 686-9494
Microbrewery

Brews: amber ale, crystal weizen, and future seasonals
Tours:: Sat., 1PM

Texas Brewing
703 McKinney Ave.
Dallas, TX 75202
(214) 871-7990
Microbrewery
Brews: Texas Bluebonnet, Outback Lager, Texas Gold
Tours: Mon.–Fri., 9AM–5PM; Sat., noon–5PM

Village Brewery
2415 Dunstan Road
Houston, TX 77005
(715) 524-4677
Brewpub
Brews: Houston Wheat, Amber Owl, Hampton Brown Ale, Armadillo Stout, Village Pale Ale. *Seasonals:* raspberry wheat, and others
Hours: Daily, 11AM–2AM

Waterloo Brewing
401 Guadalupe St.
Austin, TX 78701
(512) 477-1836
Brewpub
Brews: Clara's Clara, Ed's Best Bitter, O. Henry Porter, Guytown IPA. *Seasonals:* Heftyweizen, bock
Hours: Daily, 11AM–2AM

Yegua Creek Brewing
2920 N. Henderson
Dallas, TX 75206
(214) 824-BREW
Brewpub
Brews: Lucky Lady Lager, Ice Haus Pale Ale, O'Brien's Texas Stout, XIT Select Pilsner,

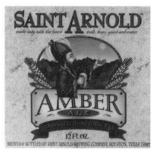

Saint Arnolds Brewing

Tucker's Golden Wheat.
Seasonals: ESB, Irish Red, brown ale

Hours: Sun.–Wed., 11AM–midnight; Thurs.–Sat., 11AM–2AM

Yellow Rose Brewing
17201 San Pedro Ave.
San Antonio, TX 78232
(210) 496-6669
Microbrewery

Brews: Yellow Rose Pale Ale, Cactus Queen Porter, Wildcatters Crude Stout, Bubba Dog Beer, Vigilante Ale, Honcho Grande

Tours: By appointment

Utah

Ebenezer's Restaurant & Naisbitt's Brewery
4286 Riverdale Road
Ogden, UT 84405
(801) 394-0302
Brewpub

Brews: Bridger Ale, amber ale, porter, raspberry ale

Hours: Mon.–Thurs., 11AM–10PM; Fri.–Sat., 11AM–11PM; Sun., 11AM–9PM

Eddie McStiff's Brewpub
57 S. Main
Moab, UT 84532
(801) 259-BEER
Brewpub

Brews: wheat, amber ale, Canyon Cream Ale, amber, McStiff Stout, raspberry wheat, blueberry wheat, spruce beer, ginger beer, cherry stout, and others

Hours: Daily, 3PM–1AM

Red Rock Brewery
254 S. 200 St. West
Salt Lake City, UT 84101
(801) 521-7446
Brewpub

Brews: pale ale, amber ale, oatmeal stout, honey wheat, Irish ale, and others, in rotation

Hours: Sun.–Thurs., 11:30AM–midnight; Fri.–Sat., 11:30AM–1AM

Salt Lake Brewing (Squatter's Pub Brewery)
147 W. Broadway
Salt Lake City, UT 84101
(801) 363-BREW
Brewpub

Brews: City Creek Pale Ale, Emigration Amber Ale, Millcreek Cream Stout.
Seasonals: Parley's Porter, Hop Head Red, Anniversary Pilsner, and others

Hours: Daily, 11:30AM–1AM

Uinta Brewing
389 W. 1700 South
Salt Lake City, UT 84115
(801) 467-0909
Microbrewery

Brews: Cut Throat Extra Pale Ale, King's Peak Porter, Uinta Hefe-Weizen, Desert Wheat

Tours: Call for information

Wasatch Brew Pub (Schirf Brewing)
250 Main St.
Park City, UT 84060
(801) 645-9500
Brewpub

Brews: premium ale, weizen beer, Slickrock lager, Irish

stout. *Seasonals:* bock, Christmas ale

Hours: Daily, 11AM–midnight

Wyoming

Jackson Hole Pub & Brewery
265 S. Millward St.
Jackson, WY 83001
(307) 739-2337

Brewpub

Brews: Snake River Lager, Snake River Pale Ale, Buffalo Brown Ale, Oatmeal Porter, Woppity Wheat; all in rotation

Hours: Mon.–Thurs., 11AM–midnight; Fri.–Sat., 11AM–1AM; Sun., noon–10PM

Otto Brothers' Brewing
1295 West St.
Wilson, WY 83014
(307) 733-9000

Microbrewery

Brews: Teton Pale Ale, Teton Ale, Moose Juice Stout. *Seasonals:* Dunkel Weizen, Old Faithful Ale

Tours: By appointment

Part IV

CENTRAL REGION

Central Region Brewery Profiles

Abita Springs Brewing Co.

There is cause to cheer the existence of the Abita Springs Brewing Company. Louisiana's first microbrewery opened in a town with a population of less than 1,500 residents. It has now been operating successfully since 1986.

Abita Springs is located just across the causeway on Lake Pontchartrain, north of New Orleans (*N'awlins,* spoken in the proper dialect). The Abita Springs Brewing Company is located in the center of town. It traces its origins to the "home-

brewers-go-wild" story that is being retold in countless other microbreweries across the country. Like most of these others, the Abita Springs Brewery is traditional with regard to its processes and ingredients, but none of the others have access to the famous water from Abita Springs. According to legend, these waters are said to have protected local Indians from yellow fever. "We do feel that we are quite influenced by our location near New Orleans and in Louisiana," says president and brewmaster Jim Patton. "Our beers are shaped by local tastes and local cuisine." Local tastes tend to run toward sweeter products — a response, perhaps, by palates weaned on Cajun and Creole cooking. For this reason, Abita Springs beers are far less hoppy than most microbrewed products. The emphasis on maltiness is influenced by both low attenuation and high original gravities (see glossary).

Currently, there are three regular beers produced at Abita Springs: Abita Golden Lager, Abita Amber, and Turbodog, which is similar to a porter. In addition, there are four seasonal/specialty brews: Abita Mardi Gras Bock, available January to May; Abita Wheat (June to September); Abita Fall Fest (October to November); and Abita Christmas Dark (December).

All of these offerings follow a 21-day production cycle, starting with a six-day primary fermentation at 48°F (9°C), followed by 15 days of aging at 32°F (0°C). With the exception of the wheat beer, malted barley is used exclusively; no adjuncts such as corn or rice are added. The malts used are produced by the English maltster, Munton and Fison. The hops are Yakima Perles from the Pacific Northwest. The yeast strain is German in origin and is used for both lagers and ales. The water source is a 2,000-foot deep Artesian well that has been tested free of manmade contaminants. These beers are available in both 12-ounce bottles and quarter- and half-barrel kegs. Current annual production is around 25,000 barrels. Abita Beer is guaranteed to be fresh. It is shipped within 48 hours of bottling.

Occasional changes have taken place throughout the past eight years, but none as comprehensive as the one undertaken in 1994. The brewery was relocated to another site, a mile away from the original location. The old building serves as the gift shop and tasting room — a wise bit of marketing. They have plans to open a brewpub on the site in the near future.

There are tours of the new brewhouse and product sampling is included in the tour. The brewery has a retail liquor license, which allows beer sales on the premises by the six-pack, case, and keg.

Birmingham Brewing Co.

Until recently, the states that comprise the Deep South were not known for their breweries or beer production. One southern beer writer in particular had written off the American Southeast as a "beer wasteland," though it was not always so.

At the turn of the century, many southern cities were producing indigenous beers to slake the thirsts of parched southerners. One city, Birmingham, Alabama, was an industrial buckle on the cotton belt. The city's industry drew workers from both North and South, and from as far away as Europe. With them came a demand for good beer. Responding to the needs of these thirsty miners, steelworkers, and railwaymen, breweries flourished in the Magic City. Until 1907, that is. In that year, long before the rest of the nation, Jefferson County, Alabama, voted to enact Prohibition. The law took effect on May 28, 1908, and on that day, 300 barrels of beer were emptied on the streets of Birmingham.

Eighty-four years passed before Alabamians would once again enjoy local beer. In June, 1992, the Birmingham Brewing Company rolled out its first barrel of Red Mountain Red Ale. It debuted at City Stages, and was closely followed by the rollout of Red Mountain Golden Lager. With the installation of a bottling line, these two beers, along with Red Mountain Golden Ale and Red Mountain Wheat Beer, were released in bottles. The Birmingham beers are currently sold at bars, restaurants, and retail stores throughout Alabama.

The Birmingham Brewing Company is the brainchild of trial lawyer Ben Hogan. Aware of the national trend towards specialty beers, Hogan became intrigued with the notion of owning and operating a microbrewery. "I'm used to risk," he says. "I try to recognize a good idea and go with it." Joining Ben in his endeavor is his brother, Tom, who handles sales and marketing. The actual brewing responsibilities fall to John Zanteson and Steve Betts. Their combined diverse brewing experience produces beer recipes that are guaranteed to please.

An ingredient that is part of every beer made at the Birmingham Brewing Company is one no other beer can match — Birmingham's top quality water. The city's water supply is recognized as one of the best in the country, due to huge limestone deposits left millions of years ago by the warm, shallow seas that once covered this region. Of 4,000 water systems tested, Birmingham's rated number five.

The brewing equipment used was handcrafted in Cincinnati and installed in the 1930s converted warehouse. It includes a 30-barrel brewkettle, hot and cold liquor tanks, a finishing tank, and seven fermentation/storage tanks. The aforementioned bottling line was made in Italy and was converted from a champagne bottling line. Because of this, the Birmingham Brewing Company is able to achieve oxygen levels 200 percent better than industry standard. This protects the taste of the beer. Initially, the bottling line was producing about 3,500 cases of beer per month. Continued growth could see as many as 5,000 to 6,000 cases rolling off the bottling line every month.

Bohannon Brewing Company

The heart and soul of Nashville is found in its rich heritage of country-western music. Just ask any of the million fans who come to this town to visit the Grand Ol' Opry or the music-inspired theme park, Opryland. But just try asking those same people where to get a good Nashville-brewed beer, and you might as well be whistlin' Dixie.

Nashville never had a reputation as a brewing town, despite the fact that it has been home to 18 breweries throughout its history. (Ironically, many of them were located right on Market Street — now known as Second Avenue — the present location of the Bohannon Brewing Company.)

Starting a microbrewery anywhere is considered a risk, but starting one in Nashville, where the concept of local handcrafted beer is as foreign as a sushi

Beer in the Twentieth-Century USA: Part I

As important as the scientific and industrial discoveries were in the 1800s, socioeconomic factors of the 1900s have been far more tumultuous for the brewing industry, starting with the single most destructive force in the history of American brewing: Prohibition. The Great Experiment managed, in 13 years, to decimate an industry that was over two centuries in the making. Of the 1,000 or so breweries that existed in America prior to 1900, only half survived to see the repeal of the 18th Amendment in 1933. Those that managed to keep their doors open did so by producing soda pop and malt syrup (ostensibly used for baking), or by brewing illegal beer for the thousands of speakeasies operated by the underworld.

When brewing beer again became legal, the laws governing its sale and distribution changed drastically. Prior to Prohibition, the "tied house" system prevailed. As part of this set-up, a brewery would own local taverns and would sell only its own brands. This gave the larger breweries an unfair advantage over the smaller ones. Lawmakers sought to break up the tied house system by instituting a three-tier system in which the brewer, the distributor, and the retailer had to be independently owned. Not even family members were allowed to own another tier in the system. This was effective in creating a free market for small brewers but would later prove to be a major obstacle for the microbrewing industry.

When the war machines thundered across Europe for the second time during this century, a new set of economic conditions charted the course for the brewing industry. A large percentage of the beer-drinking demographic was fighting the war. Robbie the Riveter was replaced by Rosie the Riveter at the munitions plant. These newly employed women were a new demographic, one with a preference for a lighter beer product. In addition, G.I. Joe was wetting his whistle with a very bland, homogenous, government-contracted beer at the PX. Between the wars, the beer can was invented, which made it possible to enjoy beer at home rather than at the corner bar. The beer can proved to be a packaging improvement as well, and those small brewers who could not afford the technological equipment necessary for canning did not survive.

In addition, an excellent refrigerated rail system, along with coast-to-coast radio advertising, ushered in the era of national breweries during the 1930s and 1940s. Americans could now find the same brand of beer in Portland, Oregon, as in Portland, Maine. Familiarity with brand names helped to sell products, and the advent of television galvanized the concept of product recognition and brand loyalty.

Three decades later, America was swept into an era of increased consciousness about health and fitness. Beer does not rank high on a fitness buff's list of desired foods. Enter light beer (the bane of a "real" beer drinker's existence). Fueled by huge advertising monies, and closely tied to sports events (with celebrities touting the advantages), the light beer revolution homogenized beer almost to ignominy. A once-proud product had become a one-dimensional, unsophisticated product created for mass market appeal.

bar, is truly a high-stakes gamble. Here in central Tennessee, just a hog toss from cotton country, the summers are as hot as a top hit song on the country music charts, and beer is believed to be best when it's cold and wet. But president and owner Lindsey Bohannon chose to focus on the positive aspects of the venture and decided it was worth the risk. The Bohannon Brewing Company became the first microbrewery in the southeastern region of the United States. Having a decidedly local flavor, it goes over well with local folks.

Lindsey Bohannon is no stranger to risk-taking. He spent five years in securities at J. C. Bradford & Company, and another two as a stockbroker at Paine Webber. Even with this promising career ahead of him, Bohannon could not shake the entrepreneurial spirit that haunted him while he earned his master's degree in finance at the University of Kentucky.

It was during a break in his studies that Lindsey Bohannon and a fellow student went on a tour of Europe. While in a German *bierstübe* enjoying fresh, locally made beer, Bohannon wondered why they couldn't find beer like that in the United States. Rather than go in search of one,

he decided to brew his own. Before jumping in headfirst, however, Bohannon did his homework. In addition to traveling extensively to find the taste he was seeking, he hired German brewmaster Julius Hummer to oversee the making of his new Nashvillian beer. The first product to hit the store shelves was Market Street Pilsner Beer, in the summer of 1989. Since then, the production schedule has expanded to include a bock beer, a wheat beer, a golden ale, a winter lager, and a gold medal–winning Oktoberfest beer. All of these Market Street beers are made from two-row barley, a blend of imported and domestic hops, and a special strain of German lager yeast from the Weihenstephan Institut near Munich.

The brewery is housed in a nineteenth century building, and tours of the 14,000 square foot, 35-barrel space are given on a regular basis. All tours conclude with a sampling of the Market Street beers in the brewery's showpiece tasting room. This room, a remnant of the old Greenbrier Distillery, has been completely restored to its original opulence. Polished dark wood, and leaded, cut glass windows provide the backdrop as one tastes one's way through the finest beers Nashville has to offer.

Boulevard Brewing Company

The Boulevard Brewing Company is the second largest brewery in the state of Missouri, second only to Anheuser-Busch in St. Louis, which happens to be the largest in the world. What's important though, is quality, not quantity — the kind of quality beer that existed in the 20 or so local breweries that flourished in this area prior to Prohibition. The Boulevard Brewing Company is dedicated to reviving Kansas City's tradition of locally made, fresh, great-tasting beers.

With support from local investors, president and brewmaster John McDonald opened the brewery in the fall of 1989. It became the first brewery to operate in Kansas City since 1903. The vertical style (gravity feed) brewhouse is located in a former warehouse on Kansas City's west side. Originally, it featured an antique German brewkettle, an American-made grist mill, fermenters, and filtering equipment. The 35-barrel kettle is steam-fired. It takes three brews to fill one 105-barrel fermenter. Eventually, they added an automatic bulk grain system (including two 30,000-pound grain silos), a new mash tun, and a quadruple-brew brite beer tank.

Since then, two more triple-brew conical fermenters have been delivered. (A triple-brew fermenter takes three batches to fill to capacity; a quadruple takes four.) The inverted, conical design allows the brewer to re-harvest the yeast from the bottom of the fermenter for use in future batches of beer. Annual output was around 7,800 barrels in 1992 and 10,000 to 11,000 barrels in 1993; it has undoubtedly increased significantly since then.

Boulevard Brewing Company combines premium domestic and European ingredients and traditional brewing processes to produce flavorful beers that are unique to the Midwest. At first the brewery's primary focus was to produce draught beer for sale in area restaurants and taverns. The initial success of Boulevard's beers created a demand for the same product in bottles. Now, four varieties of Boulevard beers are available in bottled form: an American-style pale ale, their London classic, Bully! Porter, an Irish-style red ale, and a traditional wheat beer that accounts for 25 percent of the brewery's package sales. Additionally, Boulevard Brewing Company produces other seasonal/specialty beers in draught form only. These include an unfiltered version of the wheat beer, Bob's "47" (in the fall only); and 10 Penny Mild, a low-alcohol beer with a big body. None of these beers are pasteurized and none contain additives or preservatives.

Current distribution of the product line extends to the western half of Missouri and the eastern half of Kansas, with a goal of regional distribution throughout the Midwest.

There is an on-the-premises tasting room that overlooks the brewhouse. While

normally used for tours, it is also available for private parties and special events. Don't forget to bring home a "Coast-Card," a combination coaster and postcard.

Broad Ripple Brewing Company

During the past several years, I've heard many different and unusual names bestowed upon American breweries and brewpubs. I've enjoyed a chuckle or two on behalf of *Bronco Bob's Brewery and Spewery* and the *Cudgel-in-the-Codpiece Olde Tyme Alehouse,* but when I first heard the name *Broad Ripple,* I figured someone dug pretty deep to come up with this one. Not so. Though it sounds like a cheap wine for cheap women, the Broad Ripple name is not only legitimate but well-respected.

Broad Ripple is the name given to the entertainment district in Indianapolis. This district is comfortably cradled in the bend of the White River on the city's north side. The name, *Broad Ripple,* in fact, is taken from a natural phenomenon that occurs in the river as it turns from south to north and back to south again. The neighborhood is a melange of ethnic restaurants, galleries, artsy-craftsy shops, and — count 'em — 23 bars, in an area of five square blocks.

Just off the beaten path is the object of a beer lover's desire. The Broad Ripple Brewpub, with its unassuming exterior, is like a butterfly hidden within its chrysalis. The neighborhood pub has two distinctly different personalities. One room is classic and Victorian, the other less formal in style. Out on the veranda,

there is al fresco dining. The bar area, with its ten-seat capacity, has a cozy feel to it, and a fireplace adds to the warmth of the room.

The brewpub's menu is fairly extensive, from appetizers, soups, and salads, to sandwiches, burgers, and other offerings. Many vegetarian items are available also. The real heart of the menu, though, is the traditional British pub fare: shepherd's pie, ploughman's lunch, pasties, Scotch eggs, and the ever-popular fish and chips (sorry, no haggis).

The food serving sizes, you will find, are more than sufficient to satisfy your hunger, but the meal is not complete without a sampling of the superb beers made at Broad Ripple. Brewmaster and owner John Hill has created a line of authentic, handcrafted ales that are "leisurely brewed," according to their logo. This authenticity is unquestioned.

A Sweet and Malty Ending

The fun doesn't have to end with the entree. Beer with dessert is a combination capable of ambrosial heights. Rather than trying to match sweet with sweet, contrasting tastes bring better results. A double chocolate cake would find a nice contrast in a dry Irish-style stout or a robust porter. A Belgian witbier can spice up any fruit-laced arrangement. Strawberry shortcake would mate well with a pale bock, and a box of chocolates would disappear quickly with an uncorked bottle of tart fruit beer on the table.

Then again, after a satisfying meal, a pint of malty Scotch ale is a dessert unto itself!

Mr. Hill, a native of Yorkshire, England, is well attuned to traditional British beer styles. The day-to-day brewing responsibilities fall on Ted Miller, John Hill's understudy. The regulars on his brewing schedule include Red Bird Mild, Pintail Ale, E.S.B. (extra special bitter), and Monon Porter. The seasonal beers include Wee Heavy, copper ale, dry stout, Bavarian wheat, and a Kölschbier.

Unlike brewpubs, which serve house brews exclusively, Broad Ripple pits its beers against the best of the rest in the microbrewing industry. There are over 40 "guest" beers, including fellow Indianapolis microbrew Duesseldorfer Ale. Legacy Lager and red ale from the Chicago Brewing Company and Baderbrau Pilsener from the Pavichevich Brewing Company head a list that features beers from Sierra Nevada, Capital, Oldenberg, Kalamazoo, and Pete's Brewing companies. Also served are several premium imported selections from Scotland, Belgium, and Germany. For those patrons who reserve their palate for fine wine there is also an extensive list of fruits from the vine.

Capital Brewing Company

Anyone who has tried the Garten Brau beers will likely agree — this brewery was a capital idea. Located in an old egg-processing plant, the Capital Brewery of Middleton, Wisconsin, has been in existence since 1986 and is responsible for producing some of the Midwest's finest microbrews.

Vestiges of the old plant serve the new occupant well. Some of the walls of the building are over two feet thick, providing excellent insulation for the refrigeration system which enables the brewery to produce extremely high quality lager beers. The Capital Brewery is considered to be one of the finest lager microbreweries in America. At the Great American Beer Festival in Denver, three gold medals, a silver, and a bronze were awarded to the Garten Brau beers. In the Midwest, the brewery has won gold, silver, and bronze medals at the Chicago Beer Society beer tastings and at the Great Taste of the Midwest, held in nearby Madison, Wisconsin (see page 142).

There are ten beers brewed at Capital — five are considered regulars (produced year-round) and the other five are made on a seasonal basis. All of the Garten Brau beers are brewed in accordance with the Reinheitsgebot (see page 23). The brewmaster, Kirby Nelson, has skillfully blended the traditional brewing styles of Europe with contemporary American ones, throwing in a measure of his own personal creativity along the way. The results are beers with time-honored qualities and uncommon drinkability.

Capital Brewery is only the second brewery in North America ever known to brew a wild rice beer. Using a unique and complicated brewing procedure, the beer is brewed with the assistance of special kettles used in the dairy industry. Barley malt costs $2.50 per pound, while wild rice is $4.25 a pound, making the beer more expensive. Wild rice imparts a nuttiness to the nose and palate (see glossary), similar to hazelnut, and the resulting beer is an excellent accompaniment to a traditional Thanksgiving feast.

Much of the brewing equipment was purchased from the Hoxter Brewery in Germany. The two all-copper brewkettles are the showpiece. Annual output is approximately 8,500 barrels a year and distribution of the beer reaches eight midwestern states.

The brewery offers tours and has a gift shop. In the beer garden, hop and grapevines provide the perfect backdrop for beer tasting as they thread their way along the fence.

Chicago Brewing Company

Drawing inspiration from Chicago's legacy of brewing great beer, the Chicago Brewing Company was named for Huck's Chicago Brewing Company. Huck's was the largest brewery in the world when it was destroyed by the Great Chicago Fire in 1871. The new lager beer pays respect to its predecessor.

Started in 1990 by members of the Dinehart family, the Chicago Brewing Company was the first brewery to brew and bottle their own beer in Chicago since the old Peter Hand Brewery closed down in the late 1970s. The original plans for this brewery centered around a brewpub concept, but the business partners were discouraged by the minor successes of the three brewpubs that opened in the Chicago area. (Only one of those is still operating today.) Market saturation became a concern, and the plans were revised. In choosing to become a microbrewery, the Chicago Brewing Company became — and still is — the only commercial bottling brewery in Chicago and the largest in the state of Illinois.

The current brewing operation is in an old pickle factory dating from the 1920s, on the city's near northwest side. The

Beer in the Twentieth-Century USA: Part II

The 1970s were undoubtedly the nadir for the American brewing industry. After decades of buyouts and hostile takeovers, only 40 companies produced all the beer brewed in this country. Thankfully, the pendulum had begun its reverse swing. Throughout this course of events, the phenomenon of *mystique* beers had held strong. (Mystique beers are those with a limited distribution area. They are often believed to be better than they really are by those who can't get them.) Some beer lovers went so far as to bootleg these beers across state lines to share them with family or friends. The notion that these beers were somehow better than the products on the shelves of the local liquor store helped to pave the way for the great influx of imported beer.

Foreign brewers, anxious to cash in on America's beer-drinking habits, managed to create and sustain a consumer backlash. The effects were almost immediate and profound. Several high profile brands experienced a meteoric rise in popularity, which prompted a quick reaction by foreign brewers and importers everywhere. Eventually, the market was inundated with product — the good, the bad, and the truly ugly. The belief was that any beer in a green bottle with a foreign label would sell. Most of them did.

On the other side of the coin, there were those disenchanted beer lovers in search of a better beer who looked no further than their own kitchens. Brewing beer at home was still a clandestine hobby, even though it was legal. In time the craft grew, clubs were formed, information was disseminated, and homebrewing came out of the closet — so far out of the closet, in fact, that many novice brewers attempted to brew professionally. These people became the pioneers of the microbrewing industry. Their journey on the road to success has been fraught with pitfalls. First of all, there was undercapitalization: no cash flow meant no beer flow. The second major problem was a throwback to Prohibition. The old three-tier system that prevented brewers from being retailers became a stumbling block for anyone trying to open a brewpub. After years of legal wrangling, in some states the laws have either been altered or broken down altogether. The third problem, which is gradually being overcome, was a lack of knowledge and appreciation of the lost art of craft brewing. Without consumers' understanding of beer and beer styles, the small brewer cannot continue to produce the wide range of flavorful ales and lagers now being produced across this country.

The microbrewing industry is now into its second decade. Most of the early microbrewers were from the West Coast, long noted as a trendsetting region. Northern California, Oregon, and Washington — especially the Portland and Seattle areas — have been on the cutting edge of this movement since its inception. The idea quickly caught on in the East, and, later, in the Midwest. In the beginning, the movement gravitated towards the larger cities, but there are now microbrewers and pub brewers who have found homes in rural America. The industry's popularity is such that the number of craft brewers in the United States has doubled every two years. There are over 450 such small breweries in the United States, with new start-ups reported every other week.

brewing plant is housed in a 12,000 square foot section of the building. With 26-foot ceilings, the structure's interior has been customized to accommodate the brewing equipment. The three-million-dollar brewery contains a two-stage copper brewhouse imported from the Pohlmann Brewing Company of Kulmbach, Bavaria, (a legendary brewery since the seventeenth century) that has been integrated with the most advanced brewing technology available. There are also two packaging lines for the kegged and bottled products. The building was designed as a USDA grade food plant, so only minimal construction was required at the site.

The first product introduced was Legacy Lager, a Bohemian-style Pilsner. (Since then, a new product has been introduced every year.) The Pilsner was followed closely by Legacy Red Ale, an Irish-style amber ale; Heartland Weiss, a Bavarian-style wheat beer; and Big Shoulders Porter, an English dark ale.

(The name is borrowed from Robert Frost's poem, *Chicago*.) All of these beers have been well received, but the flagship brand, Legacy Lager, continues to grab the lion's share of awards. In 1990, the Chicago Beer Society voted Legacy Lager best among a dozen brands at the annual International Tasting. In 1991 and 1992, Legacy Lager took the prestigious gold medal for European Pilsner at the Great American Beer Festival and Heartland Weiss was awarded the bronze medal in 1992. All told, the Chicago Brewing Company has won five gold, three silver, and two bronze medals in recognition for outstanding brewing achievement.

Late in 1994, a Nordic holiday brew from Chicago Brewing Company made its debut. Legacy de-Icer Ale was made in response to the onslaught of cloned ice beers on the market. The ale's secret de-icing power was found in an ancient Norse rune that described a magical spice mixture for reviving frozen Vikings.

The Importance of Glassware

Beer should always be served in a glass. The reasons for this are many. Beyond common courtesy for customers or guests, there is the visual appeal of a properly poured beer in an appropriate glass. This propriety goes beyond looks, however. Most beer glassware serves the secondary, but no less important, purpose of capturing the aromatics of the beer. When pouring beer, it is important to build a frothy head in the glass. By allowing the liquid to plop into the glass, carbonation is released, and, along with it, the volatile odorants in the beer. Just as food's savory aromas entice us, beer's piquant aromatics are also meant to attract and captivate our olfactory senses. Finally, decanting a beer rather than drinking it straight from the bottle spares the imbiber the discomfort and embarrassment that may accompany the build-up of carbonation within the gastro-intestinal tract. Look good and feel good. Decant your beer.

A blend of clove, coriander, allspice, and orange peel was added to a brew made from seven different malts. The draught-only de-Icer Ale was brewed in the spirit of Christmas; a sizable chunk of the sales of de-Icer Ale was earmarked for local children's charities.

At this writing, Chicago Brewing Company's products are available in 28 states and are being exported to several European cities including Frankfurt, Dublin, London, and Paris. Additionally, a Japanese restaurant chain has contracted with the Company to brew and bottle a beer exclusively for their Tokyo restaurants.

Columbus Brewing Company

Earlier in its history, Columbus, Ohio, had six breweries operating at the same time. This is cause for pride in our brewing heritage and cause for sadness because all that remains of these breweries are memories.

The city's brewing industry can be traced to the early 1800s when Columbus was just a borough only two years old. The first brewers were English, and their breweries were well known for their traditional ales. In the 1830s a great wave of German immigrants moved westward to settle in the Ohio Valley, and in the following decades men with names like Schlegel, Hoster, Biehl, Schlee, Blenckner, and Stoker started breweries in Columbus. Both the English ale and German lager styles of beer were popular with the towns-folk, but by 1863 the lighter, hoppier lager became the predominant style.

From the early days, when the labor-intensive brewing trade was powered by man, through the advent of steam power, and, eventually, to the fully-mechanized industry that it became, Columbus's brewing industry's success ebbed and flowed but never ceased completely until Prohibition. Most of the brewers were located in close proximity on the city's south side, which became known as the Brewery District.

Today, the Brewery District is as vibrant as ever. Totally rehabilitated and revitalized, it is a thriving business and entertainment center that spans 27 acres of vintage brewery buildings. These renovations of old family breweries house some of Columbus's finest restaurants, unique retail shops, a winery, and a couple of microbreweries serving a respectable selection of beer styles.

Located on S. Front Street, on the north end of the Brewery District, is the appropriately named Columbus Brewing Company. Founded in 1988, the Columbus brewery was Ohio's first microbrewery. This brewer of fine lager and ale has revived the European brewing traditions started by the original Columbus brewers over 150 years ago.

The brewhouse, occupying space on both levels of a two-story, red-brick building, is plainly visible through the windows on the public walkway. The brewing equipment consists of a custom-made, seven-barrel English system. It has a current capacity of 1,000 barrels per year. Brewmaster Scott Francis and brewer Ben Pridgeon brew only all-malt products, with no adjuncts or preservatives. Regularly found on tap is Columbus Pale Ale, Pilsner beer, and nut brown ale. Another product, called Columbus 1492, is contract brewed by the F.X. Matt Brewing Company in Utica, New York. The 1492 is the only product that is available in bottles.

You can find the Columbus Brewing Company behind Gibby's Bar on Front Street, adjacent to The Patio (an outdoor beer-garden-style eating, drinking, and entertainment area). Free live music is offered regularly for visitors to the Brewery District.

Frankenmuth Brewery, Inc.

The Frankenmuth Brewery in Frankenmuth, Michigan, typifies the level of success that can be attained in the microbrewing industry. This success did not come easily and it certainly did not happen overnight, but the little brewery's history reads like a blueprint for success.

The Frankenmuth Brewery is located in the small, central Michigan town of the same name. Known as "Michigan's little Bavaria," it was settled by German immigrants in 1845. The town's settlers came from the village of Franken, Germany. They added "muth," which means "courage," to the name of their new home in America. Today, there are only about 5,000 local residents, but as Michigan's most visited tourist attraction, the Bavarian hamlet draws about three million visitors a year.

Frankenmuth Brewery, Inc. was formed in 1987 by Ferdinand (Fred) Schumacher in order to renovate the old brewery building, built in 1862, that stood on Main Street. At various times it had functioned as both the Cass River Brewery and the Geyer Bros. Brewery. Renovation became a much larger project than anticipated. It was virtually destroyed by a fire in 1987.

The eventual reconstruction included the installation of an all-copper brewhouse imported from Germany. This equipment is designed with the Old World method of fire brewing (heating the beer kettles directly by fire) in mind. Some of the storage tanks used were salvaged from the old Stroh brewery in Detroit, that had been closed and demolished in 1986. Ironically, it was the Stroh brewery that was famous for its fire-brewed beers.

The Frankenmuth Brewery has a current annual brewing capacity of 50,000 barrels.

Top-of-the-line equipment, as impressive as it sounds, is only as good as those in charge of its operation. The original brewmaster at Frankenmuth was, himself, a German, and tremendously talented at brewing traditional German style beers. Fred Scheer was lured away from his position as brewmaster at another midwestern microbrewery. He was attracted by the opportunity to start up a new microbrewery and to live and work in Frankenmuth. He is also a personal friend of Fred Schumacher, and that may have had something to do with it! Schumacher was the chief operating officer at the brewery and was almost single-handedly responsible for making the Frankenmuth brewery the successful operation it is today. Schumacher sold his interest in the brewery in 1990. Their mission accomplished at the brewery, Scheer and Schumacher decided to establish their own brewing consulting firm. Fred Scheer's replacement as brewmaster was Erich Schalk, also from Germany.

Since the inaugural brew back in March, 1988, the product line has continued to expand. Currently made under the Frankenmuth label at the brewery are a Pilsner, a dark, a weisse, an Oktoberfest, and an extra light. Frankenmuth also controls the Old Detroit label, which offers Old Detroit Amber Ale and Old Detroit Red Ale. There are also several private label beers and contract brews being made there on a regular basis. Frankenmuth's beers have won a fair share of awards and recognition across the country, including three gold and two silver medals at the Great American Beer Festival in Denver. For their standards of excellence, the Frankenmuth Brewery is one of the most highly regarded micros in the nation.

Visits to the Frankenmuth brewery are always encouraged. Adjacent to the brewery is a gift shop and hospitality center. Tours of the facility are provided and samples of the Frankenmuth brands are cheerfully proffered. In case you are not able to make it up to the brewery, the Frankenmuth beers are widely available throughout the Midwest.

Goose Island Brewing Company

Chicago's oldest and largest brewpub has celebrated an anniversary every May since 1988. It was then that Goose Island made its debut, with an invitation-only grand opening party, complete with complimentary hors d'oeuvres and taster glasses of beer. That occasion set the

standard by which this brewpub has grown and prospered. Good food, great beer and an appreciation for the beer-loving patron have become the benchmark at Goose Island. The pub brewery continues to receive wide and enthusiastic acclaim due to its commitment to quality products and customer education.

The Goose Island Brewing Company set up shop in an old Turtle Wax factory on Chicago's near northwest side. The exposed brick and beam interior hints at its past and the brewpub aspires to authentic British pub atmosphere, American breweriana notwithstanding. The huge, rectangular, cherrywood bar, situated in the middle of the main floor, is the nerve center of the split-level restaurant. (Planned for the spring of 1995: a pool room.)

The brewing system was manufactured and installed by J.V. Northwest of Oregon. The all stainless steel brewhouse includes a mash tun, brewkettle, heat exchanger, and six conical fermentation tanks. Goose Island's current annual output is over 2,000 barrels, placing it first in volume in the Chicago area and fifth on the national level for brewpubs. This large volume is divided into a broad spectrum of beer styles. Last year alone, 24 different styles of beer were offered at Goose Island, two of which took awards at the Great American Beer Festival. Eighty percent of the 1,300 barrels brewed in the first year was of the lager variety, but now ales and specialty beers account for 70 percent of the beer production.

One good reason for this shift in preference can be attributed to Goose Island's efforts to educate their customers. The Brewmaster's Dinner is one such example. This collaboration between chef and brewmaster presents an array of beers and a sampling of complementary cuisine. It is essentially an educational dinner party. Occasionally, a guest chef is invited to participate in this highly successful program. Another example of patron education is the Master of Beer Appreciation (MBA) program, which encourages customers to sample a "curriculum" of styles produced at Goose Island. Sampling earns points towards premiums on such items as T-shirts.

The food menu at Goose Island favors a more elaborate cuisine than typical pub grub, which tends to be very inexpensive and simple. (In the United States this usually takes the form of sandwiches and soups; in the United Kingdom, meat pies and fish and chips are the fare; and in Germany, cheese, bread, and sausage.) The cuisine is considered eclectic, with entrees that are American, Mexican,

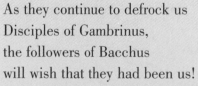

A Beer Lover's Oath

No matter how much they
    mock us,
slander, and demean us,
the proselytes of Bacchus
shall never come between us.

As they continue to defrock us
Disciples of Gambrinus,
the followers of Bacchus
will wish that they had been us!
— Marty Nachel

Belgian, English, and German in tradition and presentation.

The beer menu is extensive: German bock beers, English ales, Irish stouts and a variety of international beer styles are brewed. Regulars on tap are Golden Goose Pilsner, Lincoln Park Lager, and Honkers Ale. The list of seasonal beers includes Old Clybourn Porter, Chicago Vice Weizen, Special Brown Ale, PMD Mild Ale, Aviator Doppelbock, Hop Scotch, RAF Best Bitter, Honest Stout, Old Abeerration Barleywine, and a mugful of others that come and go.

An extensive line of breweriana — T-shirts, hats, sweatshirts — are always available for purchase. Tours are given, a regular newsletter is printed, and weekly homebrewing classes are offered at Goose Island, which also serves as the official home for homebrewers and members of the Chicago Beer Society. They hold their monthly meetings at "the Goose."

Great Lakes Brewing Company

The city of Cleveland once boasted of 29 breweries, which produced and distributed fresh, locally made beer. Prohibition, of course, changed all that. Of the ten breweries that attempted to reestablish themselves after 1933, Christian Schmidt was the sole survivor — that is, until 1984.

The Great Lakes Brewing Company emerged in 1988 as Cleveland's first microbrewery and the first brewpub in the state since Prohibition. The founders of Great Lakes Brewing, brothers Dan and Pat

Conway, created a brewery in the strong tradition of Cleveland's past brewers.

Pat Conway's love affair with good beer began while he was studying and traveling in Europe. Back in the United States, bartending helped him get through graduate school. It also gave him an important perspective of the marketplace. He was serving a lot of imported beer, which clearly indicated a shift in the American palate. People were gravitating toward a more robust, European-style beer. While in Chicago for a teaching stint in 1985, Pat began to dream of starting a microbrewery. When he returned to Cleveland, the dream became a reality, with the help of his brother, who left a secure job in banking to lend his financial expertise to the venture.

The first part of the plan was to establish the concept that this was to be "Cleveland's own" brewery. It was important to tap into the city's civic pride. One way of accomplishing this was to settle in a turn-of-the-century building, located in a blue collar district on the city's near west side. (They ignored suggestions to build their brewery on the outskirts of town.) The 10,000-square-foot Victorian building was previously a feed store and later a tavern. It exemplifies the romance of brewing days past. There are eight dining areas on three different levels, including: The Beer Cellar, with its rugged sandstone walls and sturdy wooden benches; The Market Room, with its charming Victorian decor, which overlooks the historic West Side Market; The Great Lakes Room, where the history of the region is celebrated with nautical artifacts and brewery memorabilia; The John D. Rockefeller Room, which is reported to be the millionaire industrialist's first office; and the beautifully landscaped Outdoor Beer Garden, which is said to be one of Cleveland's most charming patios. Other rooms are more functional. There is The Brewhouse, where patrons can watch the brewing process from behind glass partitions; and the infamous Tap Room, housing Cleveland's oldest bar. This arched mahogany bulwark is said to have sustained a couple of bullet wounds inflicted by none other than gang-buster Eliot Ness, who frequented the old Market Tavern.

A huge bar sets the perfect stage for the award-winning brews that appear here seven days a week. Easily one of this nation's most versatile brewers, Great Lakes produces German-style lagers, English-style ales, and Belgian-style specialty beers (see Beer Styles, pages 2–17) with equal skill and enthusiasm. The following bottled products all won medals in the Great American Beer Festival: Moon Dog Ale (gold, 1992), Burning River Ale, Dortmunder Gold (gold, 1990), Eliot Ness Amber, Commodore Perry I.P.A. (bronze, 1992), and Edmund Fitzgerald Porter (gold, 1991). The seasonal brews, found only on tap at Great Lakes, include: Cleveland Brown Ale, Christmas Ale, Rockefeller Bock, Ohio City Ale, Emmet's Stout, Holy Moses Ale, Nosferatu Red Ale, Conway's Irish Ale, Honey Ale and Best Bitter.

While good beer is always the hallmark of a good brewpub, food and service are also important. The Great Lakes Brewing Company offers a quality menu and sophisticated presentation. "Our menu is regional-eclectic with a thread of health-consciousness," says Pat. "The foods dovetail nicely with the beers."

Presently, a new brewing facility is under construction that will triple their capacity. This will allow them to expand distribution of their bottled product, which is now limited to the greater Cleveland area.

Indianapolis Brewing Company

The Indianapolis Brewing Company, in the "Circle City," was originally formed in 1889 when the merger of three regional breweries was successfully completed. Those three breweries, all located in Indianapolis, were Lieber Brewing Company, C. F. Schmidt Brewing Company, and Casper Maus Brewing Company. The new brewing triumvirate introduced the Duesseldorfer brand, which was the

result of combining the strengths and talents of these three brewing concerns. The new Duesseldorfer beer quickly made its presence known by acquiring awards for brewing excellence. Among these, the most impressive were a gold medal at the Paris World Exposition in 1900, grand prize at the St. Louis World's Fair in 1904, and a gold medal at the Belgium World Exposition in 1905. Unfortunately, these glorious days were short-lived, as the Indianapolis Brewing Company, along with hundreds of others, fell victim to Prohibition's axe.

Today's Indianapolis Brewing Company began operations in 1987 with hopes of picking up where its predecessor had left off. This microbrewing newcomer from the Hoosier state was originally known as the Naptown Brewing Company (Naptown being a little-known, self-deprecating name for Indianapolis). The first brands marketed by Naptown Brewing were Main Street Lager and Main Street Pilsner beer. Though tasty and enjoyable, neither the beer nor the brewery attracted much attention. It was for this reason that the brewery was transformed into the new and

improved Indianapolis Brewing Company and laid claim to the brewing heritage of the city.

The goal and mission of the Indianapolis Brewing Company is to produce high quality, all-malt beers and ales, in the tradition and style of pre-Prohibition brewing in the United States. The Duesseldorfer beers are: Duesseldorfer Amber Ale, Duesseldorfer Pale Ale, and Duesseldorfer Dark Ale. In addition to these, there are two seasonal beers — a bock beer and an Oktoberfest. The above are all-grain, all-malt beers that are filtered but unpasteurized, and contain absolutely no additives or preservatives. Current production is about 2,000 barrels per year, which includes a number of beers brewed under contract for other American microbreweries.

Beer is available for sampling in the tasting room after tours — there is a $1.00 charge per person mandated by state law. Six-packs and cases also are available for take out.

Lakefront Brewing Company

The dream started in the early 1980s. Jim Klisch was a year or so into his newfound hobby when he was joined by his brother, Russell, and their good friend, Carson Praefke. Homebrewing became their passion. Once they were proficient at it, they entered their brews in, and won, many competitions, including the Wisconsin Vintners Association and the Wisconsin State Fair, where their beer won Best-of-Show in 1984. Five

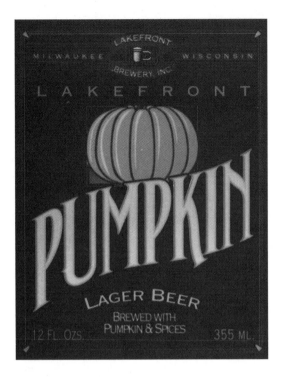

turing. At last the brewery-in-waiting had found a home, but, before the first grain could be cracked, no less than five codes had to be met: construction, plumbing, electrical, ventilation, and health.

As for the brewing equipment, Lakefront Brewery's is a hybrid system. Various discarded parts from other breweries and food industry businesses have been put to good use. The grain mill at the brewery formerly ground coffee for inmates at the state prison in Waupun. Schlitz, Pabst, Sprecher, Pepsi, and milk industry hand-me-downs helped to keep initial costs to a minimum. Total start-up costs were a mere $25,000. What is most impressive is that the whole operation was bankrolled out of personal savings and the brewery itself was built by the corporate members, with minimal help from tradesmen.

In the beginning, deliveries were made on a two-wheeled dolly. There was only one draught account — and that was right across the street at the Gordon Park Pub. There, on December 12, 1987, Klisch Lager made its debut. Soon afterwards, a second brew, Riverwest Steinbeer, was introduced. Then came Eastside Dark and Cream City Pale Ale; along with seasonal and specialty brews — Lakefront Bock in the spring, Lakefront Pumpkin Beer in the fall, and Lakefront Spice Beer for the holidays. This brew contains 190 pounds of honey, resulting in a relatively high alcohol content.

The response to these beers was so positive that it became impossible to maintain a supply to meet the demand. An expansion took place in January, 1989. Despite this, it's still difficult to keep pace with the

hundred gallons of homebrew later, they had amassed a remarkable collection of 35 ribbons in a span of three years.

Encouraged by their early accomplishments, the trio decided to incorporate and to investigate the viability of brewing commercially. By October, 1985, the fledgling corporation purchased a small building in the Riverwest neighborhood on Milwaukee's north side. By coincidence, the little brown building once housed a bakery, and now, in a poetic twist of fate, yeast once again meets grain. It proved to be an ideal situation. Not only did the building have a tall ceiling to facilitate a gravity feed system, but a large, centrally located drain as required by plumbing code. Only one major obstacle lay in their path — zoning laws that restricted the area to retail enterprise. The corporation petitioned the city and a variance was granted designating the neighborhood as light manufac-

demand. Consequently, Lakefront's beers rarely are found outside the metropolitan Milwaukee area.

Despite the expansion of personnel and equipment, the Lakefront Brewery maintains a close link with its homebrewing past. There is even a homebrew supply shop operating out of the front of the brewery. Any aspiring brewer in need of inspiration need look no further than the little Lakefront Brewery in Milwaukee. It is a monument to ingenuity and perseverance.

Oldenberg Brewery and Entertainment Complex

As breweries go, the Oldenberg Brewery and Entertainment Complex is among the most unique. Oldenberg is not just another brewery, it is a world of fun, food, history, and entertainment.

The history of Oldenberg can be traced back to 1969 and the successful home building business of Jerry Deters. In diversifying his business, Mr. Deters built a hotel on Buttermilk Pike, just off I-75, about five miles south of Cincinnati. Opened in 1970, the hotel underwent constant renovation and expansion. In the early 1980s, Jerry Deters had the idea of incorporating a microbrewery and entertainment facility with the hotel. The idea became a reality when the old Wiedemann Brewery, located a few miles away, closed. Ground was broken, and the doors to Oldenberg were opened in October 1987.

The name of the brewery comes from the Oldenberg region of Germany, the homeland of the Deters family. When Jerry Deters's great-grandfather came to Cincinnati in the mid-1800s, there was a large German population in the region and more than 50 breweries operating in the greater Cincinnati metropolitan area. Today, there is still a strong sense of German heritage and tradition in Cincinnati, but much of the brewing heritage has been lost. There was only one local brewery before Oldenberg came on the scene.

This new brewery burst forth in a big way. In addition to the brewhouse and packaging plant, the complex is comprised of several other areas of interest. At center stage — so to speak — is the Great Hall, which features a 65-foot atrium, skylights, cobblestone walkways, high-arched windows, and more than 100 tons of ornate iron work. Sitting atop the massive hall is the old Wiedemann Brewery weathervane, which graced the the Wiedemann Brewery of Newport, Kentucky for over 100 years.

Throughout the entertainment complex are thousands of brewery artifacts selected from a huge collection known as the

American Museum of Brewing History and Arts. The sheer magnitude of this collection makes it unique. There are millions of one-of-a-kind pieces, and the curators frequently change the exhibitions.

In addition to the Great Hall, there is also a traditional brewpub called J. D.'s Malt House & Eatery, and an outdoor beer garden for warm weather beer consumption. However, the real attraction is the beer itself. It is brewed daily in small, 25-barrel batches. (In a year's time this would amount to approximately 12,500 barrels. This is the capacity at Oldenberg, but it is actually the legal limit set by the state of Kentucky.) Oldenberg's present brewmaster is Ken Schierberg, and his assistant is Dave Gausepohl. They are responsible for producing all of the Oldenberg beers, as well as a couple of contract brews. Under the Oldenberg label, there are three regular production beers: Oldenberg Premium Verum (known as OPV), Oldenberg Blonde, and Oldenberg Weiss. The contract brews are Vail Ale and McGuire's Irish Old Style Ale. The remaining beers are seasonal and specialty brews: Oldenberg brand stout, Oktoberfest lager, winter ale, and Oldenberg Outrageous Bock. The regular products are distributed in Ohio, Kentucky, Indiana, and other select markets. Carryout beer can also be purchased at the gift shop, along with dozens of breweriana items.

Storing Beer

The proper handling and storage of beer is a universal concern. No one in the industry, least of all microbrewers, will deny that beer is fragile. Beer is essentially a food product; it begins its decline shortly after leaving the brewery. Although each brewer takes steps to protect the beer from the ravages of time, it is preferable to consume beer while it is as fresh as possible. Most national breweries that pasteurize the beer do not like their product to languish on store shelves for more than three months after packaging. In fact, some print coded pull dates for the retailer to follow. This period represents the shelf life of the beer. Most microbrewers only *flash pasteurize* their beers, leaving them somewhat less stable in the bottle, and thereby reducing the shelf life. Many microbrewers print pull dates in clear English to assure the consumer that the product is fresh.

Microbrewers depend on retailers to treat their products with respect, but, more often than not, cooler space is lost to those products with quick turnovers. Even if consumers do their best to handle craft beers with kid gloves, the retailer is still the weak link in the chain. The serious drinker of microbrewed beer can help by looking for pull dates and inspecting the bottle for protein flakes or other precipitate matter that suggests the beer is past its prime. Once purchased, microbrewed beer — or any beer for that matter — should be kept refrigerated for optimum freshness. If refrigeration is a problem, keeping bottled beer in a location that is cool and dark, and not subject to temperature fluctuations, is the next best thing. Immediate consumption avoids most problems. Except for well-hopped, high octane brews, beer does not handle the aging process as gracefully as wine and whiskey.

Anyone traveling in the Cincinnati and northern Kentucky area is strongly encouraged to visit the Oldenberg Brewery and Entertainment Complex. Be sure to ask about the Beer Camp program sponsored by Oldenberg.

Pavichevich Brewing Company

"Been there, done that." And now that he's here making beer, he brings a lifetime of experiences with him every day. Ken Pavichevich, that is. Ken is one of those people who, once you've met them, are not easily forgotten. He is in his mid-40s, and, if you have the time, he'll be glad to tell you all about his former careers as a model, an oil company executive, and a Chicago police officer. It was while he was a patrolman, pinned down by high-rise sniper fire, that Pavichevich convinced himself that another career move was in order. To the betterment of the microbrewing industry, Ken chose to make beer.

The Pavichevich Brewing Company came into existence in a much different way than did most other microbreweries. Equipment was not scavenged, salvaged, and reconditioned. Friends and family members were not wheedled into risking retirement savings. Location choices did not consist of shuttered factories or dilapidated warehouses.

This brand new, state-of-the-art brewing facility was built from the ground-up, in a clean and modern industrial park, and was financed by investors who took advantage of a stock offering presented to the public

in 1988. Over two million dollars was amassed and the brewery was on its way. Then Ken coaxed former Stroh brewmaster, Douglas Babcook, out of retirement, because he needed a brewmaster equal to the high expectations now placed on the fledgling brewery. No stove-top brewer would do.

Prior to building the brewery, Ken and Doug traveled extensively throughout Europe, specifically to Germany and Czechoslovakia, in order to settle on the exact type and style of beer to produce. Several return trips were made to confer with European brewmasters and to decide on final ingredients and processes. The style chosen was the original Czechoslovakian Pilsner-style beer from Bohemia (see Beer Styles, pages 2–17). The new Pavichevich brew was named Baderbrau after a good friend, Franz Bader, and, for this honor, Mr. Bader was paid the princely sum of ten dollars.)

In accordance with that style, and adhering to the Reinheitsgebot, Baderbrau is made from 100-percent malted barley. Like all classic Czech Pilsners, Baderbrau uses 95 percent Saaz variety hops from the Zatec region of Bohemia, and the remaining five percent are from Germany.

As testimony to its genuine Pilsner taste, Ken Pavichevich proudly displays a letter from Josef Tolar, brewmaster at the Budvar Brewery in Budejovice (Budweis), Czechoslovakia. In his letter, Mr. Tolar attests to the fact that ". . . he (Pavichevich) indeed knows how to produce a classic beer . . ." Additionally, Michael Jackson, the international Bard of Beer, called Baderbrau "the best Pilsner I've ever tasted in America." And, when President Bush was to visit Chicago, his staff always arranged to have a case of Baderbrau delivered to the President's suite at the Hyatt Regency. Lastly, Gunter Wasserberg, Consul General at the German Consulate in Chicago, has been serving Baderbrau at official functions since 1989.

After firmly establishing Baderbrau as one of the premium microbrews in the Midwest and the nation, the Pavichevich Brewing Company launched another outstanding European lager style, Baderbrau Bock, a Baderbrau Pilsner–quality brew, with the addition of crystal malt and chocolate malt for that full, dark, grain flavor and increased hop levels to balance the sweetness. Shortly after the bock was introduced, the Jakob Brothers Bakery in Chicago decided to feature a beer bagel for its "Bagel of the Month" program. Baderbrau Bock was chosen, and the "Baderbagel" was born.

In 1994, the brewery's ownership changed, but founder Ken Pavichevich remains the president.

Central Region Brewer Profiles

Victor Ecimovich, III

An engineering background is not a prerequisite for becoming a brewmaster, but Victor Ecimovich, III will tell you that it doesn't hurt to have one. Victor, who hails from Chicago, was working toward his engineering degree in the mid-1980s when he made a batch of pale ale with borrowed homebrewing equipment. He used a recipe from one of the few homebrewing books available at the time, and, as he recalls, it turned out pretty well. Ecimovich took notice of the rapidly expanding microbrewing industry on the West Coast and thought there might be a future in it for him. Little did he know . . .

He enrolled at the Siebel Institute in Chicago, where he studied brewing technology. The Institute, established in 1872, consists of the Siebel Institute of Technology and the United States Brewers' Academy. The Siebel Institute serves the brewing industry on a technological level, while the Brewers' Academy serves the industry on an educational level, preparing would-be brewmasters for service in the industry. (Only the Wiehenstephan Institut, near Munich, Germany, is more highly respected than the Siebel Institute.)

After completing his studies, Victor was offered a position at the Millstream Brewing Company in Amana, Iowa. This was an opportunity to work with Joe Pickett, and Victor jumped at the chance. (Pickett once owned the old Dubuque Star brewery in Dubuque and he had many years of experience in the brewing industry.) In Amana, Victor was able to convert his classroom studies to hands-on training, which he considers his most valuable experience — to this day.

In late 1987, Victor received another offer, this time to become brewmaster for the soon-to-be-opened Goose Island Brewing Company in his hometown of Chicago. Victor packed his bags and settled into the new brewhouse in time to prepare for the grand opening. He was responsible for formulating most of the beer recipes at Goose Island. Some of these garnered awards. Though his stay at Goose Island was brief, Victor is proud of his accomplishments there.

Now Ecimovich works as a consultant to the microbrewing industry. He travels to various locations to help brewers open new breweries or to help improve existing operations.

When last seen, Victor was happily promoting a new Bavarian wheat beer, Summit Hefe-weizen, which he formulated for the Summit Brewing Company in St. Paul, Minnesota.

Larry Bell

There are hundreds of brewers producing beer in hundreds of microbreweries across the nation. Each is unique, each has his own story to tell.

Meet Larry Bell. Larry's hard-won success in this business is a classic "rags-to-(relative) riches" story. It began in 1976, when Bell moved from a suburb of Chicago to Kalamazoo, Michigan, to attend Kalamazoo College. After two years of studies, Bell ran short of funds. Forced to find full-time employment, he was hired as a baker at a local bakery. While there, he had his first exposure to homebrewed beer, compliments of a fellow employee. "He wasn't a good baker and that kind of carried over into his brewing," recalls Bell with a laugh. When he moved to a house with three beer-guzzling buddies, Bell remembered homebrewing and realized he could be making all the beer they wanted — for much less money. And so he began . . .

When a microbrewery opened in nearby Ann Arbor, Bell made frequent visits there. His interest piqued, he got more serious about his avocation, reading brewing publications and increasing his batch size, learning and experimenting along the way. With a cash gift from a family member, Bell started the Kalamazoo Brewing Supply Company, and continued to nurture his dream of owning his own brewery. Bell's reputation as a homebrewer caught the attention of a local spice-extraction company executive, who wanted to try some brewing experiments with hops. One thing led to another.

Negotiations between Bell and his new financial backer resulted in the incorporation of the Kalamazoo Brewing Company in April, 1985 — the first microbrewery in the Midwest. The initial investment was $39,000, a paltry sum in the industry, even back then. With some used and reconditioned restaurant equipment and a lot of blood, sweat, and determination, the little brewhouse managed to produce 135 barrels of beer in 1986. Almost ten years and three expansions later, the Kalamazoo Brewing Company now produces an estimated 8,000 barrels annually. Bell's beer is getting lots of attention, so much so that he has opened an on-site bar called the Eccentric Cafe, where enthusiasts can try the product in draught form.

Despite the growing popularity, Larry has never lost sight of his homebrewing roots and homebrewers seem to be his most loyal fans. These ardent fans would be the first to tell you: Larry Bell's beers are not for everyone. For the most part, the Kalamazoo stable of beers — all 16 of them — are rich, chewy ales; not meant for the faint of heart.

"K-Zoo" brews can be found throughout the Midwest, as far west as North Dakota, and as far east as Virginia. They each bear the thumbprint of their creator: bold, assertive, respected, and, perhaps, even a bit eccentric.

Dave Miller

It is estimated that there are millions of homebrewers in the United States. Few of them have been brewing for 20 years. Even fewer have authored four books on the subject and are now crafting beer for a brewpub in a major American city.

Dave Miller is a native of St. Louis, Missouri, where he has been the brewmaster at the St. Louis Brewery since 1991. The path that led him there began in 1975 with his first batch of homebrewed beer. In 1981, Dave won the title of Homebrewer of the Year when his Pilsner beer won Best-of-Show at the AHA Nationals. By 1987, he had won his first blue ribbon at the National Homebrew Competition, sponsored by American Homebrewers Association.

Along the way, Dave was a charter member and vice president of the St. Louis Brews (the local AHA affiliated homebrew club) where he was in charge of the technical programs as well as writing a column in the club newsletter.

In 1981, the same year he won his national title, Miller's first book, *Homebrewing For Americans,* was published. This was among the first books to deal with all-grain brewing techniques. He then went on to write the *Complete Handbook of Homebrewing* in 1988 and *Continental Pilsner* in 1989. Miller is considered an expert on this particular style. Most recently, he has written *Brewing the World's Great Beers,* a step-by-step guide to various brewing styles, with practical, easy-to-follow recipes for those who wish to emulate them. Miller has also authored several articles on brewing for a number of publications.

Respected for his boundless expertise in the brewing sciences, Miller has also been a frequent speaker at homebrewing conferences across the country. He has been a certified beer judge for many years, and his graduation from the Siebel Institute of Brewing Technology paved the way for his position at the St. Louis Brewery. But, before there could be a brewpub in St. Louis, there had to be a change in the law restricting the operation of brewpubs in Missouri. Dave Miller was instrumental in lobbying the state legislature for passage of a bill legalizing brewpubs.

Central Region Beer Festivals

Blessing of the Bock
Milwaukee, WI
March, 3rd week
(414) 372-8800

All microbrewers and homebrewers are invited to bring their best bock beer to participate. The blessing, a ritualistic event, complete with Catholic priest, is hosted by the Lakefront Brewery, and proceeds are donated to the local war veterans memorial park.

Wisconsin Microbrewers Beerfest
Chilton, WI
May
(414) 849-2534

All-Wisconsin micro festival is hosted by Bob Rowland's Calumet Brewing Company and is held at spacious county fairgrounds. Barbecued chow and live music are included.

Southport Brewers Festival
Kenosha, WI
June, 2nd week
(414) 694-9050

This microbrewery invitational, hosted by Brewmasters Pub, takes place under a tented courtyard. There usually are approximately 20 midwestern microbrewers in attendance. It's very crowded, very loud, very tasty.

Blues & Brews Cruise
Chicago, IL
August, 4th week
(312) 692-2337

This four-hour cruise on Lake Michigan, complete with a dozen microbrews, Chicago-style barbecue, and a top name blues band, is sponsored by the Chicago Beer Society.

Great Taste of the Midwest
Madison, WI
August, 3rd week
(608) 256-1100

The biggest and best event in the Midwest, and it's always a sellout. Hosted by the Madison Homebrewers & Tasters Guild, there were more than 30 participating breweries in 1994.

Beer Across America
Midwest Brewers Oktoberfest
Chicago, IL
Late September or October
(800) 854-BEER

Originated by Goose Island Brewing Company, this event is now multi-sponsored and has been moved to a larger, more accommodating downtown location at Navy Pier. Twenty-five microbrews and live music attract a large crowd.

Taste of the Great Lakes
Frankenmuth, MI
October or November
(517) 652-3445

This event continues to grow. What started as a homebrewer's conference has expanded to include tastings, tours, and dinners, with famous speakers holding forth on all aspects of beer and brewing.

Central Region Listings

Birmingham Brewing

Alabama

Birmingham Brewing
3118 3rd Ave South
Birmingham, AL 35233
(205) 326-6677
Microbrewery
Brews: Red Mountain Red Ale, golden lager, golden ale.
Seasonals: wheat, Red Mountain Light
Tours: Call in advance

Port City Brewery
25 Dauphin St.
Mobile, AL 36602
(205) 438-BREW
Brewpub
Brews: Middle Bay Light, Gulf Coast Gold, Admiral Semmes' Stout, Azalea City Steamer.
Seasonals: Christmas ale
Hours: Mon.–Thurs., noon–2AM; Fri.–Sat., 11AM–closing; Sun., noon–6PM

Arkansas

Ozark Brewing
4430 Dickson St.
Fayetteville, AR 72701
(501) 521-BREW
Brewpub
Brews: Long Rain Ale, Six in Hand Stout, Coach Light Ale, Plowman's Pilsner. *Seasonals:* hefe-weizen, IPA, Backporch Bitter, and others
Hours: Daily, 11AM–midnight

Vino's
923 W. 7th St.
Little Rock, AR 72201
(501) 375-8466
Brewpub
Brews: 7th Street Pale, Big House Ale, Lazy Boy Stout, and others in rotation
Hours: Mon.–Wed., 11AM–10PM; Thurs.–Sat., 11AM–midnight; closed Sun.

Weidman's Old Fort Brew Pub
422 N. Third St.
Fort Smith, AR 72901
(501) 782-9898
Brewpub
Brews: Fort Smith Light, Rope Swing Red, Weizen, Hell on the Border Porter, Big Wheel Stout, Pale Ale, Munchner. *Seasonals:* Raspberry Ale, Pumpkin Ale, Emerald Isle Ale, Ozark Lambic

Hours: Mon., 11AM–2PM and 5PM–10PM; Tues.–Thurs., 11AM–11PM; Fri., 11AM–1AM; Sat., 11AM–midnight; closed Sun.

Illinois

Blue Cat Brewpub
113 18th St.
Rock Island, IL 61201
(309) 788-8274
Brewpub
Brews: Wigged Pig Wheat, River Back Jack, Wee Bit Scotch Ale, Blue Cat Porter, Big Bad Dog, Arkham Stout, Raspberry Beer, all in rotation
Hours: Mon.–Sat., 11AM–3AM; Sun., 11AM–midnight

Box Office Brewery & Restaurant
145 N. 3rd St.
DeKalb, IL 60115
(815)748-BREW
Brewpub
Brews: Box Office Premier Golden Ale, Maureen O'Hara Irish Red Ale, Coal Porter
Hours: Daily, 11:30AM–1AM

Brewbakers Ale House & Deli
425 15th St.
Moline, IL 61265
(309) 762-3464
Brewpub
Brews: light cream ale, golden ale, red pale ale, porter
Hours: Mon.–Thurs., 7AM–midnight; Fri., 7AM–2AM; Sat., 11AM–2AM; Sun., 11AM–midnight

Capitol City Brewing and Bar & Grill
107 W. Cook St.
Springfield, IL 62704
(217) 753-5725
Brewpub
Brews: pale ale, Scotch ale, Abe's Red Ale, Pilsner, honey beer, and others
Hours: Call for information.

Chicago Brewing
1830 N. Besly Ct.
Chicago, IL 60622
(312) 252-BREW
Microbrewery
Brews: Legacy Lager, Legacy Red Ale, Heartland Weiss, Big Shoulders Porter
Tours: Sat., 2PM

Doppelbockers Brewpub
10th & Commerce
Lockport, IL 60441
Brewpub
No further information available at press time

Galena Main Street Brewpub
300 N. Main St.
Galena, IL 61036
(815) 777-0451
Brewpub
Brews: Czech Honeybrew, Better Bitter Ale, Irish Clans Red Ale, Galena Graphite Double Stout, Galena Weissbier, Karl's Cream Ale, Ancestral Porter, and others
Hours: Times vary by season; call for information

Chicago Brewing

Golden Prairie Brewing
1820 W. Webster Ave.
Chicago, IL 60614
(312) 862-0106
Microbrewery
Brews: Golden Prairie Ale, Maple Stout, Honey Ginger
Tours: By appointment

Goose Island Brewing
1800 N. Clybourn
Chicago, IL 60614
#add:(312) 915-0071
Brewpub
Brews: Honker's ale, blonde ale, two dozen rotating seasonal and specialty beers
Hours: Mon.–Thurs., 11AM–midnight; Fri.–Sat., 11AM–2AM; Sun., noon–11PM

J. D. Nick's
1711 W. Hwy.50
O'Fallon, IL 62269
(618) 632-BREW
Brewpub
Brews: light, amber, Pilsner. *Seasonals:* Numbskull Amber Lager, Horst's Oktoberfest
Hours: Mon.–Thurs. and Sun., 11AM–1AM; Fri.–Sat., 11AM–2AM

Joe's Brewery
706 S. 5th St.
Champaign, IL 61820
(217) 384-1790
Brewpub
Brews: India pale ale. *Seasonals:* porter, Russian Imperial stout, doppelbock, hefe-weizen, dunkel weizen, Pilsner, Oktoberfest, oatmeal stout, barleywine, and others
Hours: Daily, 11AM–1AM

Mickey Finn's Brewery
412 N. Milwaukee Ave.
Libertyville, IL 60048
(708) 362-6688
Brewpub
Brews: wheat ale, amber ale, oatmeal stout, Hop Garden Helles, spiced wassail
Hours: Mon.–Sat., 11AM–2AM; Sun., noon–9PM

Mill Rose Brewing
45 S. Barrington Rd.
South Barrington, IL 60010
(708) 382-7673
Brewpub
Brews: Dark Star, Downtown Brown Ale, Country Inn Ale, Prairie Pilsner, W. R. Stout, General's Ale, Wheat n' Honey, Weiss
Hours: Mon.–Sat., 11AM–1AM; Sun., 11AM–10PM

Pavichevich Brewing
383 Romans Road
Elmhurst, IL 60126
(708) 617-5252
Microbrewery
Brews: Baderbrau Pilsner, Baderbrau Bock
Tours: Sat. Reservations required 24 hours in advance.

Star Union Brewing
P.O. Box 282
Hennepin, IL 61327
(815) 925-7400
Microbrewery
Brews: Star Model, Starved Rock Amber Ale
Tours: Call for information

Taylor Brewing
200 5th Ave. E
Naperville, IL 60563
(708)717-8000
Brewpub

Brews: raspberry wheat, honey wheat, summertime ale, and others in rotation. Other microbrewed beers on tap.

Hours: Mon.–Thurs., 11:15AM–midnight; Fri.–Sat., 11:15AM–1AM; closed Sun.

Weinkeller Brewery
6417 W. Roosevelt Road
Berwyn, IL 60402
(708) 749-2276
Brewpub

Brews: Berwyn Brew Pilsner, Bavarian Weiss, Aberdeen Amber Ale, Dusseldorfer Doppelbock, Dublin Stout, Berliner Weisse. *Seasonals:* Oktoberfest, Christmas ale

Hours: Mon.–Thurs., 11:30AM–1AM; Fri.–Sat., 11:30AM–3AM; Sun., 2PM–1AM

Weinkeller Brewery
651 Westmont Dr.
Westmont, IL 60559
(708) 789-2236
Brewpub

Brews: Westmont Pilsner, Bavarian Weiss, Kristall Weiss, Aberdeen Amber Ale, Dusseldorfer Doppelbock, Weinkeller ESB, Dublin Stout, Berliner Weisse, and seasonals

Hours: Mon.–Thurs., 11AM–1AM; Fri.–Sat., 11AM–2AM; Sun., noon–1AM

Indiana

Bloomington Brewing Company (Lennie's)
1795 E. 10th Street
Bloomington, IN 47407
(812) 339-2256
Brewpub

Brews: Quarrymen Pale Ale, Bloomington Red Ale, Bad Elmer's Porter. *Seasonals:* barleywine, weizen

Hours: Sun.–Thurs., 11AM–midnight; Fri.–Sat., 11AM–1AM

Broad Ripple Brewpub
840 E. 65th St.
Indianapolis, IN 46220
(317) 253-2739
Brewpub

Brews: Red Bird Mild, Pintail Pale Ale, ESB, Monon Porter. *Seasonals:* Wee Heavy, copper ale, dry stout, Bavarian wheat, Kölsch

Hours: Mon.–Thurs., 11AM–midnight; Fri.–Sat., 11AM–1:30AM; closed Sun.

Indianapolis Brewing
3250 N. Post Road
Indianapolis, IN 46226
(317) 898-1235
Microbrewery

Brews: amber ale, dark ale, pale ale. *Seasonals:* Brick Yard, bock, Oktoberfest, Pike Place IPA (on contract)

Tours: By appointment

Lafayette Brewing
622 Main St.
Lafayette, IN 47901
(317) 742-2591
Brewpub

Indianapolis Brewing

Dallas County Brewing

Brews: Kölsch, pale ale, oatmeal stout. *Seasonals:* IPA, brown ale, Christmas ale, Big Boris Barleywine

Hours: Mon.–Thurs., 11AM–midnight; Fri.–Sat., 11AM–1AM; closed Sun.

Mishawaka Brewing
3703 N. Main St.
Mishawaka, IN 46545
(219) 256-9993

Brewpub

Brews: Mishawaka Gold Lager, Lake Effect Pale Ale, South Shore Amber Ale, Founder's Classic Dry Stout, Ankenbrock Weisen, and others

Hours: Mon.–Thurs., 11:30AM–11PM; Fri.–Sat., 11:30AM–1AM; Sun., noon–9PM

Oaken Barrel Brewing
50 N. Airport Pkwy.
Greenwood, IN 46143
(317) 887-2287

Brewpub

Brews: golden ale, amber ale, porter, and seasonals

Iowa

Babe's: The Brewery
417 6th St.
Des Moines, IA 50309
(515) 244-9319

Brewpub

Brews: Wood Duck Wheat, Thoroughbred Classic Ale, Ring Neck Red Ale, Owl's Head Brown Ale, Black Angus Oatmeal Stout, and specialties

Hours: Mon.–Thurs., 11AM–1AM; Fri.–Sat., 11AM–2AM; Sun., 11AM–7PM

Dallas County Brewing
301 S. 10th St.
Adel, IA 50003
(515) 993-5064

Brewpub

Brews: light, lager, ale, porter, and seasonals

Hours: Daily, 11AM–10PM

Fitzpatrick's Alehouse
525 S. Gilbert
Iowa City, IA 52240
(319) 356-6900

Brewpub

Brews: golden lager, Celtic Ale, Mighty Stout, wheat. *Seasonals:* Christmas ale, bock

Hours: Mon.–Fri., 2PM–2AM; Sat., noon–2AM; Sun., 5PM–2AM

Front Street Brewing
208 E. River Dr.
Davenport, IA 52801
(319) 322-1569

Brewpub

Brews: Bucktown Stout, Old Davenport, Charuat Legacy, Raging River Ale

Hours: Mon.–Thurs., 11AM–midnight; Fri.–Sat., 11AM–1AM; Sun., noon–10PM

Millstream Brewing
Lower Brewery Road
Amana, IA 52203
(319) 622-3672

Brewpub

Brews: Millstream Lager, Millstream Wheat, Schild Brau Amber. *Seasonal:* Oktoberfest

Hours: Summer: Mon.–Sat., 9AM–6PM; Sun., noon–5PM; Winter: Mon.–Sat., 10AM–5PM; Sun., noon–5PM

Kentucky

Blue Grass Brewing
3929 Shelbyville Road
Louisville, KY 40207
(502) 899-7070
Brewpub
Brews: S. P. Pils, Kölsch, altbier, Dark Star Porter, raspberry mead, and seasonals
Hours: Mon.–Thurs.,
11AM–midnight; Fri.–Sat.,
11AM–1AM; Sun., noon–1AM

Oldenberg Brewery & Entertainment Complex
I-75 & Buttermilk Pike
Fort Mitchell, KY 41017
(606) 341-2802
Brewpub
Brews: Premium Verum, Oldenburg Blonde, Oldenburg Weiss, Vail Ale. *Seasonals:* stout, Outrageous Bock, Oktoberfest, Winter ale
Hours: Daily, 10AM–5AM

Silo Microbrewery
630 Barret Ave.
Louisville, KY 40204
(502) 589-BREW
Brewpub
Brews: raspberry light, Derby City Dark, Silo Wheat Light, Red Rock Ale, and seasonals
Hours: Mon.–Thurs.,
11:30AM–1:30AM; Fri.,
11:30AM–2:30AM; Sat.,
5PM–2:30AM; closed Sun.

Louisiana

Abita Brewing
21084 Hwy. 36
Abita Springs, LA 70432
(504) 893-3143
Microbrewery
Brews: Abita Golden, Abita Amber, Turbodog. *Seasonals:* wheat beer, Mardi Gras Bock, Fallfest, XXXMAS
Tours: Sat., 1PM

Crescent City Brewhouse
527 Decatur St.
New Orleans, LA 70130
(504) 522-0571
Brewpub
Brews: Red Stallion, Pilsner, Black Forest. *Seasonals:* Carnival, Maibock, Oktoberfest, Christmas bock, weissbeer
Hours: Daily, 11AM–close

Rikenjaks Brewing
9916 Hwy. 421
Jackson, LA 70748
(504) 634-2785
Microbrewery
Brews: Old Hardhead Scottish Style Ale, ESB, American Ale
Tours: By appointment

Michigan

Duster's Microbrewery
114 N. Main St.
Lawton, MI 49065
(616) 624-3771
Brewpub
Brews: Classic German wheat, red ale, stout. *Seasonal:* Classic spring wheat
Hours: Tues.–Thurs. and Sun., 1PM–11PM; Fri.–Sat., 1PM–2AM; closed Mon.

Oldenberg Brewery & Entertainment Complex

Silo Microbrewery

Abita Brewing

Frankenmuth Brewery

Kalamazoo Brewing

James Page Brewing

Frankenmuth Brewery
425 S. Main St.
Frankenmuth, MI 48734
(517) 652-6183
Microbrewery

Brews: extra light, Old German Style Pilsner, Old German Style Dark, Natural Weisse, Old Detroit Amber Ale. *Seasonals:* Old German Style Bock, Cherry Weiss

Tours: Daily, 11AM–5PM May–Oct.; Wed.–Sun., Nov.–Apr.

Grand Rapids Brewing Company
3689 28th Street SE
Grand Rapids, MI 49512
(616) 285-5970
Brewpub

Brews: Silver Foam, Thornapple Gold, River City Red, Black Dog Ale, Vienna Beer

Hours: Sun.–Thurs., 11AM–midnight; Fri.–Sat., 11AM–1AM

Hereford & Hops Brewing Co.
624 Ludington St.
Escanaba, MI 49829
(906) 789-1945
Brewpub

Kalamazoo Brewing (Eccentric Cafe)
315 E. Kalamazoo Ave.
Kalamazoo, MI 49007
(616) 382-2338

Microbrewery with on-premise saloon.

Brews: Third Coast Beer, Bell's Amber Ale, Bell's Porter, Bell's Kalamazoo Stout, Bell's Beer. *Seasonals:* Deb's Red Ale, Bell's Best Brown Ale, Bell's Solsun Ale, and others

Hours: Mon.–Fri., 9PM–10PM; Sat., noon–10PM; Sun., noon–5PM

Tours: Sat., or by appointment

Traffic Jam & Snug
511 W. Canfield at 2nd
Detroit, MI 48201
(313) 831-9470
Brewpub

Brews: West Canfield Wheat, Big Red Bitter, Detroit, Coal Porter, and others in rotation

Hours: Mon., 11AM–3PM; Tues.–Wed., 11AM–9PM; Thurs., 11AM–10:30PM; Fri., 11AM–midnight; Sat., 5PM–midnight; closed Sun.

Minnesota

James Page Brewing
1300 Quincy NE
Minneapolis, MN 55413
(612) 331-2833
Microbrewery

Brews: James Page Private Stock, Boundary Waters. *Seasonal:* Boundary Waters Bock

Tours: First Sat. of the month, 1PM–3PM

Rock Bottom Brewery
825 Hennepin Ave.
Minneapolis, MN 55402
(612) 332-BREW
Brewpub

Brews: North Star Premium, Gopher Gold Golden Ale, Rock Slide Red, Beaver Brown Ale, Stillwater Stout. *Seasonals:* Eric the Red, Itasca, and others

Hours: Mon.–Sat., 11AM–1AM; Sun., 4PM–1AM

Sherlock's Home
11000 Red Circle Dr.
Minnetonka, MN 55343
(612) 931-0203
Brewpub
Brews: Queen Anne Light, Gold Crown Lager, Bishops Bitter, Star of India IPA, Palace Porter, Piper's Pride, Stag's Head Stout, and seasonals
Hours: Mon.–Sat., 11AM–1AM; Sun., 4PM–1AM

Summit Brewing
2264 University Ave.
St. Paul, MN 55114
(612) 645-5029
Microbrewery
Brews: Summit Extra Pale Ale, Great Northern Porter.
Seasonals: winter ale, hefe-weizen, Heimertingen Maibock
Tours: Sat., 1PM. Reservations required 1 week in advance.

Mississippi

No microbreweries at press time

Missouri

Boulevard Brewing
2501 Southwest Blvd.
Kansas City, MO 64108
(816) 474-7095
Microbrewery
Brews: pale ale, wheat beer, Bully! Porter. *Seasonal:* Irish ale
Tours: Sat., 1:30PM. Reservations required 1 week in advance.

Flat Branch Pub & Brewing
115 S. 5th St.
Columbia, MO 65201
(314) 499-0400

Brewpub
Brews: Tiger Tale Ale, pale ale, Scottish, bitter, IPA, brown, Green Chili, porter, blackberry ale, and more
Hours: Sun.–Wed., 11AM–midnight; Thurs.–Sat., 11AM–1AM

Saint Louis Brewery
2100 Locust St.
St. Louis, MO 63103
(314) 241-2337
Brewpub
Brews: wheat ale, hefe-weizen, Pilsner, pale ale, cask-conditioned ale, Spark's Oatmeal Stout, and seasonals
Hours: Mon.–Thurs., 11AM–midnight; Fri.–Sat., 11AM–1:30AM; Sun., noon–midnight

75th Street Brewery
520 W. 75th St.
Kansas City, MO 64114
(816) 523-4677
Brewpub
Brews: Cow Town Wheat, Yardbird's Saxy Golden Ale, Possum Trot Brown Ale.
Seasonals: Royal Raspberry Ale, Muddy MO Stout
Hours: Mon., 4PM–1:30AM; Tues.–Sat., 11AM–1:30AM; Sun., noon–midnight

Weathervane
1027 E. Walnut
Springfield, MO 65806
(417) 831-6676
Brewpub
Brews: Golden Tail Ale, Red Rooster Ale, raspberry ale.
Seasonal: SummerFest
Hours: Daily, 11AM–1AM

Summit Brewing

Boulevard Brewing

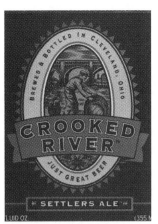

Crooked River Brewing

Great Lakes Brewing

Ohio

Barley's Brewpub
467 N. High St.
Columbus, OH 43215
(614) 228-2537
Brewpub
Brews: Pilsner, pale ale, Irish Rogue, Ivan Porter, and seasonals
Hours: Daily, 11AM–1AM

Burkhardt Brewing
3700 Massillon Road
Uniontown, OH 44685
(216) 896-9200
Brewpub
Brews: North Star, White Cliff Ale, Eclipse. *Seasonals:* bock, Holiday Honey Ale, Irish red, Mug Ale, Oktoberfest
Hours: Mon.–Sat., call for information. Closed Sun.

Captain Tony's Pizza & Pasta Emporium
23200 Chagrin Blvd.
Beachwood, OH 44122
(216) 464-TONY
Brewpub
Brews: Halloween Beer, Christmas Beer, St. Patricks
Hours: Mon.–Thurs., 11AM–11PM; Fri.–Sat., 11AM–midnight; Sun., noon–9PM

Columbus Brewing
476 S. Front St.
Columbus, OH 43215
(614) 224-3626
Microbrewery (brews can be tasted next door at Gibby's or Hagen's Ale & Tee)
Brews: gold, pale ale, nut brown ale, Black Forest Porter, 1492 Lager. *Seasonals:* Special Reserve, Oktoberfest, stout, Christmas Warmer
Tours: By appointment

Crooked River Brewing
1101 Center St.
Cleveland, OH 44113
(216) 771-BEER
Microbrewery
Brews: Settler's Ale, German lager, Oktoberfest, and seasonals
Tours: By appointment

Gambrinus Brewing
1152 S. Front St.
Columbus, OH 43207
(614) 444-7769
Microbrewery
Brews: Gambrinus Golden Lager, Augustiner Amber Lager
Tours: Call for information.

Great Lakes Brewing
2516 Market St.
Cleveland, OH 44113
(216) 771-4404
Brewpub
Brews: Moon Dog Ale, Burning River Ale, Heisman, The Elliot Ness, Commodore Perry IPA, Edmund Fitzgerald Porter, and seasonals
Hours: Mon.–Thurs., 11:30AM–midnight; Fri.–Sat., 11:30AM–1AM; Sun., 3PM–11PM

Hoster Brewing
550 S. High St.
Columbus, OH 43065
(614) 228-6066
Brewpub
Brews: Eagle Light, XX Pale, Gold Top, amber lager.

Seasonals: Independence English Ale, Oktoberfest, Maibock, Black Top Doppelbock, and others

Hours: Mon.–Sat., 11AM–2AM; Sun., 4PM–11PM

Liberty Brewing Company
1238 Weathervane Lane
Akron, OH 44313
(216) 869-BEER

Brewpub

Brews: Zeppelin, Nathan Hale Pale Ale, Nutsy Fagin Brown Ale, Dragonslayer Scotch Ale, Black Silk Porter, Liberator Doppelbock

Hours: Mon.–Fri., 11:30AM–2:30AM; Sat., noon–2:30AM; closed Sun.

Lift Bridge Brewing Co.
1119 Lake Ave.
Ashtabula, OH 44004
(216) 964-6200

Microbrewery

Main Street Brewpub
1203 Main St.
Cincinnati, OH 45210
(513) 665-HOPS

No further information available at press time.

**Melbourne's
(Strongsville Brewing)**
12492 Prospect Road
Strongsville, OH 44136
(216) 238-4677

Brewpub

Brews: Bondi Beach Blonde, Wombat Wheat Beer, Down Under Beer. *Seasonals:* stout, Oktoberfest, Christmas bock, Irish red ale

Hours: Mon.–Thurs., 11AM–midnight; Fri.–Sat., 11AM–1AM; closed Sun.

Tennessee

**Big River Grille
& Brewing Works**
222 Broad St.
Chattanooga, TN 37402
(615) 267-BREW

Brewpub

Brews: Trolleyman Wheat, Angler's Amber Ale, Imperial 375 Pale Ale, Iron Horse Stout. *Seasonal:* J. Ross' Brown Ale

Hours: Mon.–Thurs., 11AM–11PM; Fri.–Sun., 11AM–midnight

Bohannon Brewing
134 2nd Ave. N
Nashville, TN 37201
(615) 242-8223

Brewpub

Brews: Pilsner draft, golden ale, wheat beer. *Seasonals:* bock beer, Oktoberfest beer, porter, blackberry wheat, and more

Hours: Mon.–Thurs., 11AM–midnight; Fri.–Sat., 11AM–2AM; closed Sun.

**Boscos Pizza,
Kitchen & Brewery**
7615 W. Farmington #30
Germantown, TN 38138
(901) 756-7310

Brewpub

Brews: Tennessee Cream Ale, Bluff City Amber Ale, Germantown Alt, Famous Flaming Stone Beer, and seasonals

Bohannon Brewing

Brewmasters Pub
Restaurant & Brewery

Capital Brewery

Hours: Mon.–Thurs.,
11AM–11PM; Fri.–Sat.,
11AM–1AM; Sun., noon–11PM

Smoky Mountain Brewing
424 S. Gay St.
Knoxville, TN 37902
(615) 673-8400
Brewpub
Brews: Old City Ale,
Blackbear Porter,
and seasonals
Hours: Mon.–Thurs.,
11:30AM–11PM; Fri.–Sat.,
11:30AM–1AM; closed Sun.

Wisconsin

Adler Brau
Appleton Brewing
1004 S. Olde Oneida St.
Appleton, WI 54915
(414) 731-3322
Brewpub
Brews: light, lager, Pilsner,
amber all malt, porter.
Seasonals: bock, weiss brau,
Holiday, Fallfest, pumpkin
spice, oatmeal stout, cherry
lager, peachy wheat ale
Hours: Mon.–Sat., 11AM–10PM;
Sun., 4PM–10PM

Brewmasters Pub
Restaurant & Brewery
4017- 80th St.
Kenosha, WI 53142
(414) 694-9050
Brewpub
Brews: Southport Light,
Kenosha Gold, Amber Vienna
Style, Royal Dark. *Seasonals:*
Maibock, mocha stout, Nort's
Cream Ale, Oktoberfest,
Johnson's Honey Lager,
Old St. Nick
Hours: Mon.–Fri., 11AM–mid-
night; Sat.–Sun., 11AM–closing

Capital Brewery
7734 Terrace Ave.
Middleton, WI 53562
(608) 836-7100
Microbrewery with on-premise
beer hall and beer garden
Brews: Gartenbrau Lager, special, dark, weizen, Wisconsin
Amber. *Seasonals:* bock,
Maibock, Oktoberfest, wild
rice, winterfest, doppelbock
Hours: Fri., 3:30PM–8PM; Sat.,
noon–8PM, during the summer

Cherryland Brewing
341 N. third Ave.
Sturgeon Bay, WI 54235
(414) 743-1945
Brewpub

Names to Remember

If you are ever in Germantown, Tennessee, stop
in at Boscos Pizza Kitchen and Brewery and
have Boscos Famous Flaming Stone Beer. Another all-time
favorite name comes from McGuire's Irish Pub & Brewery
in Pensacola, Florida. When asked what you would like, simply respond with: "What the German on the Floor is
Having." (It's a strong ale.)

Brews: golden rail, silver rail, weizen, Cherry Rail, Irish light, apple bach, raspberry light

Hours: Daily, 10AM–4AM

Gray's Brewing
2424 W. Court St.
Janesville, WI 53545
(608) 752-3552
Microbrewery

Brews: pale ale, oatmeal stout, honey ale

Tours: First and third Sat. of the month, at 1PM and 2PM

Great Dane Brewing Company
123 East Doty
Madison, WI 53703
(608) 284-0000
Brewpub

Brews: Crop Circle Wheat, Landmark Gold, Peck's Pilsner, Devil's Lake Red Lager, Stone of Scone Scotch Ale, Emerald Isle Stout, Black Earth Porter, Barleywine

Hours: Sun.–Thurs., 11AM–2AM; Fri.–Sat., 11AM–2:30AM

Lakefront Brewery
818A E. Chambers St.
Milwaukee, WI 53212
(414) 372-8800
Microbrewery

Brews: East Side Dark, Riverwest Stein Beer, Klisch Lager, Cream City Pale Ale
Seasonals: Big Jim's Pumpkin Beer, Klisch Cherry Beer

Tours: Sat., 1:30PM and 3:30PM, to first 30 people

New Glarus Brewing
County West & Hwy. 69
New Glarus, WI 53574
(608)527-5850
Microbrewery

Brews: Edel-Pils, Uff-da Bock, Solstice Weiss, Zwickel, Staghorn, Oktoberfest
Seasonal: Belgian Red

Tours: Fri.–Sat., 12PM–4PM

Oconto Brewing Co. (Main Event Sports Bar & Grill)
121 Main St.
Oconto, WI 54153
(414) 834-4811
Brewpub

Randy's FunHunters Brewery
841 E. Milwaukee St.
Whitewater, WI 53190
(414)473-8000
Brewpub

Brews: pale ale, brown ale, amber lager, Pilsner; all rotate

Hours: Tues.–Thurs. and Sat., 11AM–10PM; Fri., 11AM–11PM; Sun., 10:30AM–9PM; closed Mon.

Rowland's Calumet Brewing (The Roll Inn)
25 N. Madison St.
Chilton, WI 53014
(414)849-2534
Brewpub

Brews: Pilsner, wheat, amber, dark. *Seasonals:* bock, rye, Oktoberfest

Hours: Tues.–Thurs., 2PM–2AM; Fri.–Sat., noon–2:30AM; Sun., noon–2AM; closed Mon.

Lakefront Brewery

New Glarus Brewing

Rowland's Calumet Brewing

Sprecher Brewing

Sprecher Brewing
701 W. Glendale Ave.
Glendale, WI 53209
(414)964-BREW
Microbrewery

Brews: special amber, black Bavarian, hefe-weiss, Milwaukee weiss, dunkel weizen. *Seasonals:* Maibock, fest, Oktoberfest, winter brew, Irish stout, and more

Tours: Sat., by appointment

Water Street Brewery
1101 N. Water St.
Milwaukee, WI 53202
(414)272-1195
Brewpub

Brews: Water Street Amber, Sporten European Lager, Water Street Weiss. *Seasonals:* bock, bitters, winter spice, brown ale, stout, red lager, Old World Oktoberfest

Hours: Sun.–Thurs., 11AM–2AM; Fri.–Sat., 11AM–2:30AM

Part V

ATLANTIC REGION

Atlantic Region Brewery Profiles

Arrowhead Brewing Company

As if proof of the widespread popularity of the microbrewing industry was needed, witness Arrowhead Brewing Company. After brewing beer as a hobby at home for over four years, Francis Mead began his march into the commercial brewing arena in 1989.

Mead was presented with the opportunity to retire early from his 21-year occupation in the pharmaceutical business. "It was time for me to move on and do something different," he says of his motivation to open a microbrewery. And nothing was left to chance. While researching the microbrewing industry for feasibility, Mead devoured all the information he could. Noting the industry's phenomenal growth on the West Coast and the dearth of small brewers in the East, he chose tiny Chambersburg, Pennsylvania, as the location for his new venture. Part of his plan included choosing a name and creating a product which could be identified strongly with America and with his home state.

Upon starting his new venture, Mead had many things in his favor. Number one was his association with Alan Pugsley.

Mead's connection with Pugsley goes back to Alan's days at the Wild Goose brewery where he was the brewmaster. Prior to Wild Goose, Alan Pugsley helped set up the D. L. Geary Brewing Company in Portland, Maine. (Ironically, this is where Fran Mead apprenticed with David Geary back in 1989.) Together, Mead and Pugsley formulated the recipe for Red Feather Ale.

Mead wanted to create a brew with a balance of maltiness and bitterness in the

traditional English pale ale style. After several test batches and ingredient adjustments, the final product is a blend of English pale malt, crystal malt, and, to a much lesser degree, chocolate malt. The grist also contains a portion of torrefied (dried up) wheat, for crispness and head retention. Hop character is achieved through separate additions of cascade, northern brewer, and Willamette hop pellets, in varying quantities. Much of the hop aroma is infused through a unique "hop percolator," devised by Pugsley, in which whole leaf hops are steeped in hot water in order to produce a hop "tea" before being added to the wort on its way to the heat exchanger. The wort is then chilled to 68°F (20°C), at which time the yeast is pitched. Primary fermentation takes about six days. Then the temperature is dropped to 48°F (9°C). The beer undergoes another three to 11 days of conditioning at 32°F (0°C). Isinglass and silica gel finings are used for clarification before being filtered through diatomaceous earth.

"People really respond favorably to it," says Mead. So much so, in fact, that the beer he produces is making a name for itself far beyond its target states (and the brewer's expectations). Red Feather Ale can now be found in New York, New Jersey, Florida, northern Virginia, and the District of Columbia. Conventional wisdom says that may be too aggressive for a relative newcomer, but, so far, the brewery has been able to support those markets.

Tours of the brewery are encouraged, but tourists are asked to call in advance of their visit — certain days on the microbrewing calendar can be more hectic than others.

Buffalo Brewing Company

The city of Buffalo once had more than 30 breweries operating at the same time, each supplying beer to a small area around the brewery. That was in the 1890s. In the 1990s, the Buffalo area has only one brewery and one brewpub — both under the same ownership. As of 1993, the Buffalo Brewing Company in Lackawanna, New York, was the twelfth largest microbrewery and the forty-ninth largest of all national breweries, including the mega-brewers.

The copper brewhouse equipment was purchased from a defunct brewery in Weissman, Germany, in 1989. It was transported overseas and installed in a former roller-rink, south of Buffalo. The additional fermenters, conditioning tanks, bottling line, and kegging equipment, were pur-

chased separately from small breweries throughout the United States and Canada.

The gleaming copper brewkettle and mash tun can be seen from anywhere in the cavernous brewpub. The company has an annual capacity of 15,000 barrels and is currently producing 10,000 barrels per year in 50-barrel batches. The brewmaster is European-born Fred Lang, who has over 30 years of brewing experience.

At Buffalo Brewing Company they use centuries-old Bavarian brewing methods. All barley and wheat malts are shipped directly from Bavaria. The yeast strains have been developed and are maintained by the prestigious Weihenstephan Brewing Institute near Munich. All hop varieties are of German origin. The beer is filtered by microfiltration. This process removes all the bacteria and provides a shelf-life almost equivalent to that of pasteurization, without the loss of flavor that pasteurization can cause. The Buffalo Brewing Company voluntarily abides by the German Purity Law of 1516 (see page 23). The only allowable exception to the law is the wheat malt used to make wheat beer.

The range of brews made at BBC is rather extensive. There is Buffalo lager, Pils, weisse, altbier, and doppelbock; Limerick's Ale, Blizzard Bock, and for the harvest season Buffalo Oktoberfest. Buffalo Oktoberfest Lager Beer is brewed to coincide with the traditional Oktoberfest celebration in Munich. It is made with two-row malt as well as caramel malt to give it a full, rich flavor and mouthfeel, true to the Märzenbier style. The alcohol content is around 5.0 percent by volume.

The Abbott Square Brewpub is of German beer hall proportions. There is seating for 400 people, banquet facilities for 1,000 guests, and a bar long enough to accommodate 40 thirsty Buffalo Bills fans, who can watch games on two wide screen televisions. (The brewpub is located just three miles south of Rich Stadium.)

There are self-guided tours of the brewery at any time, and guided tours given at 2 PM every Saturday afternoon. Check out the food menu which includes pub grub, barbecue items, steaks, and more than 20 sausage and meat pies. There are also 15 European draught beers and miscellaneous national brand beers and microbrews served.

Catamount Brewing Company

Here's proof that the microbrewing industry has indeed arrived: the AAA Tour Guide lists the Catamount Brewing Company as a recommended tour in the state of Vermont.

The Catamount Brewery's location is a large part of the reason for their success.

The population of Vermont experiences seasonal swells due to tourism, and hundreds of tourists visit the brewery every month. The tour schedule has had to be expanded more than once. Originally, there were four tours given every week, then it was six, and now there are 14! These tours help spread the word about microbrewing and they sell a lot of beer that way: retail sales on the premises account for 10 percent of their business.

The Catamount Brewing Company's history began in 1985, when Alan Davis and Steve Mason put together a business plan for the new brewery. With that completed, the pair split up briefly. Mason, a homebrewer, traveled to England to learn how to brew traditional ales on a large scale. He spent four months at the Swannell Brewery in Hertfordshire, where he became acquainted with brewery design, equipment, and procedures. Davis, meanwhile, remained stateside, searching for model microbreweries from which to learn successful marketing techniques. Reunited, Davis and Mason worked feverishly to set

Bathtub Suds

I'm just a humble homebrewer,
I've got no shiny copper.
I only brew five gallons a batch —
I just boil 'er up and hop 'er.

No foil labels, no fancy caps,
just plain glass bottle and stopper.
I pay no tax, just brew and relax
then grab a beer and pop 'er!

— Marty Nachel

up their brewery in an old meat packing plant. After much trial and error, the team honed their skills and decided on a couple of favorite recipes. Brewmaster Mason's British-influenced technique and choice of quality ingredients are evident in the Catamount line of beers. Currently producing four brews, all are true to both English styles (see Beer Styles, pages 2–17) and the German Purity Law (see page 23). The four ingredients used in the brewing process are a select yeast strain, Midwestern malted barley, and high quality domestic hops, as well as the one ingredient believed to be critical to the flavor of their beer, the pure Vermont water.

Since its beginnings, Catamount has become one of the most prolific breweries in New England. Its consistent growth in annual output has been accompanied by a marketing strategy that diverges from conventional microbrewing wisdom in several respects, including a wholesaler-based distribution strategy and exploitation of out-of-state markets. Vermont is very rural and doesn't have the population base to support a brewery producing more than 2,000 to 3,000 barrels a year. About 50

CATAMOUNT
Christmas Ale
1990
Brewed and Bottled by Catamount Brewing Company
White River Junction, Vermont

percent of the brewery's production is sold in New Hampshire, Massachusetts, Connecticut, and upstate New York.

The beers brewed at Catamount, all of which are bottled, include Catamount Amber, Ethan Allen Ale (commemorating Vermont's bicentennial in 1991), the GABF gold medal winner, Catamount Gold, and Catamount Porter, which beer writer Michael Jackson pronounced "the best porter on the East Coast." This beer originally was brewed as a Christmas beer, but overwhelmingly positive reviews of the porter convinced Davis and Mason to make it a regular on their brewing schedule. The porter has since been replaced by a seasonal Christmas ale, unique in the fact that its recipe is slightly modified each year.

So what about the brewery's name, you ask? For a clue, take a look at the bottle labels and bottle caps. That menacing looking feline is an eastern cougar, one of the great cats that once thrived in the New England highlands. It has been considered extinct for decades, but occasional sightings are still reported. Officially known as "Cat-of-the-Mountain," its name became shortened to Catamount. Ponder the concept of endangered species and you'll better appreciate the connection between cat and brewery.

Commonwealth Brewing Company

In Boston, heritage and tradition are more than advertising hyperbole. They are woven into the fabric of the city. For long-established businesses, boasting of one's heritage and tradition has a ring of redundancy. For new establishments wishing to claim heritage and tradition, skepticism lurks near. But the Commonwealth Brewing Company, with its unique approach to the brewing of beer, has managed to keep the skeptics at bay.

Founded in 1986, the Commonwealth Brewing Company was not only one of the first brewpubs in the country, but also the oldest continuously operating brewery in the state of Massachusetts. The brewery was opened by an Englishman named Richard Wrigley and two partners. Their original concept for this brewery-restaurant included a line of British-style ales in the belief that Bostonians would hail this return to authenticity. Such was not the case. Many a thirsty patron was put off by a warm, dark, and flat beer. The owners sold their interests in the business by 1992.

The new owner and president, Joe Quattrocchi, and his wife, Lisa, have been working on the brewery since mid-1991. They have taken the brewery on a slightly different tack, and have been successful. They quickly added a couple of beers that closely resembled the mass market fare to which their customers were accustomed, and thus narrowly dodged a bullet.

Today, with the proliferation of microbrews and their widespread acceptance by the beer drinking public, the Commonwealth Brewing Company continues to produce the rich, flavorful, and traditional ales envisioned by the founder nearly a decade ago.

New head brewer, Tod Mott, and his assistant, Jim Migliorini, are making a genuine effort to brew seasonal specialty beers on a continual basis, in addition to the eight regular beers kept in the brewing rotation. An attractive earth-tone spectrum of brews awaits the beer lover upon each visit to the brewery. These include blonde ale, golden ale, golden export, Burton bitter, amber ale, Famous porter, and classic stout. The specialties include Imperial stout, I.P.A., Sullivan's Irish Red Ale, smoked dunkelweizen, Heartland wheat beer, nut brown ale, Big Stiche Alt, Joe Q's Uptown Export, 90 Schilling Ale, E.S.B., and, most recently, Wassail Solstice Winter Warmer.

Boston Burton Ale is a contract-brewed and bottled version of the very popular Burton Bitter. The name Burton is taken from the brewing town of Burton-on-Trent, England, famous for its legendary pale ales. This beer has received high praise as of late. *Boston* magazine named Boston Burton Ale the best beer in Boston, and, in another local publication, *The Improper Bostonian,* Boston Burton Ale was declared "best local brew." According to the brewer, this proud beer is the result of two-row pale malt (92 percent), crystal malt (7 percent), and black malt (1 percent). The hop varieties include Clusters for bittering and Kent goldings for the ale's aromatics. The yeast is a well-guarded, top-fermenting strain. The final product is filtered but not pasteurized. Current distribution is limited to the greater Boston area. Future plans include expanding the market to all of Massachusetts, and, eventually, to all of New England.

Those fortunate enough to visit the Commonwealth Brewing Company will find it well worth their while. The 200-seat restaurant is a veritable copper depository. In addition to the huge gleaming kettles, the copper-topped tables reflect warm, recessed lighting by night, and bright sunshine by day.

High-tech Brewing

The 1800s was the time of the great Industrial Revolution. This boom in industry brought many technological advancements that helped to improve the business of brewing beer. The invention of compressed gas refrigeration was a giant leap for brewing. Where aging beer used to be stored in caves or kept cool with ice cut from frozen lakes and rivers, the lagering process could now be carried out within the brewery's four walls and throughout the four seasons. About this time, a few of Europe's finest brewers were working together to produce a new strain of yeast capable of fermentation in low temperatures. Anton Dreher of Austria, Gabriel Sedlmeyer of Germany, and Emil Hansen from Denmark shared this success. It was Hansen who furthered the research done by Louis Pasteur and isolated the first single-cell yeast culture. From this early work in microscopy came the bottom-fermenting yeast called *saccaromyces carlsbergensis,* named after the Carlsberg Brewery in Copenhagen where Hansen did much of his work. This new style of beer was lighter in color and body, and mellower in flavor due to the length of the aging process. People seemed to prefer the new lager beer, and brewers were happy to oblige.

The Commonwealth Brewing Company offers very extensive menus for lunch, lunch buffet, and dinner. Many of the food selections incorporate their beer in the recipes. Of the myriad choices available, the C.B.C. prize-winning barbecue ribs are a perennial favorite. These ribs took a $10,000 prize during a recent Great Yankee Rib Cook-off.

D.L. Geary Brewing Company

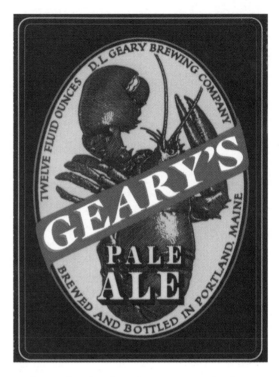

In January, 1992, Beer Across America — "Beer of the Month Club" launched its inaugural shipment of microbrewed beer to a small but enthusiastic membership. That shipment included a six-pack of Geary's Pale Ale. It was important to "come out of the gate" quickly and convincingly, and Geary's played a big part.

The D.L. Geary Brewing Company has not only contributed to the success of Beer Across America, but also to that of the American microbrewing community, in general. This Portland, Maine, brewery has been at the forefront of the movement toward fresh, flavorful, locally made beer. According to David Geary, "The United States was ready for a beer with a bite and I was anxious to offer one." When the brewery opened in 1984, there were about 20 microbreweries operating in the United States, the majority of them in California and the Pacific Northwest.

David Geary is a former medical supplies sales executive, who had no experience in the production of beer. After incorporating, he set off on a winter-long apprenticeship at breweries in Scotland and England. This learning method prepared him for the massive undertaking that lay before him. Meanwhile, his wife and business partner, Karen (to whom Geary attributes much of the brewery's success), remained stateside, setting up the framework of the business by collecting information, writing letters, and doing research.

Geary's first apprenticeship was at the Traquair House in Peebleshire, Scotland, an historic residence dating back to the 1500s that is still owned and inhabited by descendants of the original family. Geary had an invitation from Peter Maxwell Stuart, the Laird of Traquair and descendant of Scottish royalty, to help brew the rare Traquair House Ale on the grounds of the family manor. Laird Stuart also set up an itinerary for Geary to apprentice at half a dozen other breweries in the United Kingdom. In addition to this hands-on education, Geary also did a lot of "research" at local pubs, eating and drinking the local fare. One thing David Geary learned above all else was that he could not possibly learn enough in one season abroad to venture out on his own and survive. He decided that a formally trained and experienced brewmaster was needed to help start the new brewery. Fortunately, Geary met such a man in Alan Pugsley (see page 178), a tremendously talented brewer who was interested in joining the venture. An English fabricator, Peter Austin, was contracted to manufacture the brewing equipment, and New England's first microbrewery was under way. The first sale of Geary's Pale Ale took place on December 10, 1986.

In the years since then, Geary's has grown both in size and reputation. Geary's Ale is now sold in 15 states, and the Geary Brewing Company is recognized as a pioneer in America's brewing renaissance, and a model of quality and excellence for the industry.

Due to its growing popularity, expansion has become a necessity. Extra capacity is needed to keep pace with sales, which have been growing at a 30 percent annual rate. The new, 50-barrel brewing system will increase annual output to 25,000 barrels, which is up from the previous production of 10,000 barrels a year.

Since day one, David Geary has believed that making and marketing a single product and building a reputation on the quality and consistency of that product is paramount to success. His pale ale is such a product. This classic British pale ale emulates the legendary beers of Burton-on-Trent in England. The pale is copper-colored, clean, and crisp, with lots of late hop flavor blending with the complex ale fruitiness. It is made from English two-row pale malt, crystal malt, and chocolate malt. The hop bill includes Cascade, Hallertau, Tettnang, and Fuggle hops.

Building on the pale ale's established reputation, Geary finally introduced the brewery's second product: Hampshire Special Ale, a seasonal specialty brew only available from November to April. This high-gravity beer has a huge toasted malt flavor balanced by an assertive hoppiness. The finish, or aftertaste, is long and lingering, with the characteristic warmth of the winter warmer style, which is a high gravity beer with higher alcohol content. This gem is also made from two-row English malts and hopped with Cascades, Mt. Hoods, and East Kent golding hops.

Dock Street Brewing Company

The Dock Street Brewing Company is not only a prime example of American entrepreneurial success, but also the consummate American microbrewery and a good role model for the industry. What began nine years ago as a contract brewing organization (see page 201) is now a full-fledged microbrewing and brewpub operation.

Brewery president Jeff Ware, a graduate of Villanova and the Philadelphia College of Art, was involved in the restaurant industry as a chef and manager for several years prior to the 1986 founding of Dock Street. The only prod-

Alcohol Content of Beer

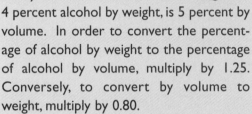

Alcohol content is based on the amount of fermentable sugars in the brew. This is called the *gravity*. Gravity is measured twice — once before the beer is fermented, and then again after fermentation. Subtracting the final reading from the initial reading reveals how much of the fermentable sugars were consumed. These consumed sugars were turned to alcohol by the yeast during the fermentation process, and, based on established measurements, alcohol content can be very accurately calculated.

Alcohol content in beer is a very confusing subject. To begin with, the federal government does not allow brewers to list alcohol content on product packaging, on the premise that beer drinkers will buy beer solely on that basis. Second, there are two methods by which alcohol content in beer is expressed, by weight or by volume. Since alcohol is lighter than the beer in which it exists, the content expressed by weight appears lower, compared to content expressed by volume. For example: a beer that is 3.2 percent alcohol by weight, is 4 percent alcohol by volume; a beer that is 4 percent alcohol by weight, is 5 percent by volume. In order to convert the percentage of alcohol by weight to the percentage of alcohol by volume, multiply by 1.25. Conversely, to convert by volume to weight, multiply by 0.80.

Further confusion is added by the dual scales by which alcohol content is measured. The two scales are the British *specific gravity* scale and the European *degrees Plato* scale. Both are used by American brewers and both are based on the concept that water, at 60°F (15°C), has a specific gravity of 1.000, or is 0° Plato. As sugars are added to the water (as is done during the mashing process), the density of the water will increase. For example: an average American light beer might have a gravity in the neighborhood of 1.034, and German doppelbock might have a gravity of 1.065. These same beers would have den-

uct initially available was Dock Street amber beer. This top-fermented ale is traditionally brewed with two-row pale and caramel malts. Cascade hops are used for bittering and for the "dry-hopped" aromatics that create the big hop nose (see glossary). The beer is fairly complex, with a decidedly fruity character. Medium-bodied and well-balanced, Dock Street Amber was voted one of America's top five beers at the Great American Beer Festival in 1986 and 1987. It has also been awarded gold medals from Monde Selection (Paris, 1994; Brussels, 1993; and Amsterdam, 1992), from the Institut International Pour Selections de la Qualité, as well as the Intitut's International High Quality Trophy in 1994.

As the perfect complement to Dock Street Amber beer, Dock Street Bohemian Pilsner was introduced in 1992. (Bohemia is on the western end of the present-day Czech Republic and is home to the original Pilsner beer.) Even the packaging of the two beers is designed to complement one another. Featured on the Pilsner six-pack carton is a female sailor — the perfect partner for the male sailor on the amber beer container. The Bohemian Pilsner is

sities of 7.5° Plato and 16.5° Plato, respectively. These are the values of the unfermented beer, and brewers often include them in their advertising or list them on their menus to give knowledgeable consumers an idea of how "big" the beer is.

There is also the problem of preconceived notions on the part of the consumer. Beers that are dark are thought to be heavier and stronger than pale beers. Ales, for whatever reason, are also expected to be thicker and more alcoholic than lagers. While there are certainly prime examples to back up these common conceptions, there are plenty of other examples to dispute them. For every dark and strong ale, there is a pale and strong lager. At the end of this box is a list of several beer styles and their approximate alcohol content by volume.

After all is said and done, alcohol content is not and should not be a measure of the quality of the beer. What is more important is to enjoy all beer — responsibly.

Beer Type	% of Alcohol
Berliner weisse	2.5–3.5
bitter	3.0–3.5
stout	3.5–5.0
California common (steam)	3.5–5.0
brown ale	4.0–5.5
Pilsner	4.0–5.0
altbier/Kölsch	4.5–5.0
Munich helles/dunkel	4.5–5.5
pale ale	4.5–5.5
weizenbier	4.5–5.5
Oktoberfest/Märzen	4.5–6.0
porter	5.0–6.5
bock	6.0–7.5
Scotch ale	6.0–8.0
Trappist ale	6.0–10.5
doppelbock	6.5–8.0
Russian Imperial stout	7.0–9.0
barleywine	8.5–12.0

made in the classic Pilsner style in its use of the delicate and expensive Saaz variety of hop from the Zatec region in Bohemia.

While about 95 percent of all the beer made in the United States is roughly in the Pilsner style, very few legitimate Pilsner beers are brewed and bottled by microbreweries. In comparison to the large industrial breweries that churn out millions of gallons of pseudo-Pilsner every four to six weeks, The Dock Street brewery takes two months to craft their Bohemian Pilsner. One key to crafting this beer is the specially purified water that emulates the very soft water (devoid of

minerals) pumped from the wells near the old Plzen brewery. Since its introduction, Dock Street Bohemian Pilsner has been awarded the gold medal at the Celebrate Annapolis Wine, Beer, Food, and Music Festival in 1992. Certainly, more awards are yet to come.

In 1994, Dock Street proudly announced the release of its first seasonal beer, Illuminator Bock, which is brewed in the style that originated in the northern German town of Einbeck. Available only in the spring and summer, it is, however, included in the Dock Street Holiday Pack sampler for November and December.

In the fall of 1990, Jeff Ware, buoyed by the success of Dock Street Amber Beer, opened the new Dock Street Brewing Company and Restaurant in downtown Philadelphia. It is an imposing space of cherry wood, polished copper brewkettles, monumental columns, and Spanish terra cotta tiles — all patterned after the great beer halls and brewhouses of Europe. The facility cost an incredible $2.2 million to build. There are tentative plans to open several more throughout the mid-Atlantic region, the first to be in Washington, D.C., at the Warner Theatre Building.

The Dock Street Brewing Company and Restaurant in Philadelphia is billed as "A Thoroughly Polished Pub," and offers a menu inspired by the classic foods of Belgium, France, England, Germany, and other countries with a rich brewing heritage. They are open for lunch, dinner, and late night. Of course, there is always a great selection of Dock Street beers brewed on the premises, including stouts, wheat beers, fruit beers, bocks, and more. Don't forget to ask for a brewery tour.

Kennebunkport Brewing Company

This Maine attraction comes from the town of Kennebunk, but calls itself the Kennebunkport Brewing Company. Fair enough, seeing as how the brewery is just across the river from Kennebunkport (famous as the summer retreat of President George Bush). Actually, the locals refer to this area along the river as "T'aint Town," because "T'aint Kennebunk and t'aint Kennebunkport!"

The brewing operations began here in June, 1992. The brewhouse is a Peter Austin-designed system and was installed by the ubiquitous Alan Pugsley, who is responsible for setting up as many as 80 small breweries worldwide, at least a dozen of which are in the United States. The British ale system typically includes brick-jacketed kettles, trademarked hop percolators, open fermentation tanks, and wooden casks. Each system is manufactured to individual specifications, to suit the needs of each brewpub or microbrewery.

At the Kennebunkport Brewing Company, brewmaster Pugsley has an able assistant in Paul Hendry. Together they perform a sort of tag-team brewing effort, since the current demand for their beer requires them to brew twice a day.

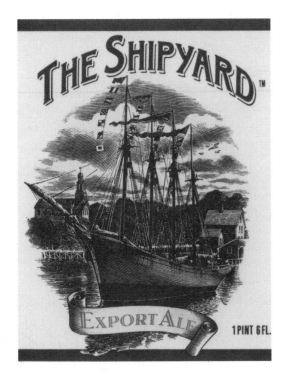

Pugsley usually starts his day at 4 A.M. By two in the afternoon, Alan finishes brew number one and Paul Hendry arrives to start the second brew, which keeps him going until past midnight.

Currently, there are five regular brews produced at Kennebunkport Brewing Company — Goat Island Light, T'aint Town Pale Ale, Brown Moose Ale, Blue Fin Stout, the flagship beer, and The Shipyard Export Ale. The Shipyard is presently available on draught in more than 100 restaurants in Maine, and can also be found in 12- and 20-ounce bottles in Maine, New Hampshire, Rhode Island, and selected areas of Massachusetts. There also are five seasonal beers: winter ale, Prelude Ale, Captain Eli's Kennebunk Porter, India pale ale, and a wheat beer. All are brewed according to traditional English brewing practices and are handcrafted from start to finish. All ingredients are

traditional, as well, right down to the top-fermenting ale yeast that originates from a strain cultured at the Ringwood Brewery 120 years ago.

Due to consumer demand, which exceeded all expectations, a second brewery has been built to serve the New England marketplace. The Shipyard Brewery is located in Portland and has a capacity of 17,000 barrels, brewed 50 barrels at a time. The same products will be brewed at both locations, but The Shipyard Brewery will be only for bottling and kegging. Unlike the Kennebunkport Brewing Company, there are no sales of beer on the premises.

The Kennebunkport Brewery shares its billing and its ales with Federal Jack's Brew Pub, at the same picturesque location along the river. Decorated in nautical and historical themes, Federal Jack's offers a full lunch and dinner menu replete with the fresh seafood for which the Maine coast is famous.

Mass. Bay Brewing Company

Adams, Revere, Attucks, Yaztremski, Bird, Doyle — all names synonymous with the city of Boston. These statesmen, revolutionaries, sports legends, and brewers have all helped to put Beantown on the map in their respective fields. But let's put aside the history books and stat sheets for a while and focus on the beer.

Though countless breweries have come and gone since the arrival of the Mayflower, one in particular harkens back

Cleaning Your Glassware

No matter which beer goes in which glass, one thing is a given: it is imperative that beer glassware be scrupulously clean. Otherwise, the beer can be affected adversely, and any efforts expended in the name of good presentation will have been for naught. The proper cleansing of beer glassware should not include any soaps or detergents that are oil-based or contain fat. The best cleansing agent is one that is unscented and contains tri-sodium phosphate. Always follow with a good hot rinse, and remember to store beer glasses upside down to keep out dust.

to Colonial times in early America, when wonderfully diverse and localized ales flourished in the new land. These hand-crafted beers were made in small batches, using the finest ingredients available. And so it is today at the Mass. Bay Brewing Company, located on Boston's waterfront. This revolutionary New England micro-brewery was established in 1987 by three young graduates with masters' degrees in business administration. Rich Doyle and George Ligeti from Harvard teamed up with Dan Kenary from the University of Chicago. The concept was conceived dur-ing a field study for a school project, the intent of which was to examine the prospects for a new brewing company. Rich Doyle dutifully executed his research at local taverns and dance clubs. Along with George Ligeti, he then traveled to the Pacific Northwest to soak in the secrets of success at the local boutique breweries. The study ultimately received a top grade, and the seeds for the Mass. Bay Brewing Company were sown.

The brewery occupies a former ship-building facility on Pier 7 in South Boston. Once a location was found, man-ufacturing problems quickly befell the budding brewers. The three partners, all of whom passed up lucrative careers in banking, now found themselves working 16-hour days and 60-hour weeks in order to attain their goal. For all their toil, they eked out meager salaries — under $20,000 each. Hard work begets hard currency, though. Just three years later, they were selling $125,000 worth of beer in five northeastern states. Between 1989 and 1990, the brewery experienced a 60 percent growth rate, producing over 4,000 barrels annually. This figure placed them in the twenty-first position among the 85 microbreweries listed by the *New Brewer* magazine in 1991. They are currently producing more than 24,000 barrels a year.

The stable of beers offered by the Mass. Bay Brewing Company is as follows: Harpoon Ale (a gold medal winner at the 1991 Great American Beer Festival), Harpoon Golden Lager, Harpoon Light, Harpoon Dark, and Harpoon India Pale Ale. There are also four seasonal beers, a stout, an Oktoberfest, a spiced winter warmer, and a new brew to be named later. (The India pale ale used to be a seasonal beer, but its popularity forced the brewers to brew it year-round.) Availability of the Harpoon beers is limited to a total of 13 New England and mid-Atlantic states, from Maine to Virginia.

One-hour tours of the brewery are given every Friday and Saturday, with no reservations required. Brewery souvenirs — T-shirts, polo shirts, sweatshirts, and more — are sold at the brewing facility, or you can call or write for a free catalogue.

The Mass. Bay brewery sponsors quarterly beer fests which spotlight each of the four seasonal beers as they are produced. These fests have attracted as many as 10,000 thirsty beer fans. The brewery also has introduced a unique way to allow neophyte beer drinkers to get acquainted with the Harpoon beers and other beer drinkers. The Harpoon 5:30 Club invites groups (minimum of 15, maximum of 80) to meet at the brewery on Tuesday, Wednesday, or Thursday evenings, to network, meet friends, and just have fun. There are more than 600

groups that have participated in this service, which offers a complete brewery tour in a relaxed, party-like atmosphere.

Keep a lookout for the Harpoon Shuttle, a brewery van offering free transportation to any patron who is unable to safely operate his or her vehicle due to over-consumption.

Old Dominion Brewing Company

"Don't drink more — drink better." So goes the slogan of the Old Dominion Brewing Company. Of course, this Virginia-based microbrewery wants you to know that *their* beer is the better beer.

The Old Dominion Brewing Company, serving our nation's capital, was established in 1989 to satisfy the tastes of beer enthusiasts on the Washington, DC metropolitan area. Dedicated to producing fresh, flavorful, full-bodied beers, they

The Foods of Eastern Europe

The cuisines of the countries from the "beer belt" of the north don't just go well with beer, they were built around it. Slavic, Czech, and Germanic foods have a natural affinity for beer. Strong, aged cheeses, pork, chicken, coarse breads, and the best of the wursts need no coaxing to find a dinner partner. Try the venerable alt-bier with sharp cheese, a malty Maibock with barbecued white meats, Munich dunkel with pumpernickel and rye, and a round, malty Oktoberfest with most sausages. For the true epicure: a Bamberger rauchbier with smoked ham or smoked sausage — pure delight!

offer not only a high quality product, but also a variety of styles.

Currently, the brewery produces 16 beers and one soft drink. These include Dominion Helles, Dominion Ale, Dominion Lager, Victory Amber Lager, Virginia Native Brite, and Tupper's Hop Pocket Ale, which is brewed exclusively for Bob and Ellie Tupper. Hard Times Select is brewed exclusively for the Hard Times Cafes throughout Virginia, as Blue Point Ale is brewed exclusively for Sutton Place Gourmet stores and the Sutton Place Cafe. There is also St. George Beer, Old Dubliner Ale, Aviator Amber Lager, and five different seasonal beers: bock, wheat, Oktoberfest, and a holiday ale in the winter. Dominion Root Beer is made from a variety of exotic ingredients including sassafras, wintergreen, honey, and yucca. The recipe for the root beer was an old, authentic recipe found in the Library of Congress and eventually perfected through many test batches.

The highly acclaimed Dominion Stout is brewed in the tradition of original Irish style stout. Two-row pale malt, chocolate, and caramel malt, wheat, and roasted barley are all included on the grain bill.

The bittering hops are cluster and Willamette, from the premier hop growing region in the United States, the Yakima Valley in Washington State. The yeast is a top-fermenting (ale) strain. The alcohol content is a medium range, 4.7 percent by volume. To fully enjoy this stout's rich chocolate/coffee character, serving it warm (50°F [10°C]) is recommended.

According to brewery president Jerry Bailey, all of the beers produced at the Old Dominion Brewing Company are made in accordance with the Reinheitsgebot (see page 23). No adjuncts or preservatives are used, and the beer is never pasteurized. The addition of a new, German-made Krones bottling machine in 1991 has improved the beer's shelf life. The machine ensures precise fill levels and a beer that is virtually oxygen-free, which is advantageous because beer (and wine, too) is especially susceptible to the changes in flavor that come about due to oxidation. Although the beer does not have to be refrigerated, it is recommended that you do so to maintain optimum freshness. In addition, all bottle labels are date-stamped, so customers can be sure they are getting the freshest product possible.

On December 23, 1993, Old Dominion brewed its one-thousandth batch of beer. To commemorate this milestone, Dominion Millenium Ale was offered on a limited basis. Dominion Millenium is a very strong ale, in the barleywine style. This beer is bottle-conditioned and has an alcohol content of 10 percent by volume. It has since become the fifth specialty beer.

If you happen to be near the District of Columbia, the Old Dominion Brewing Company conducts regularly scheduled tours of their brewing facility. These tours are offered every Saturday afternoon, and groups of 15 or more should contact the brewery in advance. Souvenir beer glasses, bottle openers, T-shirts, and sweatshirts are all for sale at the brewery hospitality suite.

Pennsylvania Brewing Company

This scenario has been played out thousands of times before: An American visits a distant land, tastes the local beer, and, upon his return to the United States, finds himself longing for that great beer taste that is now just a fond memory. For Tom Pastorius, that longing was strong enough to drive him into starting his own brewing company.

For 12 years, Pastorius and his wife, Marybeth, lived in Germany and enjoyed all the native brews. One in particular, erbacher, brewed near Heidelberg, was the object of Tom's longing; so much so that this Pittsburgh couple dedicated themselves to reproducing that beer here in the United States. It started with the

founding of the Pennsylvania Brewing Company in 1986. With the help of Dr. Joe Owades at the Institute for Brewing Studies in San Francisco, the recipe for Penn Pilsner was created. The original product was brewed and bottled at the Pittsburgh Brewing Company in Pittsburgh, and was later contracted to the Jones Brewing Company in Smithton, Pennsylvania, where it is still made.

Not satisfied with brewing just one beer, Tom Pastorius set out to open his own Pittsburgh area brewpub. First he put together a real estate partnership to acquire and restore a nineteenth century German brewing complex in the historic section of Pittsburgh's north side. A four-million-dollar restoration was required to transform the condemned buildings into a showpiece of economic revitalization. In addition to the brewery, the complex provides offices for a number of other companies as part of a business incubator program. With the restoration underway, Pastorius returned to Germany to purchase brewing equipment and to find a brewmaster for the new brewery. His

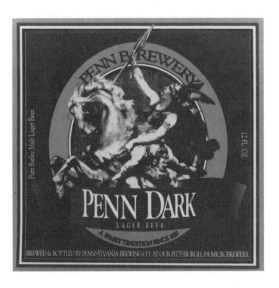

choice was Alexander Deml, a top graduate of the Weihenstephan, the world's most prestigious brewing school. The equipment — 30 hectolitre brewing kettles are solid copper — was hand-fabricated by Jacob Carl of Goeppingen.

Brewing at the new Allegheny Brewery & Restaurant began in 1989. The adjoining beer hall restaurant opened later that year. There are ten varieties of authentic, German-style beer (see Beer Styles, pages 2–17) being brewed and sold in draught form. In addition to Penn Pilsner, Penn Light Lager, Penn Dark, and kaiser are brewed all year. Seasonal specialties include an Oktoberfest, bock, Märzen, altbier, weizen, and weizenbock. After operating at capacity for two years, an ambitious expansion of the brewery and restaurant was completed this year. A second lager cellar with nine 1,600-gallon tanks tripled the brewery capacity, and the new Ratskeller party room provides additional seating for the overflow of customers who fill the restaurant and outdoor biergarten every weekend.

The former Eberhardt & Ober Brewery buildings, which have stood on this site since 1883, are now listed in the National Register of Historic Places and are sparking a revitalization in their Deutschland neighborhood. While the Pennsylvania Brewing Company made history as the first microbrewery in the state, the Allegheny Brewery is the first "tied house" (brewery-owned restaurant) in the state since Prohibition. This was made possible only after a special act of the legislature on their behalf. A note regarding the Allegheny name: the Deutschtown area, where the brewpub is located, is in what used to be the city of Allegheny until its larger, more aggressive sister city across the river forced a merger in 1907.

Now back to the beer. Although the Pennsylvania Brewing Company was founded to brew the award-winning Penn Pilsner, critical acclaim has spread to the other brews at the Allegheny Brewery. All of the beers are brewed in accordance with the Reinheitsgebot of 1516 (see page 23). A six-week lagering process is believed to be the key to the quality of Penn Pilsner. Ingredients include German hallertau hops, a blend of two-row barley, and roasted malts. The beer also is brewed in small batches to ensure freshness. It has been tested at the Weihenstephan Institute at the University of Munich and awarded certification for sale in Germany. If a beer-rich nation like Germany imports Penn Pilsner to its shores, it must be of value here at home.

Weeping Radish

It all started on a quiet island on the North Carolina coast. This area long has been a destination for vacationers from all over the United States and other points on the globe. The Outer Banks is home to Cape Hatteras and Cape Lookout National Seashore, with their abundance of wildlife, picturesque lighthouses, and seascapes. Nags Head Beach is popular among sun worshippers, and Kill Devil Hills, the site of man's first recorded flight, is just up the road. Roanoke Island was the location of Sir Walter Raleigh's ill-fated Lost Colony, now a national historic site, as is the Wright Brothers Memorial at Kitty Hawk.

In 1980, Uli Bennewitz first came from Germany to the Carolina coast. He was no tourist, however. He came to manage a 20,000-acre corn and bean farm near Manteo. He was a recent graduate of the Seale Hayne Agricultural College in Devonshire, England. The son of a Bavarian import-export agent, Bennewitz recognized the potential of a German-style brewery and restaurant on Roanoke Island. By 1986, Bennewitz and his wife, Eileen, opened the Weeping Radish Restaurant and Brewery, one of the first brewpubs in the eastern United States.

The Weeping Radish takes its name from the large, white, German radish that is typically served as an accompaniment to beer at Bavarian bierskellers and inns. It resembles an American turnip in appearance, and has a sharp flavor reminiscent of horseradish. The root is thinly sliced, lightly salted, and put back together. The salt draws out the moisture and gives the appearance that the radish is weeping. Eating this makes one thirsty, which is the whole idea of serving it with beer.

The establishment's early years were lean due to lack of advertising, but, with each year that passed, the Weeping Radish gained a reputation for good food and great beer. The key was in creating a family atmosphere. Since it is located in a tourist area, it was necessary to accommodate not just adults, but adults who were also parents — children always have been welcome here. The Weeping Radish has added a Springfest to its calendar, along with the traditional Oktoberfest in the fall. For these special occasions, they bring in a German oompah band, plenty of family entertainment, and plenty of beer. When

weather permits, events are held outside in the beer garden, with plenty of room for the kids to play and the adults to dance.

Because of its increased popularity, Bennewitz has had to expand the brewery to meet the demand for his beer. The old five-barrel system has been replaced with a new 15-barrel system, and a second brewery has been opened in Durham. Current production is about 1,500 barrels a year, most of which is consumed at the restaurant. There is also on-site sale of one-liter refillable bottles and five-liter mini-kegs. Additional 22-ounce bottles allow for minimal distribution throughout North Carolina and to the Washington, D.C./northern Virginia area.

There are three basic lager styles produced by the Weeping Radish: the helles is a light, but not low-calorie beer; the fest bier is an amber beer; and the Black Radish is in the dunkel (Bavarian dark) style. There are also four seasonal brews: Maibock in the spring, a weiss (sheat beer) in the summer, an Oktoberfest in the fall, and a dark and rich doppelbock, which is their Christmas beer.

Along with the Christmas beer, they also have released their first gift catalog of German beer steins, Weeping Radish memorabilia, and membership in the Weeping Radish Beer Club. You can call the 800 number or visit anytime. The restaurant and brewery are open seven days a week. They used to close for the holidays, but Bennewitz says they are now going to "bite the bullet" and stay open year-round. The brewery offers daily tours that conclude with free product sampling.

Wild Goose Brewing Company

In Cambridge, Maryland, hard by the shores of Chesapeake Bay, a small brewery first fired up its brewkettle in October, 1989. It began operation in the old 7,000-square-foot Phillips Packing plant, in an industrial park, away from the glare of the city lights.

The brewhouse is of British design, with a 25-barrel brewlength. Originally equipped to produce under 8,000 barrels per year, the Wild Goose Brewery is now running at peak production of 11,500 barrels per annum, and the operation is one of the top 30 microbreweries in the country. The Wild Goose brews with the finest English two-row malted barley, hops from the Yakima Valley in Washington State, and a rare Ringwood (England) ale yeast that, when combined, create fresh, rich, and tasty beers.

The first beer introduced by this brewery was the flagship Wild Goose Amber

Beer, a medium-bodied English-style pale ale. Following this debut came the premier Thomas Point Golden Ale, a classic English-style ale. This beer was named originally for the last manned screwpile lighthouse on Chesapeake Bay, but eventually it was simplified to Wild Goose Golden Ale to avoid any confusion. In time, the brewery's reputation earned it the privilege of brewing one-of-a-kind signature beers for some of Maryland's preeminent taverns. Among these brews are Blue Dog Ale for Fager's Island, Oliver's Ale for the Wharf Rat, and Samuel Middleton's Pale Ale for Middleton's Tavern.

Having firmly established a reputation as a brewer of high quality standard ales, the Wild Goose then turned its attention to producing seasonal and specialty beers. Snow Goose Winter Ale was rolled out in late 1992, Wild Goose Spring Wheat Ale in early 1993, and Wild Goose Porter made its first appearance in late 1993. The porter has since become one of the regular beers, and an India pale ale also has been added to the rotation. Within a year, the Maryland microbrewery reached its milestone five hundredth brew.

Now that the production potential has been pushed to the limit and the brewery is selling every drop of beer it produces, a recent expansion project will allow for a 40 percent increase in output this year. One reason for the dramatic increase, according to one brewery representative, is that the seasonal beers account for increased awareness of the regular beers. A consumer's curiosity about a particular specialty product could lead him or her to try the amber or the golden. An enlarged distribution area also has created a sales surge for the brewery. The core market for Wild Goose products is the mid-Atlantic states that border Maryland, but the distinctive labels can be spotted as far north as Massachusetts and as far south as South Carolina, in a total of 14 states, including Illinois, Minnesota, and Colorado. Now that's a Wild Goose chase one can appreciate!

The Wild Goose Brewing Company hosts four beer tastings every month and an annual beerfest. Free brewery tours, including product sampling, are given throughout the week. A nice line of breweriana, including T-shirts, polo shirts, rugby shirts, hats, and bumper stickers, is available for purchase at the gift shop.

Atlantic Region Brewer Profiles

Alan Pugsley

His motto is "How's the beer?" That's appropriate for Alan Pugsley — a designer and brewer of great beer — and he has a proven track record in scores of small breweries all over the world. His motto represents the consumer's perspective of any brewing operation, large or small: making good beer is what it's all about.

Alan Pugsley has been making good beer for over a decade. Shortly after he graduated from England's Manchester University in 1981, he pursued a career in science education. Within one short year, however, Pugsley's attention was drawn from teaching to brewing, putting his biochemistry degree to good use at the famed Ringwood Brewery. Ringwood was owned by Peter Austin, a staunch believer in small-batch brewing and cask-conditioned ales. With the support of CamRA (Campaign for Real Ale), Austin began opening small breweries throughout the United Kingdom. Thanks to Peter Austin and those of like mind, the British craft brewing industry has increased a hundredfold since 1981. Pugsley played a big part in this expansion, as a virtual ambassador

of ale, opening many small breweries across the globe.

In 1985, Pugsley launched a consulting business while continuing to work with Austin. His travels brought him to Canada and the United States with greater frequency as the North American microbrewing movement gained momentum. In 1990, Pugsley became the majority owner of Peter Austin & Partners, Ltd., which has now opened more than 80 breweries. The company, which subcontracts the manufacture of its brewing equipment, sells and services a variety of systems according to the customers' needs. These systems are based on simplicity: they are easy to operate and to clean. In addition to providing brewing equipment, Peter Austin & Partners can help prospective brewers choose brewery locations, design the installation, and even obtain the necessary licensing at the state and federal levels. The company will design individual beer recipes, and it can train novice brewers at one of its brewery start-ups in Maine.

Drawing on his vast knowledge and experience, Alan Pugsley has participated in the development of several patents for small brewing operations. Heating systems, specialized whirlpools, and a hop "percolator" are among the unique ideas that Alan has devised.

Pugsley's influence has been unmistakeably felt here in the United States. He has been instrumental in setting up more than a few microbrewery and brewpub operations. His credits include the D.L. Geary Brewing Company, The Kennebunkport Brewing Company, and Gritty McDuff's in Maine; the Wild Goose Brewing Company in Maryland; and the Arrowhead Brewing Co. in Pennsylvania.

Based on Alan Pugsley's view of the American microbrewing revolution, the best is yet to come. Growth of the craft-brewing industry should continue well into the next millenium, and that's from one who knows good beer.

Alan Eames

The immense importance of a pint of ale to a common person should never be overlooked."
— Canon of St. Paul's Cathedral, eighteenth century.
(From A Beer Drinker's Companion by Alan Eames)

He has been called the Indiana Jones of beer for his relentless continent-hopping pursuit of good beer. He has also been called the Beer King because he is the reigning know-it-all of beer. Alan D. Eames is well known in beer and brewing circles, not for his brewing prowess, but for his tireless research of beer history, his knowledge of ancient brewing practices, and his prolific writings on these subjects. Alan has a degree in cultural anthropology that, when combined with his love of beer, provides the impetus to risk life and limb in order to exhume the secrets of our beer past.

Eames' appreciation of the malted beverage was evident as far back as 1974, when he opened a country store in the backwoods of Massachusetts. There, he stocked hundreds of bottled beers from exotic locations around the world. In 1983, he introduced Portland, Maine, to an outstanding selection of draught beers at his nationally recognized tavern, Three Dollar Dewey's, which was located a couple of blocks from the waterfront. Brattleboro, Vermont, became the home for the second Dewey's, as it had for the Eames family in 1986. That same year Alan published his first book, *A Beer Drinker's Companion*, a collection of more than 400 quotations spanning 5,000 years of mankind's relationship with beer. Because he is a veritable encyclopedia of beer, Eames has been appointed historical consultant for *All About Beer* magazine, to which he submits regular articles on such diverse subjects as *chicha* (maize beer) in South America, and beer gods and related dieties. His latest book, *Secret Life of Beer* (Storey Publishing, 1995), details the history, poetry, songs, and literature of beer.

When not busy writing, Eames has conducted various seminars on beer and brewing at the prestigious Culinary Institute of America in New York. He also spends better than half the year on the road, traveling to breweries, restaurants, and beer festivals to record the renaissance of the American brewing industry.

In recognition of his dedication to beer, Eames was recently named director of the American Museum of Brewing History and Arts, located at the Oldenberg Brewery and Entertainment Complex in Ft. Mitchell, Kentucky. It houses the world's greatest collection of American brewery antiques and collectibles. Eames is also becoming somewhat of a media darling with the increased popularity of the microbrewing movement. His numerous television appearances include two tête-a-têtes with Bryant Gumbel on the *Today Show*.

Carol Stoudt

Carol Stoudt. This could be the perfect name for someone in the brewing business. But forget the images of hearty, Irish black beer. The spelling is pure German, and so is its owner.

Carol Stoudt's German heritage is obvious to visitors at the Stoudt Brewing Company in Adamstown, Pennsylvania. This southeastern area of the state was settled by German immigrants in the 1700s, and Stoudt's ancestors were among them. A family tree decorating a wall in the *biergarten* can attest to that fact. A better testimony than the family tree, though, is Carol Stoudt's German-style beers. *Her* beers. *She* brews them.

It was not an easy transition from school teacher to brewmaster, nor was it a short one. Carol has a master's degree in education, but, between teaching and raising children (she has five of her own), she was eager for a new challenge.

There were, indeed, challenges to opening up a brewery. One of them forced Carol and her husband, Ed, to separate — legally speaking — on behalf of the business. Pennsylvania law prohibits brewers from distributing their own beers. Ed owns and operates the family's Black Angus Restaurant, and it was his idea to open a brewery at the same location. Because of state law, Ed could neither own nor direct the new brewery. Furthermore, because Ed could not participate financially in the brewery, the Stoudts had to separate their finances, as well.

These legal inconveniences were an aggravation, but not nearly as frustrating as the sexist barriers set in place by male egos in the industry. As one woman in a male-dominated business, Carol was faced with stereotypes daily. She says that the beer industry still espouses a "belly up to the bar" attitude, where beer drinking women often elicit negative responses from men. Despite the disrespect she has been shown, Stoudt recognizes that both men and women should be educated about fine beer, and she has not been discouraged from marketing her beers with pride. "It helps to have a sense of humor, and to be tall," she says with a smile.

After she visited many European breweries, took brewing classes, and apprenticed at a New Orleans brewery, Carol eventually purchased her brewhouse and trained with a consultant/brewmaster. Since the brewery's opening in 1987, production has increased from an output of 650 barrels to one of 5,000, within seven years. In addition to all the positive reviews of the Stoudt lineup of beers, over the years Carol's efforts have received an impressive collection of 15 medals at the Great American Beer Festival, including a gold, a silver, and a bronze, all in 1994.

While professional achievement is rewarding, Carol Stoudt believes that her work also provides an important lesson for her children. "They can see that a person, a woman, can do anything that interests her or him. . . ."

Atlantic Region Beer Festivals

Boston Brewers Festival
Boston, MA
May (2nd week)
(617) 547-2233

More than 10,000 people attend this festival annually, and more than 50 breweries particpate. The Boston Brewers Festival provides a wide range of Canadian and American micro and specialty brews. Rollouts of new and hard-to-find brews are commonplace. The event is held at Boston's World Trade Center.

Great Eastern Invitational Microbrewers Festival
Adamstown, PA
June (3rd week)
(717) 484-4386

This premier weekend festival is held at Stoudt Brewery/Black Angus Hall. It showcases beers produced in the eastern United States. More than 50 specialty beers are available. Tasting sessions are held twice a day in order to accommodate the large number of participants. There is great food to eat at the adjacent Black Angus Restaurant. Tickets sell out fast!

Great New England Brewers Festival
Northhampton, MA
July (3rd week)
(413) 584-9903

This up-and-coming beerfest is sponsored by the Northhampton Brewing Company and spotlights the best brews from New England. It is held outdoors, under large tents. Only three years old, the festival has been growing annually. In 1994, approximately 20 brewers were on hand, proffering 40 beers.

Vermont Brewers Festival
Burlington, VT
September (2nd week)
(800) 864-5927

This microbrewery festival showcases the best craft-brewed beer from New England and beyond. Currently, efforts are focused on creating a brewer's coalition to support the festival. For further information, contact the Vermont Pub and Brewery in Burlington, at the number above.

New York Beerfest
(International Beer & Food Tasting
Under the Brooklyn Bridge)
New York, NY
September (3rd week)
(718) 855-7882

The third year of this event will be in 1995. It takes place under two large outdoor tents, erected on the Brooklyn waterfront. More than 50 foreign and domestic specialty beers are available for tasting. The atmosphere is typically New York — crowded, hectic and . . . festive.

Stoudt Oktoberfest
Adamstown, PA
October (1st week)
(717) 484-4386

This festival is similar to the Great Eastern Invitational (see page 182), with the addition of traditional German Oktoberfest food and music.

Atlantic Region Listings

New England Brewing

New Haven Brewing

Connecticut

Hartford Brewery
35 Pearl St.
Hartford, CT 06103
(203) 246-BEER
Brewpub
Brews: Arch Amber, Pitbull Gold, IPA, Dunkelweiss, Bacchus, Bitter. *Seasonals:* wheat beer, mild ale, pale ale, stout, porter, Kölsch, alt, Scotch ale, and others
Hours: Mon.–Thurs., 11:30AM–1AM; Fri., 11:30AM–2AM; Sat., noon–2AM; closed Sun.

New England Brewing
25 Commerce St.
Norwalk, CT 06850
(203) 866-1339
Microbrewery
Brews: Atlantic Amber, Gold Stock Ale. *Seasonals:* oatmeal stout, holiday ale, light lager
Tours: By appointment

New Haven Brewing
458 Grand Ave.
New Haven, CT 06513
(203) 772-2739
Microbrewery

Brews: Elm City Connecticut Ale, Elm City Golden Ale, Blackwell Stout, Mr. Mike's Light Ale, Belle Dock
Tours: By appointment

Delaware

No microbreweries at press time

District of Columbia

Capital City Brewing
1100 New York Ave.
Washington, D.C. 20005
(202) 628-2222
Brewpub
Brews: bitter, pale ale, nut brown ale, porter, alt, Kölsch
Hours: Daily, 11AM–2AM

Florida

Beach Brewing
5905 S. Kirkman Road
Orlando, FL 32819
(407) 345-8802
Brewpub
Brews: Honey Wheat Light, Knight Light, Beach Blonde,

Red Rock, Magic Brew

Hours: Daily, 7AM–2AM. No beer sales before noon on Sun.

The Highlands Brewery
Sebring, FL
No further information at press time

Hops Grill & Bar
4502 W. 14th St.
Bradenton, FL 34207
(813) 756-1069
Brewpub
Brews: Clearwater Light, Hops Golden, Hammerhead Red
Hours: Mon.–Thurs., 11:30AM–11PM; Fri.–Sat., 11:30AM–midnight; Sun., 11:30AM–10PM

Hops Grill & Bar
18825 U.S. Highway 19 North
Clearwater, FL 34624
(813) 531-5300
Brewpub
Brews: extra pale ale, Hammerhead Red, golden lager. *Seasonal:* Anniversary ale
Hours: Mon.–Thurs., 11:30AM–11PM; Fri.–Sat., 11:30AM–midnight; Sun., 11:30AM–10PM
Tours: By appointment

Hops Grill & Bar
9826 San Jose Blvd.
Jacksonville, FL 32257
(904) 645-9355
Brewpub
Brews: Hops Golden, Hammerhead Red, Clearwater Light
Hours: Mon.–Thurs., 11:30AM–11PM; Fri.–Sat.,

11:30AM–midnight; Sun., 11:30AM–10PM

Hops Grill & Bar
4820 S. Florida Ave.
Lakeland, FL 34744
(813) 471-6200
Brewpub
Brews: Clearwater Light, Hops Golden, Hammerhead Red
Hours: Mon.–Thurs., 11:30AM–11PM; Fri.–Sat., 11:30AM–midnight; Sun., 11:30AM–10PM

Hops Grill & Bar
33086 U.S. Highway 19 North
Palm Harbor, FL 34684
(813) 789-5678
Brewpub
Brews: Clearwater Light, Hammerhead Red, Hops Golden Lager
Hours: Mon.–Thurs., 11:30AM–11PM; Fri.– Sat., 11:30AM–midnight; Sun., 11:30AM–10PM

Hops Grill & Bar
14303 N. Dale Mabry Hwy.
Tampa, FL 33618
(813) 264-0522
Brewpub
Brews: Clearwater Light, Hammerhead Red, Hops Golden Lager. *Seasonals:* Hops Extra Pale Ale, Anniversary Ale
Hours: Mon.–Thurs. and Sun., 11:30AM–11PM; Fri.–Sat., 11:30AM–midnight

Hops Grill & Bar
327 N. Dale Mabry Hwy.
Tampa, FL 33609
(813) 871-3600
Brewpub

Brews: Clearwater Light, Hops Golden Lager, Hammerhead Red

Hours: Mon.–Thurs., 11:30AM–11PM; Fri.–Sat., 11:30AM–midnight; Sun., 11:30AM–10PM

Irish Times Pub & Brewery
9920 Alt. A1A
Palm Beach Gardens, FL 33410
(407) 624-1504
Brewpub

Brews: red ale, pale ale, lite. *Seasonals:* dry pale, Trappist Ale, raspberry beer, Oktoberfest

Hours: Daily, 11:30AM–2AM

Kelly's Caribbean Bar, Grill & Brewery
301 Whitehead St.
Key West, FL 33040
(305) 293-8484
Brewpub

Brews: Havana Red Ale, Key West Golden Ale, Paradiso Caribe, Southern Clipper

Hours: Daily, 11AM–2AM

Market Street Pub
120 SW. First Ave.
Gainesville, FL 32601
(904) 377-2927
Brewpub

Brews: Kooka Brew, Gainesville Gold, Downtown Brown. *Seasonals:* light Pilsner, wheat bier, Oktoberfest, winter special

Hours: Mon.–Thurs., 11AM–1AM; Fri.–Sat., 11AM–2AM; Sun., 1PM–9PM

McGuire's Irish Pub & Brewery
600 E. Gregory St.
Pensacola, FL 32501
(904) 433-6789
Brewpub

Brews: Irish red ale, porter stout ale, lite ale. *Seasonals:* Irish cream ale, barleywine, raspberry wheat ale, lemon shandy, Christmas ale

Hours: Daily, 11AM–2AM

Mill Bakery, Eatery & Brewery
11491 Cleveland Ave.
Fort Meyers, FL 33907
(813) 939-2739
Brewpub

Brews: honey wheat light, Scotch ale, English bitter, Red Rock, and seasonals

Hours: Mon.–Sat., 11:30AM; Sun., 8AM–2AM

Mill Bakery, Eatery & Brewery
330 Fairbanks
Winter Park, FL 32789
(407) 644-1544
Brewpub

Brews: harvest light, honey wheat, dark, Red Rock. *Seasonals:* Wheatfield Dry, holiday ale, stout

Hours: Daily, 6:30AM–2AM

Ragtime Tavern & Grill
207 Atlantic Blvd.
Jacksonville, FL 32233
(904) 241-7877
Brewpub

Brews: Redbrick Ale, A Strange Stout, Westbury Wheat,

Dolphin's Breath Lager, and seasonals

Hours: Daily, 11AM–2AM

River City Brewing
835 Museum Circle
Jacksonville, FL 32207
(904) 398-2299
Brewpub
Brews: Jag Light, Red Rooster, Jackson Pale Ale, Riptide Porter. *Seasonal:* Wet Lightning ESB
Hours: Daily, 11AM–1AM

Riverwalk Brewery
111 SW. 2nd Ave.
Fort Lauderdale, FL 33301
(305) 764-8448
Brewpub
Brews: Lauder Light, Lauder Ale
Hours: Mon.–Sat., 11AM–midnight; Sun., noon–midnight

Santa Rosa Bay Brewery
54 Miracle Strip Pkwy.
Fort Walton Beach, FL 32548
(904) 664-BREW
Brewpub
Brews: Red Irish Ale, golden ale, wheat ale. *Seasonals:* Christmas ale, summer dark wheat
Hours: Mon.–Thurs., 11AM–midnight; Fri.–Sat., 11AM–closing; Sun., 5PM–10PM

Sarasota Brewing
6607 Gateway Ave.
Sarasota, FL 34231
(813) 925-2337
Brewpub

Brews: Cobra Lite Lager, Presidential Pale Ale, Sequoia

Amber Lager, Sara DeSoto Golden Ale, Ja Mills Honey Mead Ale, Queens Porter, and seasonals
Hours: Mon., Fri., Sat., 11AM–2AM; Tues.–Thurs., 11AM–midnight; Sun., noon–midnight

Thai Orchid Restaurant & Brewery
317 Miracle Mile
Coral Gables, FL 33134
(305) 443-6364
Brewpub
Brews: Sao Noy, Ying Thai, Chang Baah
Hours: Daily, 11:30AM–3PM and 5PM–10:30PM

Georgia

Atlantic Brewing
1219 Williams St. NW
Atlanta, GA 30309
(404) 892-4436
Microbrewery
Brews: Red Brick Ale
Tours: By appointment

Marthasville Brewing
3960 Shirley Dr. SW
Atlanta, GA 30336
(404) 713-0333
Microbrewery
Brews: Martha's Pale Ale, Martha's Hefe-Weizen
Tours: By appointment

Casco Bay Brewing

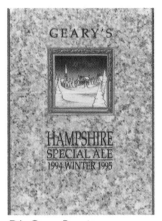

D.L. Geary Brewing

Kennebunkport Brewing

Maine

Andrew's Brewing
RFD. #1
Lincolnville, ME 04849
(207) 763-3305
Microbrewery
Brews: Andrew's Old English Ale, Andrew's Brown, Andrew's Old St. Nick Porter
Tours: By appointment

Bar Harbor Brewing
Rt. 3, Otter Creek
Bar Harbor, ME 04609
(207) 288-4592
Microbrewery
Brews: Harbor Light Pale Ale, Thunder Hole Ale, Cadillac Mountain Stout, Brewer's Choice, Ginger Mild Ale
Tours: Mon.–Fri., 3:30PM–5PM, in season

Casco Bay Brewing
57 Industrial Way
Portland, ME 04103-1071
(207) 797-2020
Microbrewery
Brews: Katahdin Golden, Katahdin Red
Tours: Call for details

D.L. Geary Brewing
38 Evergreen Dr.
Portland, ME 04103
(207) 878-2337
Microbrewery
Brews: Geary's Pale Ale.
Seasonals: Hampshire Special Ale, Geary's London Porter
Tours: By appointment

Gritty McDuff's Brew Pub
396 Fore St.
Portland, ME 04101
(207) 772-BREW
Brewpub
Brews: McDuff's Best Bitter, Portland Head Light Pale Ale, Black Fly Stout, Lion's Pride Brown Ale, Sebago Light.
Seasonals: Halloween Ale, Christmas Ale, Nuptial Ale, IPA, and others
Hours: Mon.–Sat., 11AM–1AM; Sun., noon–1AM

Kennebunkport Brewing (Federal Jack's Brew Pub)
8 Western Ave.
Kennebunk, ME 04043
(800) BREW-ALE
Brewpub
Brews: Goat Island Light, Brown Moose Ale, Shipyard Export Ale, Taint Town Pale Ale, Kennebunkporter.
Seasonals: winter ale, Blue Fin Stout, and others
Hours: Daily, noon–1AM

Lake St. George Brewing
RR. 1, Box 2505
Liberty, ME 04949-9738
(207) 589-4690 or 589-4180
Microbrewery
Brews: Dirigo Ale, amber, pale ale
Tours: By appointment

Lompoc Cafe & Brewpub (Atlantic Brewing)
34-36 Rodick St.
Bar Harbor, ME 04609
(207) 288-9513
Brewpub
Brews: Bar Harbor Real Ale,

Coal Porter, Lompoc's Pale Ale, Roger's 3 Frog Stout, spiced ale, blueberry ale

Hours: May–Oct., daily, 3PM–midnight

No Tomatoes Restaurant (Great Falls Brewing)
36 Court St.
Auburn, ME 04210
(207) 784-3919
Brewpub
Brews: pale ale, All Gone Amber, Bobcat Brown, porter
Hours: Daily, 11AM–midnight

Sea Dog Brewing
43 Mechanic St.
Camden, ME 04843
(207) 236-6863
Brewpub
Brews: Penobscot Pilsner, Owl's Head Light, Windjammer Blonde, Old Gobblywobbler Brown, Old Baggywrinkle ESB, Old East India IPA, and others
Hours: Daily, 11:30AM–1AM

Shipyard Brewery
86 Newbury St.
Portland, ME 04101
(207) 761-0807
Microbrewery
Brews: Shipyard Export Ale, Blue Fin Stout
Tours: Call for details

Sugarloaf Brewing (Theo's Pub)
RR#1, Box 2268
Carrabassett Valley, ME 04947
(207) 237-2211
Brewpub
Brews: light ale, Carrabassett

Pale Ale, Dead River Dark, and seasonals
Hours: Sun.–Thurs., 11:30AM–10PM; Fri.–Sat., 11:30AM–11PM

Sunday River Brewing (The Moose's Tale)
1 Sunday River Road
Bethel, ME 04217
(207) 824-3541
Brewpub
Brews: Pyrite Gold, Redstone, Black Bear Porter, Mollyecket IPA, Sunday River Alt, Harvest Fest
Hours: Winter: Daily, 11:30AM–1AM; Summer: Wed.–Sun., 11:30AM–1AM

Maryland

Baltimore Brewing
104 Albemarle St.
Baltimore, MD 21202
(410) 837-5000
Brewpub
Brews: Pils, dark, Märzen, weizen. *Seasonals:* alt, Maibock, wheat bock, doppelbock
Hours: Mon.–Thurs., 11:30AM–11PM; Fri.–Sat., 11:30AM–midnight; closed Sun.

Frederick Brewing
103 S. Carroll St.
Frederick, MD 21701-7899
(301) 694-7899
Microbrewery
Brews: Blue Ridge Golden Ale, Amber Lager. *Seasonals:* wheat beer, porter
Tours: Sat., 1PM and 2:30PM; Sun., 1:30PM

Wild Goose Brewery

Boston Beer Co.

Olde Town Tavern
& Brewery
227 E. Diamond Ave.
Gaithersburg, MD 20877
(301) 948-4200
Brewpub
Brews: Forest Oak Amber Ale,
Irvington Pale Ale, Windridge
Light, Belt's Bitter, Diamond
Stout, and more
Hours: Daily, 11AM–1AM

Oxford Brewing
611G Hammonds Ferry
Road
Linthicum, MD 21090
(410) 789-0003
Microbrewery
Brews: Oxford Class Amber
Ale, Oxford Raspberry Wheat,
Eleanor's Amber Ale.
Seasonals: Oxford Santa Class,
Summer Gold, Piccadilly Porter
Tours: By appointment

Sisson's
(South Baltimore Brewing)
36 E. Cross St.
Baltimore, MD 21230
(410) 539-2093
Brewpub
Brews: Stockade Amber, Marble
Golden, Cross Street Stout, So
Bo Hefe-Weizen. *Seasonals:*
Christmas ale, and more
Hours: Mon.–Sat.,
11:30AM–2AM; Sun., 4PM–2AM

Wharf Rat Camden Yards
(Oliver Breweries)
206 W. Pratt St.
Baltimore, MD 21201
(410) 244-8900
Brewpub
Brews: Oliver's Best Bitter,

Oliver's SW1, Oliver's Summer
Light, Oliver's Irish Red,
Blackfriar Stout. *Seasonals:*
Oliver's Pale Ale, Oliver's ESB.
Hours: Mon.–Sat.,
11:30AM–2AM; Sun.,
11:30AM–midnight (until 2AM
in summer)

Wild Goose Brewery
20 Washington St.
Cambridge, MD 21613
(410) 221-1121
Microbrewery
Brews: amber beer, golden ale,
India pale ale, porter
Tours: Weekdays 11AM–3PM
and weekends; reservations
required 3–4 days in advance

Massachusetts

Atlantic Coast Brewing
50 Terminal St.
Boston, MA 02129
(617) 242-6464
Microbrewery
Brews: Tremont Ale, Tremont
Best Bitter. *Seasonal:* Tremont
Porter
Tours: By reservation

Berkshire Brewing
12 Railroad St.
South Deerfield, MA 01373
(413) 665-6600
Microbrewery
Brews: pale ale, extra pale ale,
porter
Tours: By appointment

Boston Beer Co.
30 Germania St.
Boston, MA 02130
(617) 522-9080

Microbrewery
(See also Samuel Adams
Brewhouse, page 197, and
Boston Beer Co., page 206)

Brews: Samuel Adams Boston
Lager, Boston Stock Ale, Honey
Porter, Cream Sout, Triple Bock,
Boston Lightship. *Seasonals:*
Oktoberfest, winter lager, cran-
berry lambic, double bock, sum-
mer wheat, dark wheat

Tours: Thurs.–Fri., 2PM; Sat.,
noon–2:30PM, every half hour.
Call 522-9090 for a recording
giving times and directions.

Boston Beer Works
61 Brookline Ave.
Boston, MA 02215
(617) 536-2337
Brewpub

Brews: Acme Light, Kenmore
Kölsch, Boston Red, Back Bay
IPA, Buckeye Oatmeal Stout,
Hercules Strong Ale, and
seasonals

Hours: Daily, 11AM–1AM

Brewery on Martha's Vineyard
43 Oak Bluffs Ave.
Oak Bluffs, MA 02557
(508) 696-8400
Microbrewery

Brews: Gay Head Light,
Menensha Golden Ale, Oak
Bluffs Amber Ale

Tours: Call for details

The Brewery at 34 Depot St.
34 Depot St.
Pittsfield, MA 01201
(413) 442-2072
Brewpub

Brews: Gimlich's Golden Ale,
Red Room Pale Ale, Ironworks

Pale Ale, Raven's Rock Stout.
Hours: Daily 11:30AM–
midnight

Cambridge Brewing
1 Kendall Square, Bldg. 100
Cambridge, MA 02139
(617) 494-1994
Brewpub

Brews: Regatta Golden,
Cambridge Amber, Charles
River Porter, Tall Tale Pale Ale.
Seasonals: wheaten ale, winter
warmer, bock, Triple Threat

Hours: Mon.–Sat.,
11:30AM–1AM; Sun., noon–1AM

Cape Cod Brew House
720 Main St.
Hyannis, MA 02601
(508) 775-4110
Brewpub

Brews: Cape Cod Lighthouse
Lager, Dakota Dark, Chatham
Light, Nantucket Red Ale

Hours: Daily, 11:30AM–1AM

Commonwealth Brewing
138 Portland St.
Boston, MA 02114
(617) 523-8383
Brewpub

Brews: Golden Ale, Boston's
Best Beer, Burton Ale, Burton
Bitter, Amber Ale, Classic
Stout, Blonde Ale, Special Old
Ale, Famous Porter

Hours: Mon.–Thurs.,
11:30AM–midnight; Fri.–Sat.,
11:30AM–1AM; Sun., noon–
closing

Ipswich Brewing
25 Hayward St.
Ipswich, MA 01938
(508) 356-3329

Mass. Bay Brewing

Microbrewery

Brews: Ipswich Ale,
Ipswich Dark

Tours: Sat., 1PM and 3PM

John Harvard's Brewhouse
33 Dunster St.
Cambridge, MA 02138
(617) 868-3585
Brewpub
Brews: John Harvard Pale Ale,
All American Light Ale, Old
Willy IPA, Export Stout, Amber
Bockbier, nut brown ale.
Seasonals: Cristal Pilsner, and
others

Hours: Mon.–Wed.,
11:30AM–12:30AM; Thurs.–Sat.,
11:30AM–1:30AM; Sun.,
11AM–midnight

Lowell Brewing
(Brewhouse Cafe & Grill)
199 Cabot St.
Lowell, MA 01854
(508) 937-1200
Brewpub
Brews: Mill City Amber Ale,
Classic Lager, Rootbeer
Hours: Daily, 11:30AM–2AM

Mass. Bay Brewing
306 Northern Ave.
Boston, MA 02210
(617) 574-9551
Microbrewery
Brews: ale, golden lager, dark,
light, hard cider. *Seasonals:*
IPA, Oktoberfest, winter
warmer, stout, birthday reserve
Tours: Fri. and Sat., 1PM

Northampton Brewery
(Brewster Court
Bar & Grill)
11 Brewster Ct.
Northampton, MA 01060
(413) 584-9903
Brewpub
Brews: golden Pilsner, amber.
Seasonals: Steamer, Old Brown
Dog, pale ale, Hoover's Porter,
weizenheimer, Black Cat Stout,
and others
Hours: Mon.–Sat.,
11:30AM–1AM; Sun., 1PM–1AM

Old Salem Village Brewing
private residence
Danvers, MA 01923
(508) 777-2260
Microbrewery
Brews: Stone's Copper Ale,
Belgian ale, blonde ale, and
others
Tours: Call for directions and
appointment.

Ould Newbury Brewing
50 Parker St.
Ould Newbury, MA 01951
(508) 462-1980
Microbrewery
Brews: Yankee Ale, Ould
Newbury Porter
Tours: Call for reservation

New Hampshire

Martha's Exchange
185 Main St.
Nashua, NH 03060
(603) 883-8781
Brewpub
Brews: Bootleg Light, Volstead,
Untouchable Scotch Ale, Ale
Capone IPA, Bull Frog Stout.

Seasonals: White Mountain Wheat, Oktoberfest, Indian Head Red

Hours: Mon., 7AM–midnight; Tues.–Sun., 7AM–1AM

Portsmouth Brewery
56 Market St.
Portsmouth, NH 03801
(603) 431-1115
Brewpub

Brews: golden lager, amber lager, pale ale, blonde ale, Old Brown Dog, Black Cat Stout. *Seasonals:* weisenheimmer, Oktoberfest, cranberry holiday ale, and more

Hours: Daily, 11:30AM–1AM

Seven Barrel Brewing
Plainfield Road
West Lebanon, NH 03784
(603) 298-5566
Brewpub

Brews: New Dublin Brown Ale, Old #7 Pale Ale, Ice Rock Canadian Ale, Champion Reserve IPA, and others

Hours: Daily, 11AM–1AM

Smuttynose Brewery
225 Heritage Ave.
Portsmouth, NH 03801
(603) 433-2337
Microbrewery

Brews: Shoals Pale Ale

Tours: By appointment

New Jersey

Long Valley Pub & Brewery
P.O. Box 368
Long Valley, NJ 07853
(908) 832-9767
Brewpub

The Ship Inn
Millford, NJ 08848
(908) 995-0188
Microbrewery Restaurant

Triumph Brewing Co.
138 Nassau St.
Princeton, NJ 08540
(609) 924-7855
Brewpub

Brews: honey wheat, pale ale, IPA, amber ale, brown ale, Irish stout.

New York

Abbott Square Brewpub (Buffalo Brewing)
1830 Abbott Road
Buffalo, NY 14218
(716) 828-0004
Brewpub

Brews: Buffalo Lager, Buffalo Pils, Limericks Ale, Buffalo Weiss. *Seasonals:* Buffalo Oktoberfest, Buffalo Doppelbock

Hours: Daily, 11:30AM–2AM

Brown & Moran Brewing
417-419 River St.
Troy, NY 12180
(518) 273-BEER
Brewpub

Brews: golden ale, amber ale, dark porter, weizenbier. *Seasonals:* Belgian Cherry Ale, St. Nick's Nectar

Hours: Mon.–Thurs., 11AM–midnight; Fri.–Sat., 11AM–2AM; Sun., noon–midnight

Smuttynose Brewery

Buffalo Brewpub

Buffalo Brewpub
6861 Main St.
Williamsville, NY 14221
(716) 632-0552
Brewpub
Brews: Buffalo Bitter, weiss.
Seasonals: Kringle Beer,
Oktoberfest
Hours: Mon.–Thurs.,
11:30AM–midnight; Fri.–Sat.,
11:30AM–1AM; Sun., noon–
midnight

Chapter House Brewpub
400 Stewart Ave.
Ithaca, NY 14850
(607) 277-9782
Brewpub
Brews: Clement's Pilsner,
Clement's Amber, Clement's
Dunkel, Vienna Amber, Cole
Porter, nut brown ale
Hours: Mon.–Thurs., 4PM–1AM;
Fri.–Sat., 3PM–1AM; Sun.,
5PM–1AM

**James Bay
Restaurant & Brewery**
154 W. Broadway
Port Jefferson, NY 11777
(516) 928-2525
Brewpub
Brews: Kölsch, IPA, porter.
Seasonal: wheat beer, and others
Hours: Call for information

Long Island Brewing
111 Jericho Turnpike
Jericho, NY 11735
(516) 334-BREW
Brewpub
Brews: Long Island Lager,
Great South Bay Stout, Jericho
Amber, Blue Point Black

Cherry Porter, Westbury
Blueberry Ale, and others
Hours: Daily, 11AM–3:30AM

**Manhattan Brewing Co.
Restaurant**
40-42 Thompson St.
New York, NY 10013
(212) 925-1515
Brewpub
Brews: gold ale, British amber,
Bavarian wheat, extra stout,
and more; all rotate
Hours: Sun.–Thurs.,
11:30AM–midnight; Fri.–Sat.,
11:30AM–2AM

Mountain Valley Brewpub
122 Orange Ave.
Suffern, NY 10901
(914) 357-0101
Brewpub
Brews: porter, copper, pale,
copper lyte. *Seasonals:* nut
brown ale, smoked porter,
blonde dopplebock, and others
Hours: Sun.–Thurs.,
11:30AM–2AM; Fri.–Sat.,
11:30AM–4AM

Park Slope Brewing
3556 Sixth Ave.
Brooklyn, NY 11215
(718) 788-1756
Brewpub
Brews: golden ale, amber ale,
I.P.A., porter, stout, California
pale ale, Christmas spiced
beers; all in rotation
Hours: Daily, 11AM–closing

Rochester Brewpub
800 Jefferson Rd.
Henrietta, NY 14623
(716) 272-1550

Brewpub

Brews: amber ale, oatmeal stout, red ale, Nickel City Dark, Buffalo Bitter, Buffalo Pils, pale ale. *Seasonals:* Oktoberfest, kringle, weiss

Hours: Daily, 6:30AM–2AM

Rohrbach Brewing
315 Gregory St.
Rochester, NY 14620
(716) 244-5680

Brewpub

Brews: Old Nate's Pale Ale, Highland Amber, Gregory Street Lager. *Seasonals:* Pilsner, porter, wheat

Hours: Sun.–Thurs., 11:30AM–11PM; Fri.–Sat., 11:30AM–midnight; Weekends in summer: Sat., 4PM–midnight; Sun., 4PM–11PM

Syracuse Suds Factory
210-216 W. Water St.
Syracuse, NY 13202
(315) 471-2254

Brewpub

Brews: pale ale, amber ale

Hours: Mon.–Sat., 11AM–2AM; Sun., noon–2AM

Westside Brewing Company
340 Amsterdam Ave.
New York, NY 10024
(212) 721-2161

Brewpub

Brews: nut brown, porter, golden, blonde, wheat, raspberry, ESB and seasonals

Hours: Daily, noon–3AM

Woodstock Brewing
20 St. James St.
Kingston, NY 12401
(914) 331-2810

Microbrewery

Brews: Hudson Lager, St. James Ale, Big Indian Porter. *Seasonal:* Ichabod Crane

Tours: Sat., 1PM, reservations suggested

Zip City Brewing
3 W. 18th St.
New York, NY 10011
(212) 366-6333

Brewpub

Brews: helles, Pilsner, Märzen, Vienna, dunkel. *Seasonals:* Maibock, doppelbock, weiss, rauchbier, and more

Hours: Daily, 11:30AM–3AM

North Carolina

Dilworth Brewing
1301 East Blvd.
Charlotte, NC 28203
(704) 377-2739

Brewpub

Brews: Reeds Golden, Albemarle Ale, Dilworth Porter. *Seasonals:* Christmas ale, weizen, Oktoberfest

Hours: Mon.–Thurs., 11AM–midnight; Fri.–Sat., 11AM–1AM; closed Sun.

Dilworth Micro Brewery
655 R. Pressley Road
Charlotte, NC 28217
(704) 522-0311

Microbrewery

Brews: Albemarle Ale

Tours: By appointment

Dilworth Brewing

Greenshields
Pub & Brewery
214 E. Martin St.
Raleigh, NC 27601
(919) 829-0214
Brewpub

Brews: Pilsner, amber bitter, dark lager, porter, oatmeal stout. *Seasonals:* wheat beer, nut brown ale, dark wheat, Christmas bitter

Hours: Daily, 11:30AM–1AM

Loggerhead Brewing
2006 W. Vandalia Road
Greensboro, NC 27407
(919) 292-7676
Microbrewery

Brews: Loggerhead Pilsner, General Green Lager, Gate City Ale, Loggerhead Light, cherry Pilsner

Tours: Call for information

Mill Bakery,
Eatery & Brewery
122 W. Woodlawn Road
Charlotte, NC 28217
(704) 529-6455
Brewpub

Brews: Harvest Gold, Wheat Field Dry, Red October, weizen, Stout Harvest Light, Hornet Tail Ale. *Seasonals:* Wooly's Winterfest, spiced ale

Hours: Sun.–Thurs., 6:30AM–11PM; Fri.–Sat., 6:30AM–1AM (beer served at 1PM)

Spring Garden Brewing
714 Francis King St.
Greensboro, NC 27410
(919) 299-3649
Brewpub

Brews: Hummin' Bird Light, Oak Ridge Amber, Blackbeard Bock, Oktoberfest, Black Rose Lager

Hours: Mon.–Thurs., 11:30AM–1AM; Fri.–Sat., 11:30AM–1:30AM; Sun., 11:30AM–10PM

Spur Steak House & Saloon
(Toisnot Brewing)
513 N. Ward Blvd.
Wilson, NC 27893
(919) 237-0086
Brewpub

Brews: Hang 'um High Pale Ale, Geronimo's India(n) Pale Ale, Bad Bob's Brown Ale, Appalachian Ambush Amber, Red Coach Revenge Stout, and other seasonals

Hours: Mon.–Wed., 11AM–10PM; Thurs.–Fri., 11AM–11PM; Sat., 4PM–11PM; closed Sun.

Tumbleweed
Grill & Brewery
473 Blowing Rock Road
Boone, NC 28607
(704) 264-7111
Brewpub

Brews: Tumbleweed Amber Ale, Gold Rush Ale. *Seasonals:* stout, rauch, and others

Hours: Daily, 11AM–10PM

Weeping Radish
Restaurant & Brewery
Hwy. 64 E.
Manteo, NC 27954
(919) 473-1157

Brewpub (second brewery location in Durham — no tours)

Brews: helles bier, fest bier, black radish bier

Hours: Daily, 11:30AM–closing

Pennsylvania

Arrowhead Brewing
1667 Orchard Dr.
Chambersburg, PA 17201
(717) 264-0101
Microbrewery
Brews: Red Feather Pale Ale
Tours: Business hours throughout the week; weekends by reservation only.

Dock Street Brewing Brewery & Restaurant
Two Logan Square
Philadelphia, PA 19103
(215) 496-0413
Brewpub
(See also Dock Street Brewing Co., page 207)
Brews: pale ale, weiss beer, Pilsner, bitter, brown ale, and seasonals
Hours: Mon.–Thurs., 11:30AM–midnight; Fri.–Sat., noon–2AM; Sun., noon–11PM

Allegheny Brewery & Restaurant (Penn Brewing)
800 Vinial St.
Pittsburgh, PA 15212
(412) 237-9402
Brewpub
(See also Pennsylvania Brewing Co., page 206)
Brews: Penn Pilsner, Kaiser Pils, Penn dark, Penn light, lager. *Seasonals:* Oktoberfest, Celebrator Bock, Maerzen Fest, alt, weizen, weizen bock

Hours: Mon.–Sat., 11AM–midnight; closed Sun.

Samuel Adams Brewhouse
1516 Sansom St.
Philadelphia, PA 19102
(215) 563-ADAM
Brewpub
(See also Boston Beer Co., pages 190 and 206)
Brews: Ben Franklin's Gold, Poor Richard's Amber
Hours: Mon.–Thurs., 11AM–midnight; Fri.–Sat., 11AM–1AM; closed Sun.

Stoudt Brewery (Black Angus Restaurant)
Route 272
Adamstown, PA 19501
(717) 484-4386
Brewpub
Brews: Pilsner, export gold, amber, fest, bock, honey double, Maibock, double bock, ale, stout, and seasonals
Hours: Mon.–Sat., 5PM–11PM; Sun., noon–9PM

Rhode Island

Union Station Brewery
36 Exchange Terrace
Providence, RI 02903
(401) 274-BREW
Brewpub
Brews: Golden Spike Ale, amber ale, Pawsox Pale Ale, Blackbeards Ale, Red Dog Ale, Irish Red Ale, and regular specials
Hours: Mon.–Fri., 11:30AM–2AM; Sat., 5PM–2AM; Sun., 3PM–1AM

Arrowhead Brewing

Dock Street Brewing Brewery & Restaurant

Allegheny Brewery & Restaurant (Penn Brewing)

Mountain Brewers

Otter Creek Brewing

South Carolina

Palmetto Brewing
289 Huger St.
Charleston, SC 29403
(803) 937-0903
Microbrewery
Brews: Palmetto Lager
Tours: By appointment

Vermont

Catamount Brewing
58 S. Main St.
White River Junction, VT 05001
(802) 296-2248
Microbrewery
Brews: gold, amber, porter. *Seasonals:* Christmas ale, Oktoberfest, bock
Tours: Sat., 11AM, 1PM, and 3PM all year; July–Oct., Mon.–Sat., 11AM, 1PM, and 3PM

Latchis Grille (Windham Brewery)
6 Flat St.
Brattleboro, VT 05301
(802) 254-4747
Brewpub
Brews: Whetstone Golden Lager, Moonbeam Ale, Ruby Brown Ale, Raspberry Amber Lager, Strawberry Whetstone, and seasonals
Hours: Mon.–Sat., 11AM–midnight; Sun., 10AM–midnight

McNeill's Brewery
90 Elliot St.
Brattleboro, VT 05301
(802) 254-2553
Brewpub

Brews: Duck's Breath Bitter, Dead Horse IPA, Slopbucket Brown, Big Nose Blonde, doppelbock, Fire House Pale, McNeill's ESB, and others
Hours: Sun.–Fri., 4PM–2AM; Sat., 4PM–1AM

Mountain Brewers
Route 4, The Marketplace, Box140
Bridgewater, VT 05034
(802) 672-5011
Microbrewery
Brews: ale, India pale ale, Kölsch, stout, brown bag ale
Tours: Daily, noon–5PM

Norwich Inn (Jasper Murdock's Alehouse)
225 Main St.
Norwich, VT 05055
(802) 649-1143
Brewpub
Brews: Old Slippery Skin, Whistling Pig Red, Short and Stout, Stackpole Porter, Old Ale, and seasonals
Hours: Tues.–Sun., 5PM–closing; closed Mon.

Otter Creek Brewing
74 Exchange St.
Middlebury, VT 05753
(802) 388-0727
Microbrewery
Brews: Copper. *Seasonals:* summer wheat ale, Hickory Switch Smoked Amber Ale, Stovepipe Porter, Mud Bock Spring Ale
Tours: Fri., 4PM amd 5PM; Sat., 1PM, 3PM, and 5PM, and by appointment

Vermont Pub & Brewery
144 College St.
Burlington, VT 05401
(802) 865-0500
Brewpub
Brews: Burly Irish Ale, Vermont Smoked Porter, Dogbite Bitter. *Seasonals:* Rock Dunder Brown Ale, Billybuck Maibock, Grandslam Baseball Beer, and others
Hours: Sun.–Thurs., 11:30AM–12:30AM; Fri., 11:30AM–2AM; Sat., 11:30AM–1AM

Virginia

Bardo Rodeo
2000 Wilson Blvd.
Arlington, VA 22201
(703) 527-9399
Brewpub
Brews: California Common, California Red, stout, porter, Beat My Wheat, and others
Hours: Daily, 11:30AM–2AM

Blue Ridge Brewing
709 W. Main
Charlottesville, VA 22901
(804) 977-0017
Brewpub
Brews: Hawksbill Lager, Piney River Lager, Afton Ale, Humpback Stout. *Seasonal:* White Oak Weizen
Hours: Mon.–Fri., 11:30AM–2PM and 5PM–2AM; Sat., 11:30AM–2AM; Sun., 10:30AM–2AM

Legend Brewing
321 W. 7th St.
Richmond, VA 23219
(804) 232-8871

Brewpub
Brews: lager, Pilsner, brown ale, porter
Hours: Tues.–Sat., 11AM–10:30PM; closed Sun.–Mon.

Old Dominion Brewing
44633 Guilford Dr.
Ashburn, VA 22011
(703) 689-1225
Microbrewery
Brews: Dominion Ale, Dominion Lager, Dominion Stout, Portner's Lager, Victory Amber Lager, Virginia Native Brite, Hard Times Select, Blue Point, O'Bannon Dark Beer, St. George Lager
Tours: Sat., noon and 3PM

Potomac River Brewing
14141 A Parke Long Ct.
Chantilly, VA 22021
(703) 631-5430
Microbrewery
Brews: Patowmack Ale, Rappahannock Red Ale, Mt. Vernon Porter
Tours: Sat., 1PM and 3PM

Richbrau Brewery & Queen's Arms Pub
1214 E. Cary St.
Richmond, VA 23229
(804) 644-3018
Brewpub
Brews: Big Nasty, Old Nick, Golden Griffen. *Seasonals:* Queen's Sour, and others
Hours: Mon.–Tues., 11:30AM–midnight; Wed.–Sat., 11:30AM–2AM; Sun., noon–9PM

Old Dominion Brewing

West Virginia

Cardinal Brewing
927 Barlow Dr.
Charleston, WV 25331
(304) 344-2900
Microbrewery
Brews: New River Ale
Tours: By appointment

West Virginia Brewing
1291 University Ave.
Morgantown, WV 26505-5450
(304) 296-BREW
Brewpub
Brews: Cheat Mountain Gold, Appalachian Ale, Pillow Rock Pilsner, Blackwater Stout, and seasonals
Hours: Mon.–Sat., 11:30AM–closing; closed Sun.

Part VI

Contract Brewing

Contract Brewing

Contract brewing allows for the existence of nationally and regionally distributed craft brews. They are not tied to any one region. Instead, we have grouped them into a fifth national "region."

Brewing on contract is not a new idea, but the immense popularity of certain contract beers has catapulted this sector of the microbrewing industry to the forefront of the current beer renaissance.

Contract brewing, for the uninitiated, is the quickest and easiest way to join in the microbrewing revolution. All one needs is the right amount of money and a little marketing savvy to be successful. The idea is to develop a recipe for a beer (you can hire professionals to do this for you), then choose among a dozen or so breweries around the country that are willing to make your beer for you. The advertising and distribution can also be farmed out to professionals in the industry. (This is an unabashedly oversimplified explanation of the process. It stands in stark contrast to the efforts of real craft brewers who invest their time and brewing talents along with their cash, and who, for the most part, started out as passionate homebrewers on a mission to share their joy.)

Leading the charge are a few nationally distributed, high-visibility products with brand name recognition. These pseudo-microbrews have achieved this level of success for a number of reasons. Timing was a big factor: these specialty beers got in on the ground floor and rode on the coattails of the real craft brewers. Aggressive marketing was essential to their prosperity and was possible because these contract brewers did not have to be concerned about purchasing expensive brewing equipment. Not to be overlooked is the beers' high quality and drinkability — many are considered top-quality, gourmet, specialty beers. In the wake of these first successful "brewing" opera-

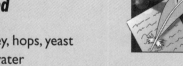

Untitled

Of barley, hops, yeast
    and water
I concoct a malty mosaic.

It's mystical powers doth numb my
    thoughts
and render my words prosaic.

— Marty Nachel

tions, dozens of others joined in the dance. According to 1994 statistics supplied by the Institute for Brewing Studies, there were 62 contract brewing companies licensed in the United States.

This segment of the industry has expanded and stratified, and is not quite as easily defined as it once was. There are nationally distributed contract beers such as Samuel Adams, Rhino Chasers, and Pete's Wicked Ales, Lagers, and so on. Initially, each of these was contracted out to a single location. Samuel Adams was produced first by the Pittsburgh Brewing Company. Then, in order to keep up with production demand, it was also contracted out to a second brewery location in Portland, Oregon, and then to a third. Additional increased sales necessitated the purchase and renovation of the old Haffenreffer Brewery, outside of Boston, in order to satisfy the demand. Then, the Samuel Adams Brewhouse — a brewpub — was opened in Philadelphia.

Some other examples of contract beers follow: Pete's Brewing Company, headquartered in Palo Alto, California, contracted its Wicked Brews to the August Schell Brewing Company in New Ulm, Minnesota. Due to consumer demand, owner Pete Slosberg was forced to turn the contract over to the larger Minnesota Brewing Company in St. Paul. Rhino Chasers beer is brewed at the F.X. Matt Brewing Company in Utica, New York, for the William & Scott Company of Culver City, California. Other well known, but more regionally distributed, beers brewed there include New Amsterdam, Olde Heurich, Dock Street, Harpoon, and

Brooklyn Beer. The esteemed Penn Pilsner is another beer contracted out of the Pittsburgh Brewing Company while the Pennsylvania Brewing Company also operates the Allegheny Brewery and Pub in Pittsburgh.

One segment of the contract brewing picture does not figure in this review, and that concerns restaurants and taverns which have a private label contract brew. In some cases, the brew is not even custom-made; in others, it is not a noteworthy beer, but just an added attraction at the restaurant. For these reasons, plus the fact that they are not regionally distributed (they are confined to the one restaurant or tavern), this kind of contract brew is not listed here even though some of them are quite well-known to the locals.

As illustrated, the success of contract beers has led to the growth of famous breweries and brewpubs. However, established pub brewing operations sometimes have worked the opposite way: by introducing contract-brewed and bottled versions of their beers to reach a wider audience. The Commonwealth Brewing Company has its Boston Burton Ale produced at The Lion, Inc., a brewery in Wilkes-Barre, Pennsylvania. Crazy Ed's Black Mountain Brewery in Arizona has a Cave Creek Chili Beer made at the Minnesota Brewing Company in St. Paul. Buffalo Bill's Brewpub in Hayward, California, and Cherryland Brewing in Sturgeon Bay, Wisconsin, have bottled products made at the Dubuque Brewing Company in Iowa. (Because of the increased frequency of this situation, when contract brewers operate a brewpub or a brewery that can be visited, a cross reference has been made to its listing in the appropriate regional section.)

There are a lot of up-and-coming contract breweries out there. The Spring Street Brewing Company in New York has a Belgian Wit beer produced in Minnesota. The only full line of fruit lagers is produced at the same location for the Beartooth Brewing Company in Boulder, Colorado, and the Brewski Brewing Company of Culver City, California, has a small stable of beers being made in Portland, Oregon.

It should come as no surprise that there are even microbreweries producing beers on contract for fellow microbreweries.

Such is the case with the Indianapolis Brewing Company, which brews Gaslight Pale Ale for Pacific Hop Exchange in Novato, California; San Juan India Pale Ale for the San Juan Brewing Company in Telluride, Colorado; and Pike Place Pale Ale for the Pike Place Brewery in Seattle, Washington. Pike Place Pale Ale also is brewed on contract at the Catamount Brewing Company in White River Junction, Vermont, while Post Road Pale Ale is made for the Old Marborough Brewing Company in Framingham, Massachusetts. Confusing, eh?

You bet. And because of the proliferation of contract brews, it is easier for large breweries to slip a few into the market

Homebrewing

Making beer and other alcoholic beverages in one's own home has gone on for centuries, but it became more common in America during Prohibition (1920–1933). After the repeal of the 18th Amendment, the practice of homebrewing continued, no longer out of necessity, but for enjoyment. Unfortunately, due to an omission in the law, it was still illegal to brew beer at home, though the law allowed the making of wine.

An act of Congress in October 1978 made homebrewing legal again, when federal legislation H.R. 1337 was signed by President Carter. This opened the doors to the microbrewing revolution. Though the federal government now allows the practice, individual state statutes may supersede federal regulations. Furthermore, homebrewers are required to follow three simple rules:

1. Homebrewers are allowed to brew no more than 100 gallons per (adult) person, per household, with a maximum of 200 gallons per household.

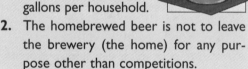

2. The homebrewed beer is not to leave the brewery (the home) for any purpose other than competitions.

3. The homebrewed beer must *never* be sold under any circumstances.

While these rules may seem unenforceable, if caught, the penalties can be severe.

It is estimated that there are more than 1.5 million homebrewers in the United States. Over 400 known homebrewing clubs account for most of the activity in the industry, and over 1,500 homebrew supply retailers generate more than $10 million in sales annually.

Homebrewers have been justly credited with the level of vitality and success in the microbrewing industry.

virtually unnoticed. Anheuser-Busch is marketing a new line of amber beer by the name of Elk Mountain; Miller has a subsidiary named Plank Road Brewery; Stroh's is parading its Augsburger brands as if they were specialty beers; and even the Genesee Brewing Company in Rochester, New York, has introduced a Honey Brown Lager — with a Dundee's Brewery label. Just because it walks like a duck and quacks like a duck . . . it could be plain foul. Let the buyer beware.

Listing of Contract Brewers

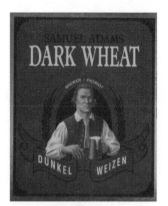

Boston Beer Co.

Pete's Brewing Co.

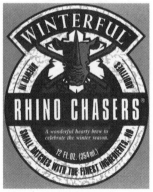

William & Scott Co.

Boston Beer Co.
30 Germania St.
Boston, MA 02130
(617) 522-9080
(See also Boston Beer Co., page 190, and Samual Adams Brewhouse, page 197)

Brews: Lightship, Samuel Adams Boston Lager, Samuel Adams Octoberfest, Samuel Adams Cream Stout, Samuel Adams Honey Porter, Samuel Adams Winter Lager, Samuel Adams Dark Wheat, Samuel Adams Double Bock, Samuel Adams Boston Ale, Samuel Adams Cranberry Lambic, Samuel Adams Wheat, and the incredible Sam Adams Triple Bock.

Pete's Brewing Co.
514 High St.
Palo Alto, CA 94301
(415) 328-7383

Brews: Pete's Wicked Ale, Pete's Wicked Lager, Pete's Wicked Winter Brew, Pete's Wicked Red

William & Scott Co.
8460 Higuera St.
Culver City, CA 90232
(800) 788-HORN

Brews: Rhino Chasers Amber Ale, Rhino Chasers American Ale, Rhino Chasers Bock, Rhino Chasers Dark Lager, Rhino Chasers Wheat, Rhino Chasers Winterful

Pennsylvania Brewing Co.
Troy Hill Road & Vinial St.
Pittsburgh, PA 15212
(412) 237-9400
(See also Allegheny Brewery & Restaurant, page 197)

Brews: Penn Pilsner

Friends Brewing Co.
P.O. Box 27
Helen, GA 30545
(404) 878-1062

Brews: Helenboch Beer, Helenboch Oktoberfest, Helenboch Peachy Wheat

Blue Hen Beer Company, Ltd.
P.O. Box 7077
Newark, DE 19714
(302) 737-8375

Brews: Blue Hen Beer

Buffalo Bill's Brewery
1082 B St.
Hayward, CA 94541
(510) 886-9823

Brews: Pumpkin Ale, Alimony Ale ("the bitterest beer in America")

Brooklyn Brewery
118 North 11th St.
Brooklyn, NY 11211
(718) 486-7422
Brews: Brooklyn Lager, Brooklyn Brown Ale

Beartooth Brewing Co.
P.O. Box 6100
Boulder, CO 80306
Brews: Beartooth Blueberry Lager, Beartooth Cranberry Lager, Beartooth Raspberry Lager

Wild Boar Brewing Co.
P.O. Box 8239
Atlanta, GA 30345
(404) 633-0379
Brews: Wild Boar Special Amber, Wild Boar Classic Pilsner, Wild Boar Winter Spiced

Red Bell Brewing Co.
P.O. Box 2168
Philadelphia, PA 19103
Brews: Red Bell Amber, Red Bell Blonde Ale

Dock Street Brewing Co.
225 City Line Avenue
Suite 110
Bala Cynwyd, PA 19004
(215) 668-1480
(See also Dock Street Brewery & Restaurant, page 197)
Brews: Dock Street Amber Beer, Dock Street Bohemian Pilsner

Olde Heurich Brewing Co.
1111 34th St. NW
Washington, D.C. 20007
(202) 333-2313
Brews: Olde Heurich Maerzen

Blue Hen Beer Company, Ltd.

Buffalo Bill's Brewery

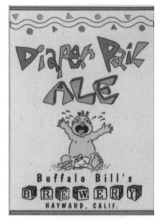

Brooklyn Brewery

Beartooth Brewing Co.

Additives and Preservatives

The federal government does not require the brewing industry to list ingredients on the labels of their products. The following is a list of the preservatives and additives the government considers safe to drink:

1. **Adjuncts employed for conversion**

   proteases and amylases derived from nontoxic strains of:

   > Aspergillus niger
   > Aspergillus oryzae
   > Bacillus subtilis
   > Diastase
   > Ficin
   > Papain

2. **Adjuncts employed for clarifying finished beer**

   proteases and amylases derived form nontoxic strains of:

   > Bromelain
   > Pepsin
   > Gallotanin

3. **Adjuncts employed to stabilize foam and to prevent gushing**

   > Alginate (propylene glycol)
   > Calcium disodium EDTA
   > Gum arabic
   > Peptone

4. **Adjuncts employed to prevent oxidation**

   > Ascorbate
   > Isoascorbate
   > Potassium metabisulfite
   > Sodium bisulfite
   > Sodium hydrosulfite
   > Sodium metabisulfite

5. **Adjuncts employed as natural and artificial flavors**

   > Acetic acid
   > Adipic acid
   > Anethole
   > Benzaldehyde
   > Citric acid
   > Ethyl acetate
   > Ethyl isobutyrate
   > Ethyl maltol
   > Gentian, extract
   > Glycerin

Grapefruit oil

Isoamyl acetate

Isoamyl butyrate

Isobutyl acetate

Juniper berries

Lemon oil

Licorice root

Lime oil

Malic acid

Methyl anthranilate

Nooktatone

Octanal

Orange oil

Quassia, extract

Sodium citrate

Sucrose octaacetate

Tartaric acid

Terpiniol

6. Adjuncts employed as artificial colors

Caramel

F.D. & C. Blue # 1

F.D. & C. Red # 40

F.D. & C. Yellow # 5

7. Adjuncts employed as microbiological inhibitors

Heptylparaben

Lest casual beer consumers be lulled into a false sense of security, it is noteworthy to mention that back in the 1960s, North American and European brewers tried using an adjunct called cobalt sulfate in an effort to improve head retention. Unfortunately, cobalt sulphate reduces the body's ability to metabolize certain substances that maintain the life of cells in the heart. Four dozen beer drinkers on two continents died as a result of drinking beer tainted with this additive; another 112 suffered unlikely heart attacks before the source of the problem was realized and eliminated.

Glossary of Terms

adjuncts. Any unmalted fermentable ingredient added to beer in an attempt to lighten or cheapen the product. The use of adjuncts is prohibited by the Reinheitsgebot (see page 23).

all grain. Refers to beers brewed with barley, barley malt, and wheat malt, and without adjuncts.

astringent. A harsh, mouth-puckering sensation, perceived as bitter taste. Usually traced to misuse of grain.

attenuate. To make thin; to dilute. With regard to fermentation, this refers to the yeasts' consumption of fermentable sugars, transforming them into alcohol and carbon dioxide gas.

barrel. A standard liquid measure in the brewing industry, equivalent to 31 gallons in U.S.

body. The sensation of fullness or thickness of a beer on the palate.

bottle-conditioned. Aged and naturally carbonated, by priming or re-yeasting in the bottle.

bouquet. Part of the aromatic profile of a beer, usually referring to hop character.

Campaign for Real Ale (CamRA). A campaign started in Britain to protect and preserve the rapidly disappearing practice of producing "real ale."

cellar temperature. Also known as British cellar temperature, 55°F (13°C). Considered by many to be optimum serving temperature for stout and other dark ales.

cloying. Particularly sweet, to the point of becoming offensive.

complex. Multi-flavored; involving many tastes and sensations on the palate.

crisp. Effervescent; highly carbonated.

diacetyl. A volatile compound produced by certain yeast strains. Diacetyl is evident in aroma and flavor and is recognized as a buttery or butterscotchy aroma and taste. It is appropriate in some ale styles, but rarely in a lager beer.

dry-hopped. The addition of hops directly to a keg of fermenting beer with the intention of imparting additional hop characteristics to the finished beer.

enteric. Pertaining to the alimentary canal; intestinal.

esters. Volatile flavor compounds that contribute to the fruity aroma of beer.

ethanol. Ethyl alcohol. Ethanol is the colorless, soluble, intoxicating element produced by the yeast during the fermentation process.

extract. Sweet wort reduced to malt extract syrup or powder by dehydration.

flash pasteurized. A shorter but higher temperature method of pasteurization; usually 170°F (77°C), for less than one minute.

finish. The aftertaste; final taste impression of the beer.

finishing hops. Hops added to the kettle late in the boiling process, intended to inbue hop aroma rather than hop bitterness in the beer.

fire brewing. The Old World method of brewing wherein the brew kettle is directly heated by fire. Most of the brew houses in American microbrewers are heated by steam coils.

fusel alcohol. Higher alcohols which are produced by certain yeast strains and at certain fermentation temperatures. Fusel alcohol is often blamed for producing aggravated hangovers.

gravity. Density or thickness of a liquid; a measure of the fermentable sugars in beer.

grist. The total mix of grain to be used in the mash.

homebrewing. The act of brewing beer in one's own home; made legal by an act of Congress in 1978. Credited with sowing the seeds of the microbrewing renaissance.

mash(ing). The process of infusing malted grain with hot water in order to extract the soluble sugars and proteins needed to make beer. The syrupy, sweet liquid that results from mashing the grain is called wort.

mouthfeel. The physical perception of beer in the mouth and on the palate; refers mainly to fullness of body and carbonic effect.

noble hops. Varieties from Germany including Hallertau, Tettnang, and Spalt.

nose. The synonym for the total olfactory perception of beer; i.e., fragrance, aroma, and bouquet.

oxydized. Off-flavor resulting from exposure to oxygen.

palate. Literally, the roof of the mouth; more commonly includes the tongue and all interior surfaces of the mouth.

phenolic. An unpleasant, chemical or medicinal odor or flavor caused by high concentrations of volatile phenol compounds in beer.

real ale. Unpasteurized and cask-conditioned ale; beer aged "in the wood."

session beer. A light-bodied, low alcohol beer, conducive to large volume consumption.

shelf life. The length of time beer can be left unrefrigerated before spoiling. (It should be noted that there are no known pathogens in beer; spoilage in beer is not harmful like spoilage in food.)

skunky. A skunk-like odor resulting from the harmful effects of light on beer. It is also known as "light-struck," and is most often caused by flourescent lighting.

slurry. A suspension of a solid in a liquid.

sparge(ing). Spraying hot water on grain bed in mash tun to recover malt sugars remaining in grain husks.

vegetal. A cooked cabbage or cauliflower-like odor produced during fermentation process.

wort. The sweet, syrupy liquid produced by the mashing process, to be fermented by the yeast during the fermentation phase; unfermented beer.

Further Reading

If you are interested in furthering your beer education, the following is a list of various publications which cover beer evaluation, homebrewing, cooking with beer, and miscellaneous information on American microbrewing, as well as the brewing industry worldwide.

Periodicals

Ale Street News. The largest circulated "brewspaper" in the United States. Bimonthly tabloid taps beer "hoppenings" in New York and New England. Subscriptions: P.O. Box 5339, Bergenfield, NJ 07621.

All About Beer. America's foremost beer publication. Bimonthly magazine covers brewing industry at large, with special focus on microbreweries. Other features on beer festivals, liquor stores, pubs, etc. Published by Chatauqua, Inc., 1627 Marion Ave., Durham, NC 27705

American Brewer Magazine. First of two magazines produced by Bill Owens, created for the serious homebrewer and aspiring microbrewer. 1049 B St., Hayward, CA 94541

American Breweriana Journal. Bimonthly magazine of the American Breweriana Association. Focus is on brewery collectibles, but also good, updated coverage of microbrewing industry. P.O. Box 11157, Pueblo, CO 81001.

Barleycorn. Bimonthly tabloid covering beer and brewing in the mid-Atlantic states. P.O. Box 2328, Falls Church, VA 22042.

BEER: the magazine. Slick, colorful, bimonthly magazine, one of two produced by Bill Owens. Promotes beer and brewing as a lifestyle. Good coverage of entire industry. 1049 B St., Hayward, CA 94541

Brew! New bimonthly magazine blends travel with beer trekking, with emphasis on the latter. All-American Publishing, 1120 Mulberry Street, Des Moines, IA 50309.

Celebrator Beer News. Celebrated tabloid brewspaper, published bimonthly. Covers West Coast beer scene. P.O. Box 375, Hayward, CA 94543

Malt Advocate. Up-and-coming magazine dedicated to the discerning consumption of beer and whisky. Beer gets the lion's share of the coverage. 3416 Oak Hill Rd., Emmaus, PA 18049.

Midwest Beer Notes. Bimonthly brewspaper serving beer lovers throughout the Midwest. Good regional coverage of micros and beer festivals. 339 Sixth Ave., Clayton, WI 54004

ON TAP: the newsletter One of the first, and still the most comprehensive newsletter on the microbrewing scene. Bimonthly newsletter covers border to border and coast to coast. ON TAP PUBlications, P.O. Box 71, Clemson, SC 29633

Pint Post. Quarterly publication of Microbrew Appreciation Society, features micros of the Pacific Northwest. 12345 Lake City Way NE, Suite #159, Seattle, WA 98125.

Southwest Brewing News. Bimonthly tabloid covers brewing industry and festivals in the South and Southwest. 11405 Evening Star Drive, Austin, TX 78739.

Yankee Brew News. "*New England's Beeriodical since 1989.*" Bimonthly paper covering microbrewing in the Northeast. P.O. Box 520250, Winthrop, MA 02152-0005

Zymurgy. Journal of the American Homebrewers Association. Published four times each year, with a fifth "special" issue. Also covers national microbrewery scene. P.O. Box 1679, Boulder, CO 80306-1679

Books

The Beer Directory: An International Guide, Publishing by Heather Wood (Storey Publishing, 1995)

The Beer Enthusiasts' Guide: Tasting and Judging Beers From Around the World, by Gregg Smith (Storey Publishing, 1994)

The Beer Log, by James Robertson (Bosak Publications, 1994)

Better Beer & How to Brew It, by M. R. Reese (Storey Publishing, 1978)

Brewing the World's Great Beers: A Step-by-Step Guide by Dave Miller (Storey Publishing, 1992)

The Complete Handbook of Home Brewing by Dave Miller (Storey Publishing, 1988)

The Complete Joy of Homebrewing, by Charlie Papazian (Avon Books, 1984)

Dave Miller's Homebrewing Guide: Everything You Need to Know to Make Great-Tasting Beer by Dave Miller (Storey Publishing, 1995)

Great Beer from Kits: Getting the Most from Kit Brewing by Joe Fisher and Dennis Fisher (Storey Publishing, 1996)

The Homebrewer's Companion, by Randy Mosher (Alephenalia Publications, 1994)

Homebrew Favorites: A Coast-to-Coast Collection of More Than 240 Beer and Ale Recipes, by Karl F. Lutzen and Mark Stevens (Storey Publishing, 1994)

Jay Harlow's Beer Cuisine, by Jay Harlow (Emeryville, CA: Harlow & Ratnor, 1991)

The New World Guide to Beer, by Michael Jackson (Philadelphia, PA: Running Press, 1988)

Secret Life of Beer: Legends, Lore, and Little-Known Facts by Alan D. Eames (Storey Publishing, 1995)

A Taste for Beer by Stephen Beaumont (Storey Publishing, 1995)

Index

Page numbers in *italics* indicated illustrations.

Casper Maus Brewing, 132–33

Maytag, Fritz, profile of, 50–51

Mead, Francis, 158–59

Mediterranean foods, beer with, 90

Melbourne's, 153

Mendocino Brewing, 20, 61, *61*

Merchant Du Vin, 40

Mexican foods, beer with, 51

Mickey Finn's Brewery, 146

Microbrewer's Conference (Denver, 1984), 30

Microbrewing industry, origins of, 125

Middleton's Tavern, 177

Migliorini, Jim, 162–63

Miles Town Brewing, 106

Mill Bakery, Eatery & Brewery (Fla.), 186

Mill Bakery, Eatery & Brewery (N.C.), 196

Miller, Dave, profile of, 141

Miller, Ted, 123

Miller Brewing, 10, 81, 205

Milling, described, 20

Mill Rose Brewing, 146

Millstream Brewing, 139, 148

Minnesota Brewing, 203

Miracle Brewing, 105–6

Mishawaka Brewing, 148

Monde Selection, 166

Montana Beverages, 106

Monterey Brewing, 61

Moonlight Brewing, 61

Moose's Tale, The, 189

Mott, Ted, 162–63

Mountain Brewers, 198, *198*

Mountain Sun Pub & Brewery, 102

Mountain Valley Brewpub, 194

Mt. Hood Brewpub, 70–71

Multnomah Brewing, 71

Munchener dunkel, described, 7

Munchener helles, described, 7

Jasper Murdock's Alehouse, 198

Murphys Creek Brewing, 61

-N-

Names of Beers information boxes, 20, 34, 64, 154, 160

Napa Valley Brewing, 61–62

Napoleon I, Emperor of France, 16

Naptown Brewing, 133

National Homebrew Competition
  1981 awards, 141
  1984 awards, 95
  1987 awards, 141
  1992 awards, 95–96

Nelson, Al, 86

Nelson, Kirby, 123–24

Ness, Eliot, 132

Nevada City Brewing, 62

New Belgium Brewing, 102, *102*

New Brewer magazine, *The*, 94, 171

New England Brewing, 184, *184*

New Glarus Brewing, 155, *155*

New Haven Brewing, 184, *184*

New York Beerfest, 183

J. D. Nick's, 146

Norman Brewing, 109

North Coast Brewing, 62

Northern Light Brewing, 76

Northhampton Brewing, 182, 192

J.V. Northwest, 34, 130

Northwest Ale Festival, profile of, 53

Northwestern Brewpub, 71

Nor' Wester Willamette Valley Brewing, 71, *71*

Northwest Microbrew Expo, profile of, 52

Norwich Inn, 198

No Tomatoes Restaurant, 189

Nutrition values of beer, 87

-O-

Oaken Barrel Brewing, 148

Oak Hills Brewpub, 71

Oasis Brewery & Restaurant, 64, 102

Oconto Brewing, 155

-W-

Walnut Brewery, 104

Ware, Jeff, 165, 168

Ware, Randolph, 86

Warner, Eric, profile of, 95–96

Wasatch Brewpub, 91, 112–13

Washington, George, 85

Wassail, described, 15–16

Wasserberg, Gunter, 138

Water for making beer, described, 19

Waterloo Brewing, 111

Water Street Brewery, 156

Weathervane, 151

Weeping Radish Restaurant and Brewery,
  196–97
  profile of, 175–76

Weidman's Old Fort Brew Pub, 144–45

Weihenstephan Institut, 95, 120, 139, 160,
  175

Weinkeller Brewery, 147

Weizenbock, described, 4

Wenceslas, King of Bohemia, 14

West Bros. Bar B-Q, 73

Westside Brewing, 195

West Virginia Brewing, 200

Wharf Rat Camden Yards, 177, 190

Wheat beer, described, 16

Whitecap Brewpub, 73

Whitefish Brewing, 106–7

Widmer Brewing, 73

Wiedemann Brewery, 135

Wild Boar Brewing, 20, 207

Wilderness Pub, 103

Wild Goose Brewing, 20, 158, 179, 190, *190*
  profile of, 176–77

Wild River Brewery, 73–74

Wild River Brewing & Pizza, 74

Wild Wild West Gambling Hall & Brewery,
  104

Wilhelm IV, Duke of Bavaria, 23–24

Willamette Brew Pub, 74

William & Scott, 203, 206, *206*

Windham Brewery, 198

Winthrop Brewing, 77

Wisconsin Microbrewers Beerfest, 142

Wisconsin State Fair, 133

Wisconsin Vintners Association, 133

Witbier, described, 16–17

Woodstock Brewing, 195

Wrigley, Richard, 162

Wynkoop, Edward Wanshear, 92

Wynkoop Billiards, 93

Wynkoop Brewery, 95, 104
  profile of, 92–93

-Y-

Yakima Brewing and Malting, 42
  profile of, 47–48

Yeast, described, 18–19

Yegua Creek Brewing, 111–12

Yellow Rose Brewing, 112

Young, Brigham, 91

-Z-

Zanteson, John, 118

Zavarone, Otto, 86

Zip City Brewing, 195

Zymurgy, 94